MULTIPLE-CHOICE AND FREE-RESPONSE QUESTIONS IN PREPARATION FOR THE AP ENGLISH LANGUAGE AND COMPOSITION EXAMINATION

(SIXTH EDITION)

By

DR. RICHARD VOGEL

D&S MARKETING SYSTEMS, INC.
1205 38th Street Brooklyn, NY 11218

w w w . d s m a r k e t i n g . c o m

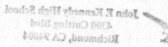

ISBN #1-878621-92-0

Printed in the U.S.A.

PREFACE

The 6th edition of *Multiple Choice & Free-Response Questions in Preparation for the AP English Language and Composition Examination* was not completed without a measure of heartache. All books exact a physical and psychological toll, and trolling endlessly through literature for potential articles and passages, developing question sets that run aground before yielding the necessary number of questions, trying to reconcile the delicate balance of gender, ethnicity, and period with the constrictive parameters of passage and exam length, and grinding through the typing, revising, editing and typesetting stages of the book is a grueling and enervating process.

This edition, however, exacted an emotional toll as well with the death in April 2005 of my co-author, Charles Winans. "Charlie," as he was affectionately known to all, was my senior English teacher in Brooklyn Preparatory High School, but his influence extended far beyond my days in the classroom. It was Charlie who persuaded me to take a turn on the stage (as Dick Deadeye in *H.M.S. Pinafore*) and who later directed me in more substantive fare as Creon in *Antigone* and Thomas á Becket in *Murder in the Cathedral*. It was Charlie who first took me to Europe, a six-country barnstorming tour with two other students that took us from Athens to Sligo. It was Charlie who first introduced me to community service through his Toy Drive that annually distributed gifts and a measure of holiday cheer to convalescent children in at least six New York hospitals. And it was Charlie who confirmed my desire to teach, who mentored me through my fledgling days in the profession, and who saw me through my graduate and doctoral studies. Writing the book with him was always a delight—long afternoons and dinners spent discussing what has always been the chief love of our lives, arguing passionately over textual ambiguities, uncovering new subtext and influences, and discovering new authors and overlooked passages. For the first time writing the book became predominantly *work*, and I found I had to fight to prevent it from becoming drudgery. Though the last years of Charlie's life were marred by the annoying impediments of age and illness and, as a result, his contribution to this book was limited, I think he would be as proud of it as I am of my nearly forty-year association with him—forever teacher, mentor, friend, and colleague.

There are others to acknowledge here as well: David Lederman, my publisher, for continuing to sponsor my AP English endeavors; Rachel and Tammi, for their invaluable assistance negotiating permissions and typesetting the book; Mary and Pamela Chesser for question evaluation and proofreading; my Social Studies colleague, Doug Young, for his help in brainstorming the synthesis essay topics; my many AP colleagues from across the country whose acumen and repartee at the June AP English Reading continue to inspire me; and the members of my last four Croton-Harmon AP English classes who graciously contributed sample essays to this edition. To all, I express my gratitude for a job well done.

All communications concerning this book should be addressed to:

D&S Marketing Systems, Inc.
1205 38th Street
Brooklyn, NY 11218
www.dsmarketing.com

MULTIPLE-CHOICE AND FREE-RESPONSE QUESTIONS as A Resource for Students and Teachers of Advanced Placement English Language

This book has been designed to help students prepare for the Advanced Placement Exam in English Language and Composition. It is not filled with definitions of literary terms nor saccharine advice on how to 'psych' students up for the examination. Rather, its passages are selected and its questions designed with the singular purpose of developing in students the habits of mind that good readers possess, that they actively employ while reading, and that they use to structure and develop their written responses to the text. Not being the examination itself, it is designed more for instruction than assessment, though it may certainly be used to measure student progress throughout the school year.

As a teacher in a relatively small public school, I have for the last twenty years enjoyed luxuries of class size and budget with which other teachers are not always blessed. I have not had to battle inordinately large enrollment, rigid forty-minute class schedules, students who take the class but not the test, censorship, or any of the other privations and problems that teachers regularly convey to me at AP English workshops. Even so, the continued success our AP English students is due less to our size than to our program, part of which involves the use of this text.

Though the book is divided into sample "exams," there is no pressing need to use it in this manner. I generally try to do one or two random selections of poetry and prose per eight-day cycle for the duration of the school year, incorporating multiple-choice and free-response practice as a regular part of my AP syllabus. Though our block-schedule gives me the opportunity to administer an entire sample examination in one class period, I seldom do, preferring to use the extra class time to discuss with students the stylistic or thematic aspects of the passage that they found interesting. Inasmuch as the book is intended to supplement, not replace, the actual AP exam, I use it to build the confidence and knowledge base of my AP English students so that they will find the exam to be more of a sequence of interesting challenges than an oppressive, three-hour literary gauntlet. Discussion of the passages and debate over the merit of a particular answer are encouraged as healthy and necessary steps toward developing higher-level thought. As we get deeper into the academic year, I gradually shift from this book to the released AP English Language exams, administering one per month, February through May. Though exam preparation never takes precedence over our core reading list, I believe that if you do not sufficiently expose students to the modes of AP questioning, you cannot expect them to answer such questions with success.

I have always maintained that teaching is really little more than a dialogue, a reciprocation of insights and ideas, an establishment of a position or a reevaluation of one. The greatest teachers throughout time have always been able to inspire such engagement, and the best AP English classrooms are forums for such exchange. If this book helps to foster insightful discussion about literature and language in your classroom, I believe it will have achieved its goal.

TABLE OF CONTENTS

Sample Examination I

Questions 1-13. Refer to the following passage.

SIR[1]—The long and intimate,
though by no means friendly, relation
which unhappily subsisted between you and
myself, leads me to hope that you will
(5) easily account for the great liberty which
I now take in addressing you in this open and
public manner. The same fact may possibly
remove any disagreeable surprise which
you may experience on again finding your
(10) name coupled with mine, in any other way
than in an advertisement, accurately
describing my person, and offering a large
sum for my arrest. In thus dragging you
again before the public, I am aware that I
(15) shall subject myself to no inconsiderable
amount of censure. I shall probably be
charged with an unwarrantable, if not
wanton and reckless disregard of the rights
and properties of private life. There are
(20) those north as well as south who entertain a
much higher respect for rights that are
merely conventional than they do for rights
which are personal and essential. Not a few
there are in our country, who, while they
(25) have no scruples of robbing the laborer of
the hard earned results of his patient industry,
will be shocked by the extremely
indelicate manner of bringing your name
before the public. Believing this to be the
(30) case, and wishing to meet every reasonable
or plausible objection to my conduct, I will
frankly state the ground upon which I
justify myself in this instance, as well as on
former occasions when I have thought
(35) proper to mention your name in public. All
will agree that a man guilty of theft,
robbery, or murder, has forfeited the right
to concealment and private life; that the
community have the right to subject such
(40) persons to the most complete exposure.
However much they may desire retirement,
and aim to conceal themselves and their
movements from the popular gaze, the
public have a right to ferret them out, and
(45) bring their conduct before the proper
tribunals of the country for investigation.

Sir, you will undoubtedly make the proper
application of these generally admitted
principles and will easily see the light in
(50) which you are regarded by me [. . . .].
I have selected this day on which to
address you, because it is the anniversary of
my emancipation; and knowing no better
way I am led to this as the best mode of
(55) celebrating that truly important event. Just
ten years ago this beautiful September
morning, yon bright sun beheld me a
slave—a poor degraded chattel[2]—trembling
at the sound of your voice, lamenting that I
(60) was a man, and wishing myself a brute. The
hopes which I had treasured up for weeks
of a safe and successful escape from your
grasp, were powerfully confronted at this
last hour by dark clouds of doubt and fear,
(65) making my person shake and my bosom to
heave with the heavy contest between hope
and fear. I have no words to describe to you
the deep agony of soul which I experienced
on that never-to-be-forgotten morning for
(70) I left by daylight. I was making a leap in
the dark. The probabilities, so far as I could
by reason determine them, were stoutly
against the undertaking. The preliminaries
and precautions I had adopted previously,
(75) all worked badly. I was like one going to
war without weapons—ten chances of
defeat to one of victory. One in whom I had
confided, and one who had promised me
assistance, appalled by fear at the trial hour,
(80) deserted me, thus leaving the responsibility
of success or failure solely with myself.
You, sir, can never know my feelings.
As I look back to them, I can scarcely realize
that I have passed through a scene so
(85) trying [. . . .].

---

[1] Captain Thomas Auld. Douglas addressed him in an open letter
  in the *North Star* on September 8, 1868.

[2] a personal property or possession

1

1. In the opening sentence of his letter to his former master, Douglass does which of the following?

   (A) apologizes for his audacity in contacting him
   (B) flaunts his recently attained liberty
   (C) understates the nature and condition of their previous relation
   (D) addresses his master in a confrontational and disrespectful tone
   (E) acknowledges his master's understandable bewilderment at his disappearance

2. In describing the potential effects of his correspondence, Douglass does all of the following EXCEPT

   (A) readily admit it will further inflame public sentiment about him
   (B) humorously envision his master's shock at seeing their names mentioned together in anything but a 'Wanted' poster
   (C) metaphorically link his master's public chagrin with his own public humiliation at the slave market
   (D) wryly speculate what additional 'charges' may be precipitated by his decision to write the letter
   (E) confidently anticipate his former master's viewing him in a more sympathetic light

3. By the phrase "rights that are merely conventional [. . .]" (lines 21-22), Douglass is referring to the

   (A) rights granted him by the Constitution
   (B) rights protecting his master's property interests
   (C) rights protecting his master's privacy
   (D) "higher laws" of religion and ethics
   (E) arbitrary nature of local statutes

4. The essential implication about those individuals "who entertain a much higher respect for rights that are merely conventional [. . .]" (lines 20-22) is that they are

   (A) sincere
   (B) ignorant
   (C) callous
   (D) hypocritical
   (E) unorthodox

5. In lines 35-46, "All will agree [. . . .] for investigation," Douglass does all of the following EXCEPT

   (A) appeal to the reason of all men by presenting what he feels is an undeniable truth
   (B) suggest that those who commit a public crime open themselves to public exposure
   (C) levy specific charges against his former master
   (D) buttress indirectly the moral grounds for his letter
   (E) presage a potential reckoning for the crimes of enslavement committed by his master

6. Douglass' argument for exposing his master's reprehensible conduct (lines 29-50) is founded upon

   (A) causal reasoning
   (B) generalization
   (C) contrast
   (D) analogy
   (E) inductive reasoning

7. In the second paragraph Douglass suggests that the imminent nature of his escape triggered antithetical feelings of

   (A) anticipation and apprehension
   (B) satisfaction and regret
   (C) elation and depression
   (D) tranquility and anger
   (E) clarity and confusion

8. Douglass' "lamenting that [he] was a man, and wishing [him]self a brute" (lines 59-60) was likely motivated by a(n)

   (A) inordinate amount of self-pity
   (B) acute consciousness of the degradation of his enslavement
   (C) paralyzing depression that impeded his taking action
   (D) misguided belief that a beast could better endure such harsh labor
   (E) embarrassing lack of fortitude

9. Douglass uses the phrase "treasured up" (line 61) to convey which of the following?

    I. The rarity of a successful escape from bondage.
    II. The extent to which the dream of escape sustained him.
    III. The duration of his clandestine planning.

    (A) I only
    (B) II only
    (C) I and II
    (D) II and III
    (E) I, II and III

10. The "one" mentioned in lines 77 and 78 is most likely

    (A) Douglass' master
    (B) Douglass' conscience
    (C) a fellow slave
    (D) an abolitionist
    (E) God

11. Which of the following is NOT characteristic of the author's style?

    (A) an analogy that subtly shifts culpability from slave to master
    (B) a forceful tone that is tempered by restraint and civility
    (C) a simile that highlights the seeming futility of an escape endeavor
    (D) a highly imagistic depiction of the sufferings of enslavement
    (E) an ironic juxtaposition of the exhilaration of his escape and the uncertainty of his future

12. The author juxtaposes his bold daytime escape with which of the following *figurative* expressions?

    I. The "dark clouds of doubt and fear" (line 64) that shook his resolve.
    II. The "leap in the dark" (lines 70-71) that he made in striking out for the North.
    III. The vulnerable feeling he experienced of "going to war without weapons" (lines 75-76)

    (A) I only
    (B) III only
    (C) I and II
    (D) II and III
    (E) I, II and III

13. Overall, Douglass' letter is BEST classified as a(n)

    (A) *ad hominem* attack upon his former owner's character
    (B) defiant celebration of the anniversary of his emancipation
    (C) retrospective reflection on the nature and motivation of Southern slave-holders
    (D) ironic apology for his inconsiderate and illicit escape
    (E) measured verbalization of his master's culpability for his physical and psychological suffering

Questions 14-25. Refer to the following passage.

"Next then," I said, "take the following parable of education and ignorance as a picture of the condition of our nature. Imagine mankind as dwelling in an underground cave [. . . .]."[1]

—Plato

Where are the songs I used to know,
    Where are the notes I used to sing?
I have forgotten everything
    I used to know so long ago.

—Christina Rossetti[2]

[. . . .] there came upon me an overshadowing bright Cloud, and in the midst of it the figure of a Woman, most richly adorned with transparent Gold, her Hair hanging down, and her Face as the terrible Crystal for brightness [and] immediately this voice came, saying, Behold I am God's Eternal Virgin-Wisdom [. . .]. I am to unseal the Treasures of God's deep Wisdom unto thee, and will be as Rebecca was unto Jacob, a true natural Mother; for out of my Womb thou shalt be brought forth after the manner of a Spirit, Conceived and Born again.

—Jane Lead[3]

Although Plato does not seem to have thought much about this point, a cave is—as Freud pointed out—a female place, a womb-shaped enclosure, a house of earth, secret
(5) and often sacred. To this shrine the initiate comes to hear the voices of darkness, the wisdom of inwardness. In this prison the slave is immured, the virgin sacrificed, the priestess abandoned. "We have put her
(10) living in the tomb!"[4] Poe's paradigmatic exclamation of horror, with its shadow of solipsism, summarizes the Victorian shudder of disgust at the thought of cavern confrontations and the evils they might
(15) reveal—the suffocation, the "black bat airs," the vampirism, the chaos of what Victor Frankenstein calls "filthy creation." But despite its melodrama, Poe's remark summarizes too (even if unintentionally)
(20) the plight of the woman in patriarchal culture, the woman whose cave-shaped anatomy is her destiny. Not just, like Plato's cave-dweller, a prisoner of Nature, this woman is a prisoner of her own

(25) nature, a prisoner in the "grave-cave" of immanence[5] which she transforms into a vaporous Cave of Spleen.

In this regard, an anecdote of Simone de Beauvoir[6] forms a sort of counter-parable to
(30) Plato's:

"I recall seeing in a primitive village of Tunisia a subterranean cavern in which four women were squatting: the old one-eyed and toothless wife, her face horribly devastated,
(35) was cooking dough on a small brazier in the midst of an acrid smoke; two wives somewhat younger, but almost as disfigured, were lulling children in their arms—one was giving suck; seated before a loom, a young
(40) idol magnificently decked out in silk, gold and silver was knotting threads of wool. As I left this gloomy cave-kingdom of immanence, womb and tomb, in the corridor leading upward toward the light of
(45) day I passed the male, dressed in white, well-groomed, smiling, sunny. He was returning from the marketplace, where he had discussed world affairs with other men; he would pass some hours in this retreat of his
(50) at the heart of the vast universe to which he belonged, from which he was not separated. For the withered old women, for the young wife doomed to the same rapid decay, there was no universe other than the
(55) smoky cave, whence they emerged, only at night, silent and veiled [. . . .]."

---

1 from the *Republic*—this famous allegory, in which prisoners in a subterranean cave are only able to see shadows of things in the world above, explores the differences between perception and reality.

2 Victorian poetess

3 17th century English mystic who experienced a vision that compelled her to abandon her secular world for a more spiritual and reflective lifestyle.

4 uttered, in Poe's Gothic classic "The Fall of the House of Usher," by Roderick Usher after burying his sister Madeline alive

5 state of being present in the natural world

6 20th century feminist and existentialist

14. The trio of complementary epigraphs that precede the passage does all of the following EXCEPT

(A) allude to the premise of a famous classical allegory
(B) intimate the level of ignorance and unhappiness to which many women have been reduced
(C) cite a literary text in which an allegorical female character symbolizes enlightenment and empowerment
(D) allude to Biblical episodes in which women are given significant maternal roles
(E) suggest that some women repress the unpleasant experiences of their pasts

15. Taken together, the trio of epigraphs that precede the passage serves to

(A) provide antithetical perspectives on the state of women in contemporary society
(B) validate the creativity and intellect of women writers
(C) presage the author's articulation of the state of women in a male-dominated culture
(D) depict the social conditions that have effected female oppression
(E) note the sustaining role of religion for women of all ages

16. The arrangement of the three epigraphs suggests that women need to progress through which sequence of stages?

(A) birth—life—death
(B) chaos—confusion—clarity
(C) ignorance—questioning—enlightenment
(D) atheism—agnosticism—belief
(E) poverty—toil—affluence

17. The third epigraph and footnote are primarily intended to establish a connection between

(A) spirituality and self-actualization
(B) beauty and prosperity
(C) nature and maternity
(D) virginity and sanctity
(E) divinity and humanity

18. Which of the following is LEAST drawn upon by the authors in developing their argument?

(A) psychoanalysis
(B) philosophy
(C) history
(D) literature
(E) mysticism

19. Throughout the course of their argument, the authors *figuratively* depict the cave as a(n)

(A) powerful life-engendering organ
(B) place of physical incarceration
(C) nightmarish gothic enclosure
(D) secluded sanctuary
(E) tomb for the aspirations of women

20. By the words, "To this shrine the initiate comes to hear the voices of darkness, the wisdom of inwardness" (lines 5-7), the authors imply which of the following?

(A) That women of past ages are themselves to blame for their ignorance and submission.
(B) That the path to empowerment begins with introspection.
(C) That for many women knowledge remains illicit and taboo.
(D) That many early women sought knowledge through participation in clandestine cults.
(E) That since Eden the pursuit of knowledge by women has been categorized as evil.

21. Lines 17-27—"But despite its melodrama [. . . .] a vaporous Cave of Spleen"—suggest all of the following EXCEPT

(A) women may be socially confined by their capacity for reproduction
(B) women have become embittered by their subordinate status
(C) women's lot is even worse than the intellectual benightedness of Plato's cave-dwellers
(D) women's subordinate place has essentially been predetermined
(E) the plight of women was a major concern of Edgar Allen Poe

22. What likely motivates the authors to label the anecdote of Simone de Beauvoir (lines 31-56) a "counter-parable" is its

    (A) geographical setting
    (B) domestic focus
    (C) restricted enlightenment
    (D) repulsive characters
    (E) feminist bent

23. The authors imply that the aging and physical disfigurement of the Tunisian cave-dwellers is a consequence of their

    (A) exposure to contagion
    (B) unhealthy diet
    (C) poor sanitation
    (D) inalterable domestic lot
    (E) uncivilized environment

24. Which of the following contribute(s) to the passage's concluding irony?

    I. The common fate shared by the withered old woman and the young wife.
    II. The smoky nature of the cave.
    III. The time and nature of the women's sole emergence from their subterranean abode.

    (A) I only
    (B) II only
    (C) I and III
    (D) II and III
    (E) I, II and III

25. The most defining aspect of the passage is the author's

    (A) intimate first-person perspective
    (B) multiplicity of allusions
    (C) penchant for parenthetical commentary
    (D) stream-of-consciousness construct
    (E) misandrogynistic tone

Questions 26-38. Refer to the following passage.

In this passage the author recounts an equestrian warmup he witnessed while attending a circus.

In attempting to recapture this mild spectacle, I am merely acting as a recording secretary for one of the oldest of societies—the society of those who, at one
(5) time or another, have surrendered, without even a show of resistance, to the bedazzlement of a circus rider. As a writing man, or secretary, I have always felt charged with the safekeeping of all
(10) unexpected items of worldly or unworldly attachment, as though I might be held personally responsible if even a small one were to be lost. But it is not easy to communicate anything of this nature. The
(15) circus comes as close to being the world in microcosm of anything I know; in a way, it puts all the rest of show business in the shade. Its magic is universal and complex. Out of its wild disorder comes order; from
(20) its rank smell rises the good aroma of courage and daring; out of its preliminary shabbiness comes the final splendor. And buried in the familiar boasts of its advance agents lies the modesty of most of its
(25) people. For me the circus is at its best before it has been put together. It is at its best at certain moments when it comes to a point, as through a burning glass, in the activity and destiny of a single performer out of so
(30) many. One ring is always bigger than three. One rider, one aerialist, is always greater than six. In short, a man has to catch the circus unawares to experience its full impact and share its gaudy dream.
(35) The ten minute ride the girl took achieved—as far as I was concerned, who wasn't even striving for it—the thing that is sought by performers everywhere, on whatever stage, whether struggling in the
(40) tidal currents of Shakespeare or bucking the difficult motion of a horse. I somehow got the idea that she was just cadging a ride, improving a shining ten minutes in the diligent way all serious artists seize free
(45) moments to hone the blade of their talent and keep themselves in trim. Her brief tour included only elementary postures and tricks, perhaps because they were all she was capable of, perhaps because her

(50) warmup at this hour was unscheduled and the ring was not rigged for a real practice session. She swung herself off and on the horse several times, gripping his mane. She did a few knee-stands—or whatever they are
(55) called—dropping to her knees and quickly bouncing back up on her feet again. Most of the time she simply rode in a standing position, well aft on the beast, her hands hanging easily at her sides, her head erect,
(60) her straw-colored ponytail lightly brushing her shoulders, the blood of exertion showing faintly through the tan of her skin. Twice she managed a one-foot stance—a sort of ballet pose, with arms outstretched.
(65) At one point the neck strap of her bathing suit broke and she went twice around the ring in the classic attitude of a woman making minor repairs to a garment. The fact that she was standing on the back of a
(70) moving horse while doing this invested the matter with a clownish significance that perfectly fitted the spirit of the circus—jocund, yet charming. She just rolled the strap into a neat ball and stowed
(75) it inside her bodice while the horse rocked and rolled beneath her in dutiful innocence. The bathing suit proved as self-reliant as its owner and stood up well enough without benefit of strap.
(80) The richness of the scene was in its plainness, its natural condition—of horse, of ring, of girl, even to the girl's bare feet that gripped the bare back of her proud and ridiculous mount. The enchantment grew
(85) not out of anything that happened or was performed but out of something that seemed to go round and around with the girl, attending her, a steady gleam in the shape of a circle—a ring of ambition, of
(90) happiness, of youth [. . . .]. In a week or two, all would be changed, all (or almost all) lost: the girl would wear makeup, the horse would wear gold, the ring would be painted, the bark would be clean for the feet
(95) of the horse, the girl's feet would be clean for the slippers that she'd wear. All, all would be lost [. . . .].

Pages 52-54 from "THE RING OF TIME" FROM THE *POINTS OF MY COMPASS* by E.B. WHITE

26. Of the following, which BEST represents the speaker's impression of the circus as expressed by the opening paragraph?

   (A) That it is inferior as spectacle to other forms of performance.
   (B) That it has little enduring impact upon its audience.
   (C) That prior to its opening it contains no magical impact.
   (D) That it is a purely American phenomenon with no universal appeal.
   (E) That it is an amalgam of contradictions that inexplicably fuse into compelling entertainment.

27. The primary purpose of the opening sentence is to

   (A) dismiss the significance of the equestrian routine
   (B) reveal the profession of the narrator
   (C) convey the indelible effect the circus has upon its audience
   (D) permit the narrator to assume a perhaps unwarranted position as spokesperson for a particular group
   (E) confess the fallibility of the speaker's memory

28. The speaker perceives the routine of the young girl as

   (A) epitomizing the practice of artistic refinement
   (B) revealing her limited knowledge of equestrian acrobatics
   (C) contributing to the intolerable tedium of the afternoon
   (D) reflecting the increasingly immoral content of all performing arts
   (E) violating child labor statutes

29. The characterization and subsequent actions of the young rider stress her

   (A) egotism and vanity
   (B) deference and politeness
   (C) agility and concentration
   (D) innocence and naiveté
   (E) hedonism and seductiveness

30. Which of the following would be an inappropriate substitution for the word "tour" in line 46?

   (A) exhibition
   (B) warm-up
   (C) circuit
   (D) inspection
   (E) routine

31. The young girl's reaction to the broken strap (lines 65-68) is BEST described as

   (A) nonplussed
   (B) mortified
   (C) petulant
   (D) indifferent
   (E) discombobulated

32. All of the following abet the sense of loss experienced by the author in the final paragraph EXCEPT

   (A) a temporal reference that highlights the transience of the moment
   (B) subtle changes in descriptive detail
   (C) the archetypal symbol of the circle
   (D) a series of anticlimactic and ironic parallel clauses
   (E) the repetition of the word "all"

33. The "all" that the author mentions in the final paragraph refers to which of the following?

   I. The unvarnished image of horse and rider.
   II. An ephemeral symbol of perfection that will not endure.
   III. The moment when one catches the circus "unawares."

   (A) I only
   (B) II only
   (C) I and III
   (D) II and III
   (E) I, II and III

34. The "enchantment" of the author's experience is *symbolically* reinforced by the

    (A) sultriness of the day
    (B) youthful vulnerability of the rider
    (C) variety of postures and tricks the young rider performs
    (D) circular cantering of horse and rider
    (E) slippers the rider will wear during the show

35. In the third paragraph the speaker's attitude shifts from

    (A) disappointed to disenchanted
    (B) bored to engaged
    (C) captivated to regretful
    (D) riveted to distracted
    (E) appreciative to nostalgic

36. The author uses either simile or metaphor to convey each of the following EXCEPT

    (A) the arresting spectacle of the single performer
    (B) the challenge of mastering Shakespearean language
    (C) the efforts of actors to refine their craft
    (D) the standing maneuvers of the young equestrian
    (E) the manner in which the young girl managed her wardrobe malfunction

37. In light of the entire passage, the speaker likely uses the term "gaudy dream" (line 34) to reflect which of the following dichotomies of the circus?

    I. Its "preliminary shabbiness" and its "final splendor."
    II. The warm-up session of the young rider and her actual performance.
    III. The impact of the circus on a youth and on an adult.

    (A) I only
    (B) II only
    (C) I and II
    (D) I and III
    (E) I, II and III

38. The author's overall attitude is BEST characterized as that of a(n)

    (A) acerbic critic
    (B) shameless apologist
    (C) avaricious promoter
    (D) passionate advocate
    (E) stern moralist

Questions 39-51. Refer to the following passage.

What a monstrous spectre is this man, the disease of the agglutinated dust, lifting alternate feet or lying drugged with slumber; killing, feeding, growing, bringing forth small
(5) copies of himself; grown upon with hair like grass, fitted with eyes that move and glitter in his face; a thing to set children screaming;— and yet looked at nearlier, known as his fellows know him, how surprising are his
(10) attributes! Poor soul, here for so little, cast among so many hardships, filled with desires so incommensurate and so inconsistent, savagely surrounded, savagely descended, irremediably condemned to prey upon his
(15) fellow lives: who should have blamed him had he been of a piece with his destiny and a being merely barbarous? And we look and behold him instead filled with imperfect virtues: in-finitely childish, often admirably valiant, often
(20) touchingly kind; sitting down, amidst his momentary life, to debate of right and wrong and the attributes of the deity; rising up to do battle for an egg or die for an idea; singling out his friends and his mate with cordial affection;
(25) bringing forth in pain, rearing with long-suffering solicitude his young. To touch the heart of his mystery, we find in him one thought, strange to the point of lunacy: the thought of duty; the thought of something
(30) owing to himself, to his neighbour, to his God: an ideal of decency, to which he would rise if it were possible; a limit of shame, below which, if it be possible, he will not stoop. The design in most men is one of conformity; here and
(35) there, in picked natures, it transcends itself and soars on the other side, arming martyrs with independence; but in all, in their degrees, it is a bosom thought [. . . .], it sways with so complete an empire that merely selfish things come
(40) second, even with the selfish; that appetites are starved, fears are conquered, pains supported; that almost the dullest shrinks from the reproof of a glance, although it were a child's; and all but the most cowardly stand amid the risks of
(45) war; and the more noble, having strongly conceived an act as due to their ideal, affront and embrace death. Strange enough if, with their singular origin and perverted practice, they think they are to be rewarded in some
(50) future life; stranger still, if they are persuaded of the contrary, and think this blow which they solicit will strike them senseless for eternity. I shall be reminded what a tragedy of miscon-ception and misconduct man at large
(55) presents,—of organized injustice, cowardly violence, and treacherous crime, and of the damning imperfections of the best. They cannot be too darkly drawn. Man is indeed marked for failure in his efforts to do right. But
(60) where the best consistently miscarry, how tenfold more remarkable that all should continue to strive; and surely we should find it both touching and inspiriting, that in a field from which success is banished, our race
(65) should not cease to labour [. . . .].

39. Which of the following BEST approximates the author's thesis?

   (A) That the "monstrous" nature of humanity precludes any attempt by humans to rise above it.
   (B) That the evil that humans do lives on in perpetuity while the good they accomplish is often forgotten.
   (C) That humanity's pervasive violence is driven by a consciousness of its fleeting existence.
   (D) That despite its barbarous heritage, humanity surprisingly continues to aspire to more noble practices.
   (E) That humanity's violent actions are justified by the greater social good that compels them.

40. The structure of the author's argument regarding the nature of man involves

   (A) utilizing an extended metaphor to provide internal unity
   (B) moving from a generalization about humanity to a specific human
   (C) establishing an initial impression and then debunking it
   (D) posing questions and subsequently answering them
   (E) identifying a cause and examining its effect

41. Which of the following descriptors is inconsistent with the author's opening comments about man?

   (A) blighted
   (B) treacherous
   (C) devouring
   (D) murderous
   (E) vain

42. The passage's opening sentence is marked by all of the following characteristics EXCEPT

   (A) an initial inversion that introduces the ignoble qualities of man
   (B) a parallel series of participial phrases
   (C) active and passive descriptions of human physical traits
   (D) a summative rhetorical question
   (E) a wry allusion to the Book of Genesis

43. Which of the following does NOT seemingly contribute to the author's labeling man a "Poor soul" (line 10)?

   (A) his inescapable mortality
   (B) his alienation in a hostile universe
   (C) his bestial origin and disposition
   (D) his compelling but fickle impulses
   (E) his tendency toward despondency

44. In the context in which it appears, the phrase, "irremediably condemned" (line 14), could plausibly be interpreted as which of the following?

   I. Remanded to the gallows.
   II. Incapable of reforming his characteristic barbarity.
   III. Forfeiting his chance at spiritual salvation.

   (A) I only
   (B) II only
   (C) I and III
   (D) II and III
   (E) I, II and III

45. In the context in which it appears, the BEST equivalent of the phrase, "of a piece with his destiny" (line 16), would be

   (A) conforming to
   (B) apart from
   (C) set against
   (D) troubled by
   (E) ignorant of

46. The tone of the words, "And we look and behold him [. . .] rearing with long-suffering solicitude his young" (lines 17-26), is BEST classified as being one of

   (A) scathing condemnation
   (B) begrudging wonder
   (C) puzzling inquiry
   (D) exasperated resignation
   (E) subdued sarcasm

47. The antecedent of the pronoun "it" in lines 35 and 37 is most persuasively argued to be

    (A) "mystery" (line 27)
    (B) "duty" (line 29)
    (C) "design" (line 33)
    (D) "conformity" (line 34)
    (E) "independence" (line 37)

48. The most "imperfect" of humanity's virtues might be considered its

    (A) tendency to be "infinitely childish" (lines 18-19)
    (B) willingness "to debate of right and wrong and the attributes of the deity [. . .]" (lines 21-22)
    (C) "rising up to do battle for an egg [. . .]" (lines 22-23)
    (D) "bringing forth in pain, rearing with long-suffering solicitude, his young" (lines 25-26)
    (E) "thought of something owing to himself, to his neighbour, to his God [. . .]" (lines 29-30)

49. The speaker's labeling man "a tragedy of misconception and misconduct" (lines 53-54) may be interpreted as which of the following?

    I. Humanity's failure to understand the immorality of its heritage of violence.
    II. Humanity's strange belief that its actions warrant salvation or damnation in some after-life.
    III. Humanity's "imperfect" design by its creator.

    (A) I only
    (B) III only
    (C) I and II
    (D) II and III
    (E) I, II and III

50. The phrase, "They cannot be too darkly drawn" (lines 57-58), suggests that humanity's legacy of evil

    (A) should not be unduly exaggerated
    (B) cannot be understated
    (C) should be categorically absolved
    (D) cannot be fairly presented by individuals ignorant of historical fact
    (E) will reap a still greater violence: their own damnation for eternity

51. The author's style in the passage is marked by all of the following EXCEPT

    (A) an impressive control of parallel syntax
    (B) a philosophical and reflective tone
    (C) diction that alternately deplores and marvels at the nature of the human
    (D) a disproportionate presentation of man's virtues and vices
    (E) a concluding sentence that implies the author's own part in the human struggle

Section II

Question One

(Suggested time—40 minutes. This question counts as one-third of the total essay section score.)

In the following passage a therapist reflects upon the problems manifested by adolescent girls. Read the passage carefully. Then, in a well-organized essay, identify the nature and source of these problems and discuss how the author uses elements of language to convey their potentially dire consequences.

Something dramatic happens to girls in early adolescence. Just as planes and ships disappear mysteriously into the Bermuda Triangle, so do the selves of girls go down in droves. They crash and burn in a social and developmental Bermuda Triangle. In early adolescence, studies show that girls' IQ scores drop and their math and science scores plummet. They lose
(5)   their resiliency and optimism and become less curious and inclined to take risks. They lose their assertive, energetic, and "tomboyish" personalities and become more deferential, self-critical and depressed. They report great unhappiness with their own bodies.

Psychology documents but does not explain the crashes. Girls who rushed to drink in experiences in enormous gulps sit quietly in the corner. Writers such as Sylvia Plath, Margaret
(10)   Atwood, and Olive Schreiner have described the wreckage. Diderot, in writing to his young friend Sophie Volland, described his observations harshly: "You all die at 15."

Fairy tales capture the essence of this phenomenon. Young women eat poisoned apples or prick their fingers with poisoned needles and fall asleep for a hundred years. They wander away from home, encounter great dangers, are rescued by princes and are transformed into passive
(15)   and docile creatures.

The story of Ophelia, from Shakespeare's *Hamlet*, shows the destructive forces that affect young women. As a girl, Ophelia is happy and free, but with adolescence she loses herself. When she falls in love with Hamlet, she lives only for his approval. She has no inner direction; rather she struggles to meet the demands of Hamlet and her father. Her value is determined utterly by
(20)   their approval. Ophelia is torn apart by her efforts to please. When Hamlet spurns her because she is an obedient daughter, she goes mad with grief. Dressed in elegant clothes that weigh her down, she drowns in a stream filled with flowers.

Girls know they are losing themselves. One girl said, "Everything good in me died in junior high." Wholeness is shattered by the chaos of adolescence. Girls become fragmented, their
(25)   selves split into mysterious contradictions. They are sensitive and tenderhearted, mean and competitive, superficial and idealistic. They are confident in the morning, and overwhelmed by anxiety by nightfall. They rush through their days with wild energy and then collapse into lethargy. They try on new roles every week—this week the good student, next week the delinquent and the next, the artist. And they expect their families to keep up with these changes.

(30)   My clients in early adolescence are elusive and slow to trust. They are easily offended by a glance, a clearing of the throat, a silence, a lack of sufficient enthusiasm or a sentence that doesn't meet their immediate needs. Their voices have gone underground—their speech is more tentative and less articulate. Their moods swing widely. One week they love their world and their families, the next day they are critical of everyone. Much of their behavior is unreadable. Their
(35)   problems are complicated and metaphorical—eating disorders, school phobias and self-inflicted injuries. I need to ask again and again in a dozen different ways, "What are you trying to tell me?" [. . . .].

"Saplings in the Storm", from REVIVING OPHELIA by Mary Pipher, Ph.D., Copyright © 1994 by Mary Pipher, Ph.D. Used by permission of G.P. Putnam's Sons, a division of Penguin Group (USA) Inc.

<u>Question Two</u>

(Suggested time—40 minutes. This question counts as one-third of the total essay section score.)

"There is no odor so bad as that which arises from goodness tainted."

Walden—Henry David Thoreau

Henry David Thoreau / *Walden* and *Civil Disobedience* / Copyright © 1960 / by Houghton Mifflin Company.

Consider the above statement. Then, write a well-organized essay in which you explore the meaning of Thoreau's statement using examples from your reading, experience, studies and/or observation to illustrate your interpretation.

Question Three

(Suggested time—55 minutes. This question counts as one-third of the total essay section score.)

Directions:

The following prompt is based on the accompanying six sources.

This question requires you to integrate a variety of sources into a coherent, well-written essay. *Refer to the sources to support your position; avoid paraphrase or summary. Your argument should be central; the sources should support this argument.*

Remember to attribute both direct and indirect citations.

Introduction:

The summer of 2005 saw widespread devastation wreaked on the city of New Orleans by Hurricane Katrina. The colorful, Mississippi Delta city, home to world-renowned restaurants, jazz and blues' clubs, and universities, saw many of its neighborhoods inundated, even washed away by flood waters that breached the barrier of its levees. The extent of this calamity has triggered fierce debate over how the city should be rebuilt in light of its population displacement, economic crisis, and continued below sea-level vulnerability. In fact, there are some who think that the potential for a similar disaster in the future begs the question whether the city should be rebuilt at all.

Assignment:

Peruse the following sources (including any introductory information) carefully. **Then, in an essay that synthesizes at least three of the sources for support, take a position that defends, challenges or qualifies the claim that the unique history of the city of New Orleans demands that it be returned to its former grandeur**.

(It is recommended that you spend 15-20 minutes of the allotted time examining the sources and devote the remaining time to writing your essay.)

Document A

Percy, William Alexander. *Lanterns on the Levee.* Baton Rouge: Louisiana State UP, 1968: 13-14.
(Note: originally published in 1941).

And the river? It is changed and eternally the same. The early settlers soon began to rebuff its yearly caress, that impregnated and vitalized the soil, by building small dikes around their individual plantations. This was a poor makeshift and in time, not without ruction and bitter debate, was abandoned in favor of levee districts which undertook to levee the river itself at the cost of the benefited landowners within the districts. After Reconstruction no more vital problem perplexed Delta statesmen than how to convince the Federal government of the propriety of contributing to the cost of building levees. At first they failed, but later niggardly aid was doled out—a bit some years, others none. Only within the last fifteen years has the government accepted the view urged for half-a-century by our people that the river's waters are our nation's waters and fighting them is the nation's fight. The United States Engineers under the War Department are now in full charge of levee and revetment work from one end of the river to the other.

But this work has not changed the savage nature and austere beauty of the river itself. Man draws near to it, fights it, uses it, curses it, loves it, but it remains remote, unaffected. Between the fairy willows of the banks or the green slopes of the levees it moves unhurried and unpausing; building islands one year to eat them the next; gnawing the bank on one shore till the levee caves in and another must be built farther back, then veering wantonly and attacking with equal savagery the opposite bank [. . . .]. The gods on their thrones are shaken and changed, but it abides, aloof and unappeasable, with no heart except for its own task, under the unbroken and immense arch of the lighted sky [. . . .].

Document B

Piazza, Tom. *Why New Orleans Matters*. New York: Regan Books, 2005: xviii-xix.

The past in New Orleans cohabits with the present to an extent not even approximated in any other North American city. Walking through the Tulane University campus, way uptown, you can see the old gymnasium where King Oliver's Creole Jazz band, with a young Louis Armstrong on cornet, played for dances. If you are adventuresome and you know where to go, you can find the houses of Jelly Roll Morton and Buddy Bolden, and Papa Jack Laine and the rest of the earliest generations of jazz musicians. In the French Quarter you can cut out of Jackson Square, ringed by the Pontalba Apartments, the oldest apartment building in North America, walk down narrow Pirate's Alley, where Jean Lafitte used to hang out, between St. Louis Cathedral on your right and the huge bulk of the Cabildo on your left, at one time the seat of Spanish government in the territory and the place where the Louisiana Purchase was signed, and half a block down encounter a great bookstore in the house where William Faulkner wrote his first novel, *Soldier's Pay*. A few blocks way, Tennessee Williams lived and wrote, amid scenes made famous by Walker Percy, George W. Cable, and other writers too numerous to mention.

These elements of New Orleans possess an astonishing vitality that has spoken to people around the world and shaped much of the best of what we think of still as American culture. Jazz music, rhythm and blues, and rock and roll, Creole cooking, Mardi Gras, the architecture of the French Quarter [. . . .]. It is not something that you find only in a tourist guide; it is a reality lived by its inhabitants every day, and as often as possible by those who love visiting [. . . .].

Document C

Harris, Bonnie and Jane Norman. "Rebuilding New Orleans: Iowans Join the Debate."
Online http://desmoinesregister.com/apps/pbcs.dll/article?AID=/20050909/NEWS 04/509090384/1006.

It will be put back together.

In shambles now, New Orleans will eventually be rebuilt, one way or another. Its history will once again inspire visitors, its ports will continue to be a pulse-point for commerce in Iowa and the rest of the country.

But will it be fixed so that the next huge hurricane doesn't blow away the billions of dollars' worth of work?

Those who know about such things—engineers, urban planners, politicians, scientists and economists—say they aren't sure.

"So much has to happen, so many things have to come together," said Craig Colten, a Louisiana State University geography professor and author of 'An Unnatural Metropolis: Wresting New Orleans From Nature.'

"Rebuilding here means so much more than walls and roofs and levees," he said.

There is no shortage of ideas on how to rebuild the city, even from people who have never been to New Orleans but feel, as many do now, that they know it. Few have been as blunt as Speaker of the House Dennis Hastert, the Illinois Republican who last week suggested that "a lot of that place could be bulldozed." He retreated amid scoldings.

Since then, some have proposed mass buyouts in the city's worst-hit areas, to be replaced with wetlands or green spaces. Others suggest building up those areas so that manufactured homes could be built and displaced residents could return. Many are calling for stricter building codes.

And, as always, attention has turned to strengthening and rebuilding the levee system, because, as Colten said, "that has always been the first resort. Policy is framed so that you respond to the last event." He noted that an Army Corps of Engineers spokesman told reporters this week that it could take the next 20 years to fortify the levees and flood walls against a Category 5 hurricane. Katrina was a Category 4.

Others say the soul of New Orleans cannot be ignored in the rebuilding efforts. Just as the city lives below the normal water level of the Mississippi River and Lake Pontchartrain, an alarming number of its residents—nearly one in three—live below the poverty level.

"Katrina, in just a few hours, managed to show us the New Orleans we'd been refusing to see," said Dave Schultz, director of Northwestern University's Infrastructure Technology Institute. "And that's how desperately poor most of the city really is" [. . . .].

Document D

Koterba, Jeff. "Eye to Eye." Daryl Cagle's Professional Cartoonists Index.
Online http://www.cagle.com/news/HurricaneKatrina/4.asp *Omaha World Herald*.

Jeff Koterba/*Omaha World Herald*

Document E

Campanella, Thomas J. "Recovering New Orleans." Online
http://architecture.about.com/gi/dynamic/offsite.htm?zi=1/XJ&sdn=architecture&
zu=http%3A%2F%2Fwww.planetizen.com%2Fnode%2F17448. 21 Sept 2005.

If history is any guide, there is little doubt this city will be rebuilt in some form. But will New Orleans be recovered as a real and robust metropolis? And whose New Orleans shall it be? Recovering a wrecked city involves much more than bricks, mortar and asphalt—or bits, bytes and electricity. As we pointed out in *The Resilient City*, it also "fundamentally entails reconnecting severed familial, social and religious networks of survivors. Urban recovery occurs network by network, district by district, not just building by building; it is about reconstructing the myriad social relations embedded in schools, workplaces, childcare arrangements, shops, places of worship, and places of play and recreation."

Public attention will undoubtedly be focused on the rehabilitation of iconic New Orleans—cleaning up Jackson Square and the Vieux Carré, replanting the palm trees on Canal Street, reopening the French Market and the convention center, perhaps building a new Superdome. But aside from some arson and looting, the New Orleans of the tourist and entertainment circuit made it through Katrina relatively unscathed. This New Orleans will rebound quickly and vigorously, and will even benefit from a surge of "sympathy tourism," much as New York did following 9/11. As Diane Davis put it in her chapter on Mexico City, post-disaster reconstruction follows "a logic of money and power." And in New Orleans tourism is big money, a backbone of the local economy.

It's altogether another story for the "other" New Orleans, the city far from the beaten tourist track, the city of the Lower Ninth Ward, Treme and Bywater and other communities inundated by Pontchartrain's floodwaters. The residents of these places may have been poor, but they were an essential part of the Crescent City's extraordinary tapestry of cultural life and traditions. They made New Orleans what it was, and were as much part of the soul of the place as the gracious homes of the Garden District or the Mississippi River itself. Moreover, to take a more harshly pragmatic tack, they were also the folks who cooked and cleaned and served all the tourists and conventioneers that the local economy is so dependent upon. If New Orleans is to become again a robust and authentic place, these former residents must be welcomed back and accommodated as enthusiastically as might new corporate investors, real estate developers or Mardi Gras revelers [. . . .].

Document F

Shafter, Jack. "Don't Refloat: The Case Against Rebuilding the Sunken City of New Orleans." Online http://www.slate.com/?id=2125810&nav=tap1/. 7 Sept 2005.

The city's romance is not the reality for most who live there. It's a poor place, with about 27 percent of the population of 484,000 living under the poverty line, and it's a black place, where 67 percent are African-American. In 65 percent of families living in poverty, no husband is present [. . . .].

New Orleans' public schools which are 93 percent black, have failed their citizens. The state of Louisiana rates 47 percent of New Orleans schools as "Academically Unacceptable" and another 26 percent are under "Academic Warning." About 25 percent of adults have no high-school diploma.

The police inspire so little trust that witnesses often refuse to testify in court. University researchers enlisted the police in an experiment last year, having them fire 700 blank gun rounds in a New Orleans neighborhood one afternoon. Nobody picked up the phone to report the shootings. Little wonder the city's homicide rate stands at 10 times the national average [. . . .].

New Orleans puts the "D" into dysfunctional. Only a sadist would insist on resurrecting this concentration of poverty, crime, and deplorable schools. Yet that's what New Orleans' cheerleaders—both natives and beignet-eating tourists—are advocating. They predict that once they drain the water and scrub the city clean, they'll restore New Orleans to its former "glory" [. . . .].

love the Great *quotes*

Sample Examination One: Explications and Answers

Explication of Passage One: From Frederick Douglass' Letter to His Former Master, Captain Thomas Auld, published in the *North Star* on September 8, 1868.

Exorcising a traumatic experience can be a painful but necessary part of the process of healing and recovery. Whether it be a rape victim confronting her abuser in court or an inmate testifying against war crimes in a tribunal, many individuals feel a need for personal confrontation with the agent of their suffering.

In the public letter written to his former master, Captain Thomas Auld, Frederick Douglass confronts the individual responsible for his enslavement. Written on the ten-year anniversary of his successful escape from bondage, Douglass endeavors to educate his master as to the immorality of his actions. In a civil but forceful manner, Douglass exercises his right to engage his master as an equal in the public forum of a newspaper. In so doing, Douglass is aware of the "disagreeable surprise" which his master may experience upon seeing their names again joined in "any other way than in an advertisement, accurately describing [Douglass'] person, and offering a large sum for [Douglass'] arrest" (lines 8-13). He expresses his understanding that slaveholders, "who, while they have no scruples of robbing the laborer of the hard earned results of his patient industry," will nevertheless be "shocked by the extremely indelicate manner of bringing [his master's] name before the public" (lines 24-29). He thus articulates his rationale for doing so.

The remainder of Douglass' letter provides a carefully crafted defense of both his escape from enslavement and his decision to address his master in public. Through an analogy equating his master with "a man guilty of theft, robbery, or murder, [who] has forfeited the right to concealment and private life [. . .]" (lines 36-38), Douglass defends his right to ferret his master out and "bring [his] conduct before the proper tribunals of the country for investigation" (lines 45-46). Flashing back to the actual day of his flight, an escape carried out somewhat brazenly during the day, Douglass recalls the tremendous cauldron of emotions which he experienced on the morning of his imminent escape; how his hope and exhilaration "were powerfully confronted at this last hour by dark clouds of doubt and fear, making [his] person shake and [his] bosom to heave with the heavy contest [. . .]" (lines 63-66). Douglass' daylight escape attempt, an ironically Kierkegaardian "leap in the dark" (lines 70-71), was further complicated by the abandonment of an accomplice who "appalled by fear at the trial hour, deserted [him] [. . .]" (lines 79-80). The less than promising odds prompt Douglass' appropriate simile, "I was like one going to war without weapons—ten chances of defeat to one of victory" (lines 75-77).

Though Douglass' letter surprisingly does not catalog the sufferings he experienced as a slave (something much more prominent in his *Autobiography*), it does effectively convey the oppressive, almost paralyzing anxiety that he experiences as a fugitive. His final lines—"You, sir, can never know my feelings. As I look back to them, I can scarcely realize that I have passed through a scene so trying [. . . .]" (lines 82-85)—reflect both the courage it took for Douglass to express these sentiments directly to his former master but also the sad acknowledgment that Captain Auld, like all oppressors, can never himself comprehend the deep harm he has inflicted upon his victim.

1. In the opening sentence of his letter to his former master, Douglass does which of the following? **(C) understates the nature and condition of their previous relation**.

   By using the words "long and intimate" to describe their relation, Douglass employs ironical understatement to depict the master-slave relation that they actually shared. Even the qualifier "though by no means friendly" fails to hint at the long enslavement he suffered at the hands of his master. This is perhaps intentionally done to establish them as equals.

2. In describing the potential effects of his correspondence, Douglass does all of the following EXCEPT **(E) confidently anticipate his former master's viewing him in a more sympathetic light**.

   That Douglass admits that by "dragging [his master] again before the public" he will "subject [him]self to no inconsiderable amount of censure" (lines 13-16) confirms choice A. That he envisions his master's "disagreeable surprise" at seeing their names coupled "in any other way than in an advertisement, accurately describing [his] person, and offering a large sum for [his] arrest" (lines 10-13) validates B. In a more metaphorical sense, the phrase "dragging you again before the public" (lines 13-14) echoes the chagrin that Douglass himself must have felt in the slave market, confirming C, while his observation that he shall "probably be charged with an unwarrantable, if not wanton and reckless disregard of the properties of private life" (lines 16-19) validates D. This leaves E as the exception.

3. By the phrase "rights that are merely conventional [. . .]" (lines 21-22), Douglass is referring to the **(C) rights protecting his master's privacy**.

   The "conventional" rights to which Douglass alludes are the antithesis of those that are "personal and essential." Since conventions are social customs, and since Douglass has already indicated that he would likely be censured for dragging his master's name through the mud in the public forum of a newspaper, C seems the most logical selection.

4. The essential implication about those individuals "who entertain a much higher respect for rights that are merely conventional [. . .]" (lines 20-22) is that they are **(D) hypocritical**.

   The choice of D as the answer is supported partly by the explication of the previous question and also by the double standard suggested by lines 23-29, "Not a few there are in our country, who, while they have no scruples of robbing the laborer of the hard earned results of his patient industry, will be shocked by the extremely indelicate manner of bringing your name before the public." Though a generalization, this seems an appropriate indictment of those slaveholders who have made their fortune from the cotton picked by slave laborers.

5. In lines 35-46, "All will agree [. . . .] for investigation," Douglass does all of the following EXCEPT **(C) levy specific charges against his former master**.

Douglass' opening affirmation that "All will agree that a man guilty of theft, robbery, or murder, has forfeited the right to concealment and private life" supports both A and B, while his claim that "the public have a right to ferret them out, and bring their conduct before the proper tribunals of the country for investigation" confirms D and E, leaving choice C as the exception.

6. Douglass' argument for exposing his master's reprehensible conduct (lines 29-50) is founded upon **(D) analogy**.

The choice of D is supported by the comparison of Douglass' master, who has stolen both his freedom and the productive years of his life, to "a man guilty of theft, robbery, or murder [. . .]" (lines 36-37).

7. In the second paragraph Douglass suggests that the imminent nature of his escape triggered antithetical feelings of **(A) anticipation and apprehension**.

Douglass' recollection in lines 60-64, that "The hopes which [he] had treasured up for weeks of a safe and successful escape from [his master's] grasp, were powerfully confronted at this last hour by dark clouds of doubt and fear [. . .]," is sufficient to make A the best choice.

8. Douglass' "lamenting that [he] was a man, and wishing [him]self a brute" (lines 59-60) was likely motivated by a(n) **(B) acute consciousness of the degradation of his enslavement**.

In line 58 Douglass refers to himself as "a poor degraded chattel," or an abused possession. The choice of the word "chattel" suggests such a degree of dehumanization or depersonalization that his wishing he was an insensate brute is quite understandable.

9. Douglass uses the phrase "treasured up" (line 61) to convey which of the following?

    I. The rarity of a successful escape from bondage.
    II. The extent to which the dream of escape sustained him.
    III. The duration of his clandestine planning.

(D) II and III

The phrase "treasured up" connotes both accumulation and value. That he has been doing this "for weeks" suggests both the length of his planning (III) and the fact that this imminent escape kept him going (II); thus, the selection of D as the answer.

10. The "one" mentioned in lines 77 and 78 is most likely **(C) a fellow slave**.

Though an indefinite pronoun, the "one" in these two lines may be identified as a fellow slave by Douglass' use of the words "confided" and "promised me assistance." In addition, the phrase "appalled by fear at the trial hour, deserted me" (lines 79-80) suggests that Douglass had an accomplice who elected at the last second not to go.

11. Which of the following is NOT characteristic of the author's style? **(D) a highly imagistic depiction of the sufferings of enslavement**.

As has been suggested in the explication of questions #5 and #6, Douglas draws an analogous connection between his master and a criminal, supporting A. Douglass' public letter to his master in the newspaper indicts him as a criminal but never descends into impolitic invective, even addressing him as "Sir" throughout. This confirms choice B. The simile, "I was like one going to war without weapons—ten chances of defeat to one of victory" (lines 75-77), validates C, while the "dark clouds of doubt and fear" (line 64) that confront him on the threshold of his escape support E. There is no imagistic catalog of Douglass' suffering in the passage.

12. The author juxtaposes his bold daytime escape with which of the following *figurative* expressions?

    I. The "dark clouds of doubt and fear" (line 64) that shook his resolve.
    II. The "leap in the dark" (lines 70-71) that he made in striking out for the North.
    III. The vulnerable feeling he experienced of "going to war without weapons" (lines 75-76).

(C) I and II.

I and II, by virtue of their mention of the dark, are antithetical to the "beautiful September morning" on which Douglass escapes.

13. Overall, Douglass' letter is BEST classified as a(n) **(E) measured verbalization of his master's culpability for his physical and psychological suffering**.

The fact that Douglass condemns his master's actions, not his character, rules out the possibility of an *ad hominem* attack. Though Douglass sends the letter on the tenth anniversary of his liberation, and though his publication of it in the newspaper may, in a sense, be viewed as defiant, he does not speak to his master in a gloating way, but in a reflective, intellectual manner, laying out the reasons for his escape and the legitimacy of them. This elevates E over choices A and B as the best answer.

Explication of Passage Two: From Sandra M. Gilbert's and Susan Gubar's *The Madwoman in the Attic*

This passage, from a seminal text of feminist literary criticism, begins with a tantalizing trio of epigraphs that hint at the chapter discussion to follow. The first, from Plato's *Republic*, features the introductory lines from the famous "Allegory of the Cave," in which prisoners in an underground cavern can see only shadows of the world above that are cast in silhouette against a rock wall. The resulting distortion in shape and size makes it impossible to distinguish illusion from reality. The second, from a poem by Victorian poetess Christina Rossetti, features an *ubi sunt* theme, a lamentation over songs and notes that have been forgotten. The third and most expansive of the three is from the writings of 17th century mystic Jane Lead and recounts her vision of a beatific figure she calls "God's Eternal Virgin-Wisdom," who appears to her in much the same fashion as the angels appear to Sarah and Mary in the Old and New Testaments. This visitation, however, does not announce an unexpected conception but implies that the recipient herself will be illuminated and born again.

Beginning with the author's allusion to Freud's observation of the similarities between a cave and the female anatomy—"a female place, a womb-shaped enclosure, a house of earth, secret and often sacred" (lines 3-5)—and wandering through a seemingly random collection of female images of the virgin sacrificed, the oracle priestess alone in her cave, and Madeline Usher prematurely entombed, this erudite and highly allusive text gradually crystallizes itself into a symbolic statement about "the plight of the woman in patriarchal culture [. . .]" (lines 20-21). The common threads between the various images are confinement, burial, immurement and suffocation, leading to the intimation that this has been women's lot over the ages.

The concluding anecdote, from twentieth century feminist Simone de Beauvoir, offers a striking real-life parallel to the epigraph from Plato. Her recollection of a "subterranean cavern" (line 32) that she once visited in Tunisia invokes disturbing images of poverty, premature aging, disease, and arduous domestic toil, all carried out by women of different generations. The sole male depicted in the anecdote is said to be "dressed in white, well-groomed, smiling, sunny [who] was returning from the marketplace, where he had discussed world affairs with other men [. . .]" (lines 45-48). She adds that he would "pass some hours in this retreat of his at the heart of the vast universe to which he belonged, from which he was not separated" (lines 49-52). The symbolic implication—that men have free roam of the world of commerce and enlightenment, and women have been banished to an underworld of domesticity and ignorance—is clear, as is the bleak fact that this exile is a permanent one.

The excerpt, couched within a study of nineteenth-century women writers, offers a challenging but accessible insight into the oppressed social status of women throughout all time. Its concluding statement, that "there was no universe other than the smoky cave, whence they emerged, only at night, silent and veiled [. . . .]" (lines 54-56), offers its own resonances in the contemporary age and depicts the plight of women as existential—creatures abandoned in an absurd, unfair and patriarchal universe in which their only choices are to cook dough, nurse infants, or weave clothing—that is, until they liberate their selves, their souls, and their minds.

14. The trio of complementary epigraphs that precede the passage does all of the following EXCEPT **(E) suggest that some women repress the unpleasant experiences of their pasts**.

Choice A is validated by the first epigraph from Plato's *Republic*, choice B by the speaker in the second epigraph who laments forgotten songs and notes and suggests she has "forgotten everything." Epigraph three validates choices C and D through the visitation of the mystical Virgin-Wisdom who will bring about the rebirth of the speaker, and through the allusions to Rebecca and Mary, the mother of Jesus. There is no defense for choice E in the passage.

15. Taken together, the trio of epigraphs that precede the passage serves to **(C) presage the author's articulation of the state of women in a male-dominated culture**.

The initial portrait of the ignorant, subterranean cave-dwellers in Plato's famous allegory, the *ubi sunt* (literally, "where are they?") sentiment of the speaker in Rossetti's poem, and the mystical figure of Virgin-Wisdom which descends to illuminate the speaker anticipate the author's discussion of the state of women in a patriarchal culture. Gilbert's and Gubar's argument uses the symbol of the cave to suggest the darkened and confined lot of the nineteenth century woman, "the woman whose cave-shaped anatomy is her destiny" (lines 21-22). The relation between cave and womb (as well as cave and tomb) suggests that men have entombed women in a maternal and domestic existence in which child-bearing, cooking, and weaving are the staples of their existence, from cradle to grave. The Tunisian experience recounted by Simone de Beauvoir provides a more contemporary example of the plight of women.

16. The arrangement of the three epigraphs suggests that women need to progress through which sequence of stages? **(C) ignorance—questioning—enlightenment**.

This is consistent with the explication of question #16. The Platonic world suggests the tenebrous world of ignorance, the poetic stanza from Rossetti the first stirrings of feminine consciousness, and the appearance of the Virgin-Wisdom in Jane Lead's vision the need for a moment of revelation and enlightenment.

17. The third epigraph and footnote are primarily intended to establish a connection between **(A) spirituality and self-actualization**.

The mystical vision of the Virgin-Wisdom calls to mind the various "annunciations" in the Bible, in which heavenly angels reveal themselves to women in order to convey important news. This vision, richly bedecked in gold and characterized by an insufferable brightness, suggests that out of the speaker's womb shall be brought a "Spirit, Conceived and Born Again." This suggests that women must reinvent themselves through their own efforts.

18. Which of the following is LEAST drawn upon by the authors in developing their argument? **(C) history**.

    The authors' allusions to Freud confirms A, their allusion to Plato and Simone de Beauvoir validate B. The references to Poe's "The Fall of the House of Usher" and Mary Shelley's *Frankenstein* support D, while the allusion to Jane Lead in the third epigraph backs E. Other than an oblique reference to the Victorian Age, the author does not draw upon history.

19. Throughout the course of their argument, the authors *figuratively* depict the cave as a(n) **(E) tomb for the aspirations of women**.

    Each of the four other choices—the womb, the prison, the bat cavern and the sanctuary—are treated literally. In figurative terms, however, women are seen as living in "the 'grave-cave' of immanence" (lines 25-26), essentially locked into their maternal and domestic roles for life.

20. By the words, "To this shrine the initiate comes to hear the voices of darkness, the wisdom of inwardness" (lines 5-7), the authors imply which of the following? **(B) That the path to empowerment begins with introspection**.

    Here the "voices of darkness, the wisdom of inwardness" suggest something that comes from inside and is a product of self-reflection and introspection. Like the prisoners in Plato's cave, before women can change their lot they must become conscious of it.

21. Lines 17-27—"But despite its melodrama [. . . .] a vaporous Cave of Spleen"—suggest all of the following EXCEPT **(E) the plight of women was a major concern of Edgar Allen Poe**.

    Lines 21-22 suggest that a "cave-shaped anatomy is [woman's] destiny," clearly alluding to the womb, her reproductive organ: this confirms choices A and D. The reference to a "vaporous Cave of Spleen" suggests that their experience has embittered them, while the authors' observation that women are not only prisoners of Nature but of their own nature suggests they are worse off than their Platonic counterparts. These facts confirm B and C. There is no basis for choice E in the passage.

22. What likely motivates the authors to label the anecdote of Simone de Beauvoir (lines 31-56) a "counter-parable" is its **(E) feminist bent**.

    Unlike Plato's allegory which broadly examines the human condition, Simone de Beauvoir's anecdote functions much more along gender lines. The Tunisian women, regardless of their generation, are all engaged in domestic tasks: cooking, nursing, weaving. Moreover, they are described as "toothless" (line 34), "disfigured" (line 37), and "withered" (line 52), and the clear intimation is that these conditions are the consequence of their lives as permanent denizens of this "gloomy cave-kingdom" (lines 42). The sole male depicted is "dressed in white, well-groomed, smiling and sunny" (lines 45-46), afforded the liberty of abandoning the Stygian cave for the enlightened world above, where he can discuss world affairs with other men. Like his male peers, he has a "retreat" (line 49), a place far distant from this "smoky cave" (line 55). This anecdote clearly captures the plight of women in a patriarchal culture; hence, the selection of E as the best answer.

23. The authors imply that the aging and physical disfigurement of the Tunisian cave-dwellers is a consequence of their **(D) inalterable domestic lot**.

This is consistent with the explication of the previous question. As de Beauvoir concludes. "For the withered old women, for the young wife doomed to the same rapid decay, there was no universe other than the smoky cave, whence they emerged, only at night, silent and veiled [. . . .]" (lines 52-56). The final images, of the women's voiceless and veiled nocturnal emergence, offer a cruel satirical commentary on the universal lot of women who have been muted, masked and kept in subordinate ignorance by males.

24. Which of the following contribute(s) to the passage's concluding irony?

  I. The common fate shared by the withered old woman and the young wife.
  II. The smoky nature of the cave.
  III. The time and nature of the women's sole emergence from their subterranean abode.

(C) I and III.

Choice C is the preference here because both women, young and old, suffer the same unfortunate fate, and because the sole moment of their liberation occurs not in the enlightened day but in the veiled and ignorant dark.

25. The most defining aspect of the passage is the author's **(B) multiplicity of allusions**.

From the philosophical, poetic and mystical epigraphs, to the literary references to Shelley and Poe, to the references to Freud and Simone de Beauvoir, the passage is replete with allusion, the preponderance of which leads to the choice of B as the answer.

Explication of Passage Three: From E.B. White's "The Ring of Time"

E.B. White's oft-anthologized essay offers an interesting counterpoint to the other passages in sample exam I in its poignant reminiscence of a circus experience. The inaugural baseball game, the first visit to an amusement park, and the initial introduction to the colorful world of clowns, animals and the Big Top often make indelible marks upon the young, and though the speaker here seems older, the ephemeral ride of the young rider nevertheless strikes a pensive and profound chord in him. Much as the compass in John Donne's "A Valediction Forbidding Mourning" completes the perfect geometrical circle, the young girl's circuit about the ring is a symbol of perfection, freezing like Keats' urn the unvarnished beauty of circus and youth in a perfect ten-minute moment.

Labeling himself a "recording secretary for one of the oldest of societies—the society of those who, at one time or another, have surrendered, without even a show of resistance, to the bedazzlement of a circus rider" (lines 2-7), the author relates how, like the order of the Genesis world emerging out of Chaos, the spectacle that is the circus too emerges out of a "wild disorder" (line 19) and a "gaudy dream" (line 34). As in all other performing arts, the rehearsal is not the performance but a prelude to or progress towards it. Thus, there is nothing jaw-dropping or polished about the girl's warm-up; rather, as the author relates,

> Her brief tour included only elementary postures and tricks, perhaps because they were all she was capable of, perhaps because her warmup at this hour was unscheduled and the ring was not rigged for a real practice session. She swung herself off and on the horse several times, gripping his mane. She did a few knee-stands—or whatever they are called—dropping to her knees and quickly bouncing back up on her feet again. Most of the time she simply rode in a standing position [. . .]" (lines 46-58).

Still, despite these simple executions the author reveals that the young rider "achieved [. . .] the thing that is sought by performers everywhere, on whatever stage, whether struggling in the tidal currents of Shakespeare or bucking the difficult motion of a horse" (lines 36-41). What he seems to be referring to is that idyllic moment of immersion and concentration in which the performer becomes so lost in the refinement of her craft as to be oblivious to the audience around her. As the author relates,

> The richness of the scene was in its plainness, its natural condition—of horse, of ring, of girl, even to the girl's bare feet that gripped the bare back of her proud and ridiculous mount. The enchantment grew not out of anything that happened or was performed but out of something that seemed to go round and around with the girl, attending her, a steady gleam in the shape of a circle—a ring of ambition, of happiness, of youth [. . . .] (lines 80-90).

For the author and the other onlookers, the circular motion weaves its own enchantment, and they become captivated by her youth and innocence and undaunted ambition. However, as Frost sagely reminds, "Nothing gold can stay," and the author comes to the somber realization that "In a week or two, all would be changed, all (or almost all) lost: the girl would wear makeup, the horse would wear gold, the ring would be painted, the bark would be clean for the feet of the horse, the girl's feet would be clean for the slippers that she'd wear. All, all would be lost [. . . .]" (lines 90-97).

Ultimately, the essay seems to be about evanescence, about the fading away of all things: youth, beauty, childhood experience. That the girl will wear makeup suggests already the painted face of adolescence, designed to allure. That the ring and the horse would both be decorated suggests, too, the need for a facade. The world of childhood is like Prufrock's kingdom under the sea—a charming, fantastic, mermaid world—"until human voices wake us and we drown." The milling crowd, the raucous barker, the ubiquitous sound of the calliope, they provide the "bedazzlement" of the professional circus performance, but the author of the passage longs for the unvarnished perfection of the practice, the audition, of performance for performance's sake, not for the applause or the paycheck. Unfortunately— or perhaps fortunately, depending upon one's perspective—that pristine moment can only be retained in his mind. The words of Keats' "Ode on a Grecian Urn" again seem most appropriate:

> Bold Lover, never, never canst thou kiss,
> Though winning near the goal—yet do not grieve;
> She cannot fade, though thou hast not thy bliss,
> For ever wilt thou love, and she be fair.

26. Of the following, which BEST represents the speaker's impression of the circus as expressed by the opening paragraph? **(E) That it is an amalgam of contradictions that inexplicably fuse into compelling entertainment**.

Lines 19-22, "Out of its wild disorder comes order; from its rank smell rises the good aroma of courage and daring; out of its preliminary shabbiness comes the final splendor," convey how these polar opposites somehow magically transform by opening night into the "gaudy dream" that is the circus.

27. The primary purpose of the opening sentence is to **(C) convey the indelible effect the circus has upon its audience**.

The key component of this sentence is the speaker's admission that he is part of a universal community that "at one time or another, have surrendered, without even a show of resistance, to the bedazzlement of a circus rider" (lines 4-7). The fact that this is being told in retrospect confirms the permanence of the circus' impact upon the speaker.

28. The speaker perceives the routine of the young girl as **(A) epitomizing the practice of artistic refinement**.

The speaker makes the observation that "The ten minute ride the girl took achieved [. . .] the thing that is sought by performers everywhere, on whatever stage, whether struggling in the tidal currents of Shakespeare or bucking the difficult motion of a horse" (lines 35-41). In these lines he links the young girl with all performers who work to develop their craft.

29. The characterization and subsequent actions of the young rider stress her **(C) agility and concentration**.

The description of the young rider illustrates how she "swung herself off and on the horse several times, gripping his mane" (lines 52-53), how she executed a few "knee-stands" (lines 54), and how she "rode in a standing position, well aft on the beast, her hands hanging easily at her sides [. . .] " (lines 57-59). The author also describes how "Twice she managed a one-foot stance—a sort of ballet pose, with arms outstretched" (lines 63-64). Choice C captures these movements best.

30. Which of the following would be an inappropriate substitution for the word "tour" in line 46? **(D) inspection**.

The word "tour," in the context in which it appears, means "a trip around the riding ring." Choices A, B, C and E all capture this in one shape or form, leaving D as the exception.

31. The young girl's reaction to the broken strap (lines 65-68) is BEST described as **(A) nonplussed**.

When the strap of her bathing suit snaps, the young girl displays no signs of panic. Rather, the author notes how she "went twice around the ring in the classic attitude of a woman making minor repairs to a garment" (lines 66-68). This is best represented by choice A, which means "unbothered."

32. All of the following abet the sense of loss experienced by the author in the final paragraph EXCEPT **(C) the archetypal symbol of the circle**.

The speaker's observation in lines 90-91 that "In a week or two, all would be changed, all (or almost all) lost [. . .]" confirms A, while the changes in descriptive detail cataloged in lines 92-96—"the girl would wear makeup, the horse would wear gold, the ring would be painted, the bark would be clean for the feet of the horse, the girl's feet would be clean for the slippers that she'd wear"—provide evidence for choice B. The series of parallel clauses, each a simple declarative sentence that depicts the changes that would take place before the actual performance, also supports D, while the phrase that closes the excerpt, "All, all would be lost [. . . .]" (lines 96-97), verifies E. The symbol of the circle, and its geometric associations with perfection, do not contribute to this sense of loss but rather reaffirm the exceptional nature of the moment.

33. The "all" that the author mentions in the final paragraph refers to which of the following?

   I. The unvarnished image of horse and rider.
  II. An ephemeral symbol of perfection that will not endure.
 III. The moment when one catches the circus "unawares."

(E) I, II and III

The speaker makes it clear in lines 80-84 that "The richness of the scene was in its plainness, its natural condition—of horse, of ring, of girl, even to the girl's bare feet that gripped the bare back of her proud and ridiculous mount." This, coupled with his observation that "her warmup at this hour was unscheduled and the ring was not rigged for a real practice session" (lines 49-52), supports both I and III. His subsequent comment that "The enchantment grew not out of anything that happened or was performed but out of something that seemed to go round and around with the girl, attending her, a steady gleam in the shape of a circle—a ring of ambition, of happiness, of youth [. . . .]" (lines 84-90), provides ample defense for II. This makes E the correct choice.

34. The "enchantment" of the author's experience is *symbolically* reinforced by the **(D) circular cantering of horse and rider**.

Much as the witches circle about their cauldron nine times in *Macbeth* until their "charm's wound up," so the circular motion of the young horse and rider weaves its spell upon the speaker. As he notes in the final paragraph, "The enchantment grew not out of anything that happened or was performed but out of something that seemed to go round and around with the girl, attending her, a steady gleam in the shape of a circle—a ring of ambition, of happiness, of youth [. . . .]" (lines 84-90).

35. In the third paragraph the speaker's attitude shifts from **(C) captivated to regretful**.

In the second paragraph the focus of the speaker is upon the action in the practice ring, and the speaker is mesmerized by the acrobatics that the young girl performs while on horseback. However, in paragraph three the author begins to rue the fact that the unvarnished routine of the young girl would soon vanish, replaced by the more polished, public version. Everything—girl, horse ring, bark—would assume a different identity, and the innocent, natural condition would be lost. Choice C captures this shift in attitude most effectively.

36. The author uses either simile or metaphor to convey each of the following EXCEPT **(D) the standing maneuvers of the young equestrian**.

Choice A is confirmed by lines 26-28, "It is at its best at certain moments when it comes to a point, as through a burning glass [. . .]." Choice B is supported by the implied metaphor in line 40, "tidal currents of Shakespeare." Choice C gets support from the implied metaphor in line 45, "to hone the blade of their talent," choice E by lines 66-68, "she went twice around the ring in the classic attitude of a woman making minor repairs to a garment." This leaves D as the exception.

37. In light of the entire passage, the speaker likely uses the term "gaudy dream" (line 34) to reflect which of the following dichotomies of the circus?

   I. Its "preliminary shabbiness" and its "final splendor."
  II. The warm-up session of the young rider and her actual performance.
 III. The impact of the circus on a youth and on an adult.

(C) I and II

This virtually oxymoronic phrase echoes the speaker's earlier observations about how the circus emerges from disorder into order, from shabbiness into splendor. His fascination with the pre-performance warm-up of the young rider is also in concert with this theme. The phrase, "gaudy dream," itself connotes both the love of the stage, spotlight and audience that drives all performers, and also the facade that is applied to both performer and space before the actual performance. The words in choice C fits this best.

38. The author's overall attitude is BEST characterized as that of a(n) **(D) passionate advocate**.

The author's description of himself as the "recording secretary" of this society shows that he is an advocate of the circus. Similarly, his repeated use of diction having to do with magic—"bedazzlement" (line 7), "magic" (line 18), "enchantment" (line 84)—suggests that he views the experience in an extremely positive light and wishes to convey that enthusiastically to his audience.

Explication of Passage Four: From Robert Louis Stevenson's *Pulvis Et Umbra*

The concluding passage in examination one is drawn from a Robert Louis Stevenson essay, *Pulvis et Umbra*, a Latin phrase from a Horatian ode meaning "dust and shadow." Thus, it is unsurprising that Stevenson's essay is a meditation on the nature of man and his finitude. Beginning with the opening lines in which man is sequentially labeled a "monstrous spectre" (line 1) and a "disease of the agglutinated dust" (line 2), the depiction of man is hardly flattering. Unlike Shakespeare, who in *Hamlet* decrees him "paragon of the animals," Stevenson portrays man at his most bestial: slumbering, feeding, growing, copulating. Even the hair growing like grass upon his face recalls his dust-to-dust destiny (and a line from Whitman's *Leaves of Grass*, "the beautiful uncut hair of graves"). To Stevenson man is a piteous, ephemeral creature—"Poor soul, here for so little, cast among so many hardships, filled with desires so incommensurate and so inconsistent, savagely surrounded, savagely descended, irremediably condemned to prey upon his fellow lives" (lines 10-15)—one whose sapient thought is incongruous with his primal origins.

Yet despite these fallibilities, there is something mysterious and noble about him, what Stevenson labels his "imperfect virtues" (line 18):

> infinitely childish, often admirably valiant, often touchingly kind; sitting down, amidst his momentary life, to debate of right and wrong and the attributes of the deity; rising up to do battle for an egg or die for an idea; singling out his friends and his mate with cordial affection; bringing forth in pain, rearing with long-suffering solicitude his young (lines 18-26).

This mystery Stevenson identifies as his "thought of duty; the thought of something owing to himself, to his neighbour, to his God: an ideal of decency, to which he would rise if it were possible; a limit of shame, below which, if it be possible, he will not stoop" (lines 29-33). It is this ironic, almost absurd, sense that Stevenson believes motivates the parent, the hero, and the martyr to give himself up in selfless sacrifice, sometimes even to death. To the author, man remains a paradox, something he on one hand laments as a "tragedy of misconception and misconduct" (lines 53-54), and on the other admires for his unwillingness to yield in total to his baser instincts. So evil can man be that Stevenson remarks that man "cannot be too darkly drawn" (lines 57-58). Yet though he may be capable of "organized injustice, cowardly violence, and treacherous crime, and of the damning imperfections of the best" (lines 55-57), and though he seems "marked for failure in his efforts to do right" (lines 58-59), he continues to strive to act correctly even in the face of egregious failure. In a candid admission of his own fallibility, Stevenson subtly shifts in his final sentence to the collective pronouns "we" and "our." His final observation in lines 58-65 recalls similarly uplifting words uttered by William Faulkner in his Nobel Prize speech:

> I decline to accept the end of man. It is easy enough to say that man is immortal simply because he will endure: that when the last ding-dong of doom has clanged and faded from the last worthless rock hanging tideless in the last red and dying evening, that even then there will still be one more sound: that of his puny inexhaustible voice still talking. I refuse to accept this. I believe that man will not merely endure; he will prevail [. . . .].

Stevenson, like Shakespeare, Faulkner and Thomas Wolfe to name three, ponders the mystery of man, and in this initially depressing piece finds in his remarkable persistence and resilience reasons to believe in him. Though his body seems undeniably immanent, his soul suggests a yearning for transcendence. And though the potential for such a flawed creature's being rewarded in an afterlife after such "perverted practice" (line 48) seems remote, there seems to the author something noble "that in a field from which success is banished, our race should not cease to labour [. . . .]" (lines 63-65).

39. Which of the following BEST approximates the author's thesis? **(D) That despite its barbarous heritage, humanity surprisingly continues to aspire to more noble practices**.

Despite his catalog of the shortcomings and imperfections of the human race, the author nevertheless observes in lines 8-10, "and yet looked at nearlier, known as his fellows know him, how surprising are his attributes!" His description of a being "[. . .] filled with desires so incommensurate and so inconsistent, savagely surrounded, savagely descended, irremediably condemned to prey upon his fellow lives" (lines 11-15) is countered by his later observation that "Man is indeed marked for failure in his efforts to do right. But where the best consistently miscarry, how tenfold more remarkable that all should continue to strive; and surely we should find it both touching and inspiriting, that in a field from which success is banished, our race should not cease to labour [. . . .]" (lines 58-65). This is best matched by choice D.

40. The structure of the author's argument regarding the nature of man involves **(C) establishing an initial impression and then debunking it**.

This is consistent with the explication of question #39. The author first paints man as a barbarous creature, then finds in him ennobling characteristics that contradict this perception and suggests that, despite his imperfections and mortality, man struggles towards some ideal or salvation.

41. Which of the following descriptors is inconsistent with the author's opening comments about man? **(B) treacherous**.

Man is characterized as a "disease of the agglutinated dust" (line 2), who feeds and grows (line 4), is "irremediably condemned to prey upon his fellow lives" (lines 14-15), and who "bring[s] forth small copies of himself" (lines 4-5). This information confirms choices A, C, D, and E, leaving B as the exception.

42. The passage's opening sentence is marked by all of the following characteristics EXCEPT **(D) a summative rhetorical question**.

Inversion is evident in the author's opening statement, "What a monstrous spectre is this man [. . .]" (line 1); parallel participial constructions and active and passive descriptions of his traits in lines 2-7, "lifting alternate feet or lying drugged with slumber; killing, feeding, growing, bringing forth small copies of himself; grown upon with hair like grass, fitted with eyes that move and glitter in his face." The wry allusion to Genesis appears in the phrase "disease of the agglutinated dust" (line 2) since it is from dust that man is first fashioned. This confirms choices A, B, C and E. There are no rhetorical questions in evidence.

43. Which of the following does NOT seemingly contribute to the author's labeling man a "Poor soul" (line 10)? **(E) his tendency toward despondency**.

Man is said to have a "momentary life" (line 21), said to have been "cast among so many hardships" (lines 10-11), said to be "savagely descended" (line 13) and "barbarous" (line 17), and described as having "imperfect virtues: infinitely childish, often admirably valiant, often touchingly kind; sitting down, amidst his momentary life, to debate of right and wrong and the attributes of the deity; rising up to do battle for an egg or die for an idea; singling out his friends and his mate with cordial affection; bringing forth in pain, rearing with long-suffering solicitude his young" (lines 18-26). This validates choices A, B, C and D. He is, on the contrary, seen to be persevering and defiant, not despondent.

44. In the context in which it appears, the phrase, "irremediably condemned" (line 14), could plausibly be interpreted as which of the following?

  I. Remanded to the gallows.
  II. Incapable of reforming his characteristic barbarity.
  III. Forfeiting his chance at spiritual salvation.

(D) II and III

Choice I is simply too literal to be a possibility. The phrase "irremediably condemned" suggests on one hand that he cannot change his being (II), and on another, inferential level, that he is damned because of this barbarism (III). This is supported by lines 47-49 in which the author observes "Strange enough if, with their singular origin and perverted practice, they think they are to be rewarded in some future life."

45. In the context in which it appears, the BEST equivalent of the phrase, "of a piece with his destiny" (line 16), would be **(A) conforming to**.

The complete line, "who should have blamed him had he been of a piece with his destiny and a being merely barbarous?," provides the determining context. Here the rhetorical question essentially asks, "Who could blame him if he had accepted being a barbarian?" Choice A provides the best paraphrase of this thought.

46. The tone of the words, "And we look and behold him [. . .] rearing with long-suffering solicitude his young" (lines 17-26), is BEST classified as being one of **(B) begrudging wonder**.

This echoes the Latin phrase, *Ecce homo*, or "Behold the man," said of Christ upon the Cross. The intimation in these lines is that man, despite his litany of shortcomings, still persists in striving toward some uncertain salvation or abiding by some inexplicable sense of duty that seems incongruous with his barbarous origins and/or nature. As the author observes in lines 58-65, "Man is indeed marked for failure in his efforts to do right. But where the best consistently miscarry, how tenfold more remarkable that all should continue to strive; and surely we should find it both touching and inspiriting, that in a field from which success is banished, our race should not cease to labour [. . . .]."

47 The antecedent of the pronoun "it" in lines 35 and 37 is most persuasively argued to be **(C) design (line 33)**.

The author suggests in lines 33-34 that "The design in most men is one of conformity." It is this that occasionally "transcends itself and soars on the other side, arming martyrs with independence" and that remains in them "a bosom thought." This echoes Thoreau's observation that "The mass of men lead lives of quiet desperation" and Emerson's advocation that it is self-reliance that enables self-actualization.

48. The most "imperfect" of its virtues might be considered humanity's **(C) "rising up to do battle for an egg [. . .]" (lines 22-23)**.

Each of the other four choices—his childishness, his willingness to explore the mysteries of the divine, his child-rearing, and his sense of duty—suggests either a minor flaw or a somewhat admirable trait. Choice C, however, suggests that he will spontaneously fight over something trivial. Whether the egg is an objective correlative for the source of a quarrel or a military conflict, it seems the most imperfect of humanity's 'virtues.'

49. The speaker's labeling man "a tragedy of misconception and misconduct" (lines 53-54) may be interpreted as which of the following?

   I. Humanity's failure to understand the immorality of its heritage of violence.
  II. Humanity's strange belief that its actions warrant salvation or damnation in some after-life.
 III. Humanity's "imperfect" design by its creator.

(E) I, II and III

According to the author, man conducts himself barbarously in many ways, and yet somehow thinks he is deserving of some after-life judgment. The word "misconception" also connotes a mistake at birth. Choice E touches all these bases.

50. The phrase, "They cannot be too darkly drawn" (lines 57-58), suggests that humanity's legacy of evil **(B) cannot be understated**.

This line is preceded by a catalog of man's barbarous behavior, his "organized injustice, cowardly violence, and treacherous crime [. . .]" (lines 55-57). The author is suggesting that because of these indignities one cannot depict him in a bad enough light.

51. The author's style in the passage is marked by all of the following EXCEPT **(D) a disproportionate presentation of man's virtues and vices**.

The parallel syntax, evidenced by lines such as "lifting alternate feet or lying drugged with slumber; killing, feeding, growing, bringing forth small copies of himself" (lines 2-5), is ubiquitous, while the meditative nature of the entire passage attests to its philosophical and reflective tone. The passage's diction paints man as "savagely surrounded, savagely descended" (line 13) and "barbarous" (line 17), but also associates him with duty, decency, bravery, perseverance and transcendence. And, consistent with the overall explication of the passage, Stevenson includes himself in this depiction by switching to the collective pronoun "our" in the final sentence. This information validates choices A, B, C and E. However, while there is a significant catalog of man's imperfections in the passage, there is also a pretty ample depiction of the positive things he accomplishes, too much to label it "disproportionate."

Explication of Free-Response Question One: From Mary Pipher's *Reviving Ophelia*

The first essay in Sample Examination One—from Mary Pipher's *Reviving Ophelia,* a case study of the difficulties faced by adolescent girls—is from the opening pages of the book and thus introduces the reader to the author's subject. It also clarifies the title by providing a synopsis of the unfortunate lot of Shakespeare's Ophelia, permitting the reader to perceive the author's interest in saving adolescent girls from a similar fate. The prompt asked students to "identify the nature and source of these problems and discuss how the author uses elements of language to convey their potentially dire consequences."

Clearly, adolescence is a troubling time for teenage girls. Pipher indicates how "IQ scores drop and math and science scores plummet," how girls "lose their resiliency and optimism and become less curious and inclined to take risks" (lines 4-5). She adds that they "lose their assertive, energetic and 'tomboyish' personalities and become more deferential, self-critical and depressed" (lines 5-7) and become disenchanted with their bodies. Moreover, their personalities "become fragmented, their selves split into mysterious contradictions" (lines 24-25). Their moods swing radically from pole to pole, and "Much of their behavior is unreadable" (line 34). Adds Pipher, "Their problems are complicated and metaphorical—eating disorders, school phobias and self-inflicted injuries" (lines 34-36). So complicated and unfathomable do they become that Pipher confesses "I need to ask again and again in a dozen different ways, 'What are you trying to tell me?' [. . . .]" (lines 36-37).

Pipher describes the complications faced by adolescent girls by initially comparing this phase of their lives to the Bermuda Triangle, a place associated with the mysterious disappearance of planes and boats. Using words and phrases such as "go down in droves" (line 2), "crash and burn" (line 3) and "plummet" (line 4), Pipher endeavors to convey the dramatic turn for the worse that teenage girls experience in this period. She also alludes to contemporary female writers (e.g., Sylvia Plath, Margaret Atwood, Olive Schreiner) who have described the "wreckage" (line 10) of this period. Pipher also alludes to fairytales and to Shakespeare's *Hamlet.* She uses the former to show how terrible calamities befall the heroines of these stories—poisonings, sleeps of unnatural duration, and wanderings—and how they are "rescued by princes and are transformed into passive and docile creatures" (lines 14-15). This image satirizes the system which 'rescues' a woman through marriage only to condemn her to an indentured servitude of housewifery. The latter reference, to *Hamlet,* uses Ophelia to epitomize what can happen to young girls when their problems become overwhelming. Those familiar with the play know that Ophelia becomes a convenient scapegoat for Hamlet who, depressed by his father's murder and his mother's incestuous marriage to his uncle Claudius, directs his frustrations squarely at her. Ophelia, who has been warned by both her father and brother to keep Hamlet in the rear of her affections and stay out of the bow range of his desire, now finds the young Dame who has courted her affections treating her disdainfully and uttering such blanket condemnations as "Frailty, they name is woman." When Hamlet mistakes her father for the king and stabs him through the arras, one can only imagine what a maelstrom of emotion Ophelia must be. As Pipher points out,

> As a girl, Ophelia is happy and free, but with adolescence she loses herself. When she falls in love with Hamlet, she lives only for his approval. She has no inner direction; rather she struggles to meet the demands of Hamlet and her father. Her value is determined utterly by their approval. Ophelia is torn apart by her efforts to please. When Hamlet spurns her because she is an obedient daughter, she goes mad with grief. Dressed in elegant clothes that weigh her down, she drowns in a stream filled with flowers (lines 17-22).

Pipher uses Ophelia almost as an objective correlative; her name, already nearly synonymous with rejection, grief, and suicide, becomes an appropriate icon for the adolescent girl and her avalanche of troubles.

In addition to diction and allusion, Pipher employs antithesis and parallelism to convey the radical emotional swings, these "mysterious contradictions" (line 25) experienced by adolescent girls: "They are sensitive and tenderhearted, mean and competitive, superficial and idealistic. They are confident in the morning, and overwhelmed by anxiety by nightfall. They rush through their days with wild energy and then collapse into lethargy" (lines 25-28). In the final paragraph Pipher becomes more personal, making reference to "[her] clients" whom she says are "elusive and slow to trust" (line 30). Using a list, she catalogs the seemingly trivial actions that can tip their delicate emotional balance: "They are easily offended by a glance, a clearing of the throat, a silence, a lack of sufficient enthusiasm or a sentence that doesn't meet their immediate needs" (lines 30-32). Suffering a death of their selves, Pipher notes how their "voices have gone underground—their speech is more tentative and less articulate" (lines 32-33). Like Ophelia they are literally and metaphorically sinking below the surface.

Though Pipher's enlightening book is limited to young girls, the troubles of adolescents are not limited by gender, and other authors have examined the particular difficulties young males experience during this awkward period of adolescence, Pipher's insightful and empathetic examination should spur a compelling and important discussion in the high school classroom.

This question has been reprinted for your convenience.

<u>Question One</u>

In the following passage a therapist reflects upon the problems manifested by adolescent girls. Read the passage carefully. Then, in a well-organized essay, identify the nature and source of these problems and discuss how the author uses elements of language to convey their potentially dire consequences.

Something dramatic happens to girls in early adolescence. Just as planes and ships disappear mysteriously into the Bermuda Triangle, so do the selves of girls go down in droves. They crash and burn in a social and developmental Bermuda Triangle. In early adolescence, studies show that girls' IQ scores drop and their math and science scores plummet. They lose

(5)   their resiliency and optimism and become less curious and inclined to take risks. They lose their assertive, energetic, and "tomboyish" personalities and become more deferential, self-critical and depressed. They report great unhappiness with their own bodies.

Psychology documents but does not explain the crashes. Girls who rushed to drink in experiences in enormous gulps sit quietly in the corner. Writers such as Sylvia Plath, Margaret

(10)   Atwood, and Olive Schreiner have described the wreckage. Diderot, in writing to his young friend Sophie Volland, described his observations harshly: "You all die at 15."

Fairy tales capture the essence of this phenomenon. Young women eat poisoned apples or prick their fingers with poisoned needles and fall asleep for a hundred years. They wander away from home, encounter great dangers, are rescued by princes and are transformed into passive

(15)   and docile creatures.

The story of Ophelia, from Shakespeare's *Hamlet*, shows the destructive forces that affect young women. As a girl, Ophelia is happy and free, but with adolescence she loses herself. When she falls in love with Hamlet, she lives only for his approval. She has no inner direction; rather she struggles to meet the demands of Hamlet and her father. Her value is determined utterly by

(20)   their approval. Ophelia is torn apart by her efforts to please. When Hamlet spurns her because she is an obedient daughter, she goes mad with grief. Dressed in elegant clothes that weigh her down, she drowns in a stream filled with flowers.

Girls know they are losing themselves. One girl said, "Everything good in me died in junior high." Wholeness is shattered by the chaos of adolescence. Girls become fragmented, their

(25)   selves split into mysterious contradictions. They are sensitive and tenderhearted, mean and competitive, superficial and idealistic. They are confident in the morning, and overwhelmed by anxiety by nightfall. They rush through their days with wild energy and then collapse into lethargy. They try on new roles every week—this week the good student, next week the delinquent and the next, the artist. And they expect their families to keep up with these changes.

(30)   My clients in early adolescence are elusive and slow to trust. They are easily offended by a glance, a clearing of the throat, a silence, a lack of sufficient enthusiasm or a sentence that doesn't meet their immediate needs. Their voices have gone underground—their speech is more tentative and less articulate. Their moods swing widely. One week they love their world and their families, the next day they are critical of everyone. Much of their behavior is unreadable. Their

(35)   problems are complicated and metaphorical—-eating disorders, school phobias and self-inflicted injuries. I need to ask again and again in a dozen different ways, "What are you trying to tell me?" [. . . .].

"Saplings in the Storm", from REVIVING OPHELIA by Mary Pipher, Ph.D., copyright © 1994 by Mary Pipher, Ph.D. Used by permission of G.P. Putnam's Sons, a division of Penguin Group (USA) Inc.

Scoring Rubric for Free-Response Question One: From Mary Pipher's *Reviving Ophelia*

9   Essays earning a score of 9 meet all the criteria for 8 papers and in addition are especially thorough in their analysis or demonstrate a particularly impressive control of style.

8   Essays earning a score of 8 identify a wide range of problems faced by young girls during adolescence and an equally wide range of issues that may trigger them. They present a carefully organized response which eloquently involves the diverse elements of language that the author uses to convey the gravity of this problem. Their prose demonstrates an impressive control of the elements of effective writing, though it is not flawless.

7   Essays earning a score of 7 fit the description of 6 essays but feature either a more thorough discussion or a greater command of prose style.

6   Essays scoring 6 identify a substantial number of problems faced by young girls during adolescence and some of the major issues that may trigger them. These responses, while adequately supported and generally sound in nature, are nevertheless not as persuasive as papers earning scores of 7 or better due to their being less developed or less cogent. Though these papers may occasionally lapse in organization, diction or syntax, they are generally clear and effective.

5   Essays scoring 5 generally understand the task but are either limited in scope or insufficiently developed. Though they may be marked by shortcomings in organization, syntax or diction, they nevertheless reflect a certain level of competence.

4   Essays scoring 4 respond inadequately to the question's task, often misunderstanding, misinterpreting, or oversimplifying the problems faced by adolescent girls, or providing insufficient evidence of the diverse elements of language that the author uses to convey the gravity of this problem. Though the prose is often adequate enough to convey the writer's points, it generally suggests a limited control over organization, diction and syntax.

3   Essays earning a score of 3 meet the criteria for a score of 4 but are either less thorough in documenting the problems faced by adolescent girls, or display a more limited control over the elements of effective composition.

2   Essays scoring 2 achieve little success in identifying the problems faced by adolescent girls or in illustrating how the author uses elements of language to convey the gravity of this problem. They may on occasion misread the passage, fail to develop their argument to any significant degree, summarize rather than analyze the passage, or display significant weaknesses in organization, clarity, fluency or mechanics.

1   Essays earning a score of 1 meet the criteria for a score of 2 but are either overly simplistic or marred by severe deficiencies in the elements of composition.

0   Essays scoring 0 offer an off-topic response that receives no credit, or a mere repetition of the prompt.

—   Indicates a blank or completely off-topic response.

Sample Student Essay One

In the passage, the therapist uses several elements of language to portray, in her opinion, the acute nature of the problems that face girls in early adolescence such as IQ and self-confidence drops. These elements include the negative use of examples, hyperbole of her patterns, and her dramatic tone.

Many of the therapist's examples are designed to illustrate her pessimistic view of the development of girls once they reach early adolescence. She believes that at this stage girls change and develop drastically, but without any positive effects. To emphasize this she cites examples from Shakespeare and fairy tales. However, the choice of examples is paramount to her point. The therapist focuses entirely on the one Shakespearean play, Hamlet, in which the female undergoes a dramatic turn for the worse as she reaches adolescence, disregarding all other plays which mention young women, such as <u>A Midsummer Nights Dream</u>, <u>The Merchant of Venice</u>, <u>Othello</u>, <u>King Lear</u>, and <u>Romeo and Juliet</u>, just a few of the Shakespearean plays where the heroine(s) has/have clear cut intents and pursue their honest goals, normally involving love and/or matrimony, to the result of a happy union or another fate determined by forces entirely out of their control. None of these heroines encounters odd changes of the heart as Ophelia does. Similarly, the therapist centers her fairy tales among those in which women start of with some semblance of intellect and then encounter a weird catastrophe and end up marrying a prince as a docile creator, such as Sleeping Beauty or Snow White. Fairy Tales such as <u>Cinderella</u> and <u>The Little Mermaid</u>, where the young women must use her own determination to follow her dreams, and does go through with her plans, are entirely ignored. This choice of example, therefore, is a strong element in shaping the author's arguments.

Just as the therapist ignores many examples countering her argument, she also uses an incredible amount of hyperbole to disregard "exceptions" and prove her point that upon reaching adolescence every girl completely loses herself. All girls are lumped together into "theys" and "girls." One girl who says that everything good in her died in junior high proves that <u>all</u> girls feel shattered as they enter adolescence. The feelings of her clients, girls who have been sent to a therapist because they have problems, are representative of the entire female half of adolescent society. This hyperbole, if read as the author wishes it to be read, surely conveys how acutely and widespread she feels this issue of adolescent girls to be.

In fact, it is the reality of the author's profession as a therapist, and the tone it lends her work, that really emphasizes her point the most. She does not talk as an objective observer, but as a participant, one who is in the midst of the problem. She has met the girls, seen their problems, and tried to help them. The tone that this lends to the piece is therefore one of dramatics, an over-eager attempt to convince her readers of what she is so sure of already. And this assuredness truly conveys how acute she feels the problems faced by adolescent girls are. Through this sincerity the therapist tries to convince her audience.

The therapist no doubt believes very strongly that upon reaching adolescence all girls go through some kind of changeover, losing their intelligence and self-respect in the maze of middle school. To emphasize this point she brings in very clear examples, a strong use of hyperbole, and a very convinced tone.

You Rate It!

1. How thorough a job did the student do in terms of <u>identifying the nature of the problems</u> faced by adolescent girls? List the ones the student identified:

_____

_____

_____

_____

2. To what degree did the student identify the <u>source(s) of these problems</u>? List the ones the student identified:

_____

_____

_____

3. What <u>elements of language</u> did the student identify that were used by the author to convey the gravity and potentially dire consequences of these problems? List the lines the students paraphrased or cited that exemplify these elements:

_____

_____

_____

_____

4. On a 0-9 scale, how would you rate this response? Explain why.

_____

_____

_____

_____

Sample Student Essay Two

In this passage the author addresses the issue of the problems manifested by girls during adolescence. The passage depicts these changes as the death of the girls' souls. In this passage [the author] uses categorical syntax to illustrate the incessancy of the manifestation and allusion to further portray the development of these problems. The author also carries a negative tone throughout the passage that parallels a lack of hope that these girls' problems cannot be solved.

The author uses lists to portray the grave endlessness of the girls' problems. In the first paragraph he categorizes all of the symptoms of this loss of self, from the tangible (drops in test scores and IQ levels), to the intangible (loss of "tomboyish personalities" and "resiliency"). The author touches upon all the facets of loss that he sees the girls experience. The author's use of categorical syntax also serves to portray the clashing of the girls' emotions and actions at this age. He explains these contradictions, "they are sensitive and tenderhearted, mean and competitive, superficial and idealistic". The author also chooses to use parallelism in his syntax to convey this contradiction that goes on inside these young girls.

The author uses allusion to make the development of these problems more tangible. He alludes to stories such as Snow White and Sleeping Beauty to suggest the clouded mind girls experience under this "spell" of adolescence. He then goes into further detail in an allusion to Shakespeare's Hamlet, which serves to describe the decay of a girl's self. By addressing how Ophelia morphed from "a girl [. . .] happy and free" to a hopelessly-in-love woman vying for Hamlet's and her father's approvals. The author suggests that a young woman loses her "inner direction" as she continues down a path where she feels it a necessity to please. The author uses this story, which ends in Ophelia's death, to portray a metaphorical death that he observes in his adolescent patients.

Finally, the author's tone offers a great deal of insight into the nature of the problems manifested by adolescent girls. His serious tone, which lacks any hint of optimism, serves as a parallel to the grave and negative condition of these girls.

Throughout the passage the author fails to be compassionate or make any attempt to sympathize with these girls. Perhaps it his lack of understanding that allows for such a cynical outlook on the issue of young girls' problems, problems that stem from the beginning of adolescence.

You Rate It!

1. How thorough a job did the student do in terms of <u>identifying the nature of the problems</u> faced by adolescent girls? To what degree did the student identify the source(s) of these problems? List the ones the student identified:

_____

_____

_____

_____

2. What <u>elements of language</u> did the student identify that were used by the author to convey the gravity and potentially dire consequences of these problems? List the lines the students paraphrased or cited that exemplify these elements:

_____

_____

_____

_____

3. How effective was the writer's plan of organization? The fluency of his/her writing? The overall correctness of the paper?

_____

_____

_____

_____

4. On a 0-9 scale, how would you rate this response? Explain why.

_____

_____

_____

_____

Sample Student Essay Three

As a girl becomes a woman, she goes through a variety of psychological changes that alter her personality completely. According to one therapist, girls entirely crash and lose their determination and become docile, self-deprecating and confused. The author makes it clear through her use of repetition and diction that a female becomes completely lost and estranged as she enters her adolescent years. Then, by using tone, she allows the audience to feel the hopelessness of an adolescent ever becoming the blissful girl she once was.

The writer's specific use of repetition has great importance in its proving that a girl's positive traits are completely untenable and a girl soon becomes stripped of any decency she once had. In the first paragraph, the repeated use of "they lose" begins the passage with this traumatic view. As these words are reused the list of personality changes seems infinite, therefore beginning to give the audience a hopeless feeling. Then, the author reiterates "they" and "their" when describing each aspect of a female and the way in which she is lost. The use of these vague terms is significant because it leaves the adolescents without an identity and forces the audience of the passage to think of the females as distant from the readers themselves. Without a distinct name it becomes apparent that these adolescents are lost and unable to be found. This leaves complete hopelessness for these mysterious females and the realization that they are unfixable and estranged from society.

The use of diction is a significant way in which an adolescent's plummeting personality becomes evident. Immediately in the passage, the author uses the words "crash and burn" to describe a female adolescent and her social changes. This makes it evident from the beginning that a terrible alteration occurs. She then goes further into detail and describes the adolescents as unreadable, shattered and lost. When compared to the assertive, energetic and optimistic personalities the author gives the girls in the first paragraph of the passage, the changed adolescents can be seen in no other light than completely altered and unattainable, and the adolescent suddenly becomes an unsolvable mystery.

After successfully proving to the audience that these adolescents are estranged, the author uses a critical, exaggerating tone as a way to convince the reader that there is no way to make the adolescents the girls they once were. The author primarily states that a girl dies at age fifteen, as if to show that the personality changes are so drastic they destroy a person entirely. She then criticizes and amplifies the mood swings of an adolescent by claiming that these females will change from loving to critical in no time at all, or be offended by a person clearing his throat. The female is regarded as elusive and slow to trust, giving a mocking tone that relates a female with an enigmatic alien. These exaggerations are successful in that they make females seem completely out of line, to the point where they do not seem fit for society. At this point, there is no possibility that these alienated women may return to society, and tone has been used to convince the reader of this.

Repetition, diction, and tone have been means for this author to communicate her view on the deterioration of adolescents at the age fifteen and the impossibility of their return. It seems as though the female is completely out of touch with society at this point in their lives and it raises an important question: is there any way a female can become docile in her older age?

You Rate It!

1. How thorough a job did the student do in terms of <u>identifying the nature of the problems</u> faced by adolescent girls? List the ones the student identified:

_____

_____

_____

_____

2. To what degree did the student identify the <u>source(s) of these problems</u>? List the ones the student identified:

_____

_____

_____

_____

3. What <u>elements of language</u> did the student identify that were used by the author to convey the gravity and potentially dire consequences of these problems? List the lines the students paraphrased or cited that exemplify these elements:

_____

_____

_____

_____

4. On a 0-9 scale, how would you rate this response? Explain why.

_____

_____

_____

_____

Author's Response to Sample Student Essays on *Reviving Ophelia*

Sample Student Essay One:

This was a very unusual essay in that the writer disagreed with Pipher's position on adolescent girls. Though many times such an oppositional stance is counter-productive—particularly in light of the fact that these issues are very legitimate ones—this writer's claims have a degree of merit in that they contend that Pipher may be using the experience of a small group to make an unfair generalization about *all* adolescent girls. I particularly liked her observation that "All girls are lumped together into "theys" and "girls," as well as her strong claim that "girls who have been sent to a therapist because they have problems, are representative of the entire female half of adolescent society." The writer counters Pipher's allusion to *Hamlet* and to fairy tales in which girls suffer unpleasantries with other plays and tales in which they do not, and notes that Pipher does "not talk as an objective observer, but as a participant, one who is in the midst of the problem."

On the down side, the syntax in the introduction and conclusion obfuscates the writer's points about elements of language. The writer mentions appropriate Shakespearean plays but without citing any concrete examples from them (she does noticeably better with the fairy tales). To some degree the writer is guilty of the same shortcoming for which she censures the author: not being sufficiently objective. While I admire the conviction with which this paper was written and enjoy the novelty of the response, I find it too readily dismisses the credential of the author and the potential of—if not the reality of–this problem's pervasiveness. I judge this an upper-half paper, but one that dismisses a little too much evidence in order to make a passionate point. Still, it is insightful and somewhat daring in its contradiction and is rewarded as such.

Author's Score: 7

Sample Student Essay Two:

This student essay, even though it responds more diligently to the task, succeeds to a lesser degree than the previous paper. To be fair, there are some good traits to be recognized. The student, for example, neatly summarizes the symptoms into the "tangible" and "intangible;" she notes that young girls are full of "contradictions;" she sees the Ophelia story as a metaphor for the death of all young girls who are plagued by these problems; and she suggests that the pessimistic tone parallels the "grave and negative condition of these girls."

The paper has rough edges as well, particularly in its diction (which is occasionally ponderous— e.g., "incessancy of the manifestation") and its handling of literary terms (e.g., "categorical syntax"). The author understands the task, but does not develop the argument terribly far. Even so, this seems better than the median and is appropriately rewarded.

Author's Score: Low 6

Sample Student Essay Three:

The third sample essay offers reason for optimism at the start, but also a glimpse of its potential shortcomings. Though the writer seems to understand the task and be able to articulate the adolescent girls' problem (as conveyed by the adjectives in the second sentence), she also fails to define the specific tone that she says "allows the audience to feel the hopelessness of an adolescent ever becoming the blissful girl she once was." Later in the essay the writer labels this as a "critical, exaggerating tone" and a "mocking tone."

Positive points are the writer's recognition of the repeated chorus of "they lose," her suggestion that the "list of personality changes seems infinite, therefore beginning to give the audience a hopeless feeling," and, to a lesser degree, her notation of the anonymity suggested by the use of "they" and "their". Some fair observations arc madc about the diction, though the writer's failure to put words used in the passage in quotation marks makes it appear that these words are part of her prose instead. In the fourth paragraph the syntax and word choice become troublesome, hindering understanding. Constructs such as "giving a mocking tone that relates a female with an enigmatic alien," "that make females seem completely out of line, to the point where they do not seem fit for society," and "is there any way a female can become docile in her older age?" frustrate a clear understanding of the writer's points.

Overall, I felt this essay displayed the characteristic of a writer not totally devoid of insight but lacking upper-half control of compositional skills.

Author's Score: 5

Explication of Free-Response Question Two: Thoreau's "Goodness Tainted"

Free-response question two asked students to respond to a line from Thoreau's *Walden*, "There is no odor so bad as that which arises from goodness tainted." The intimation inherent in this observation is that nothing is as rank as the corruption of goodness.

This question lends itself particularly well to literature and history. Certainly a persuasive argument can be made for the appropriateness of tragedy, though some plays work more successfully than others. In Shakespeare, for example, a play such as *MacBeth* seems a natural fit, given the protagonist's love for and loyalty to Duncan, the king he later murders to ascend the throne. Similarly, Claudius' insidious actions in Hamlet also seem a reasonable choice. Arthur Miller's *Death of A Salesman* and *The Crucible* also seem quite appropriate in light of the adulteries committed by Willy Loman and John Proctor, moral failings which return to complicate their lives. In all four plays betrayal figures prominently in tainting the goodness of the main characters. The novel, too, provides ample possibilities. A student might gravitate toward the political corruption of Willie Stark in Robert Penn Warren's *All the King's Men*, toward Jay Gatsby's bootlegging and racketeering in F. Scott Fitzgerald's *The Great Gatsby*, or toward Hester Prynne's self-ostracizing adultery in Nathaniel Hawthorne's *The Scarlet Letter*. Or students may opt for Herman Melville's *Billy Budd* or Harper Lee's *To Kill A Mockingbird* to show how goodness may be tainted by things as diverse as an impulsive, inadvertent action and the bigotry of a jury. Even exposés such as Upton Sinclair's *The Jungle* or Ken Kesey's *One Flew Over the Cuckoo's Nest* may be used to answer this question persuasively.

In terms of history, the ubiquitousness of corruption throughout time makes this particularly fertile ground. From Benedict Arnold to William Calley to Bill Clinton, crimes of perfidy, savagery and infidelity have certainly besmirched prominent individuals. From Tammany Hall to Watergate to Enron, political and financial scandals have shamed the halls of governance. Whether individual or institutional, students should find no shortage of past and contemporary examples with which to address the topic of goodness tainted.

<u>Question Two</u>

(Suggested time—40 minutes. This question counts as one-third of the total essay section score.)

"There is no odor so bad as that which arises from goodness tainted."

Walden—Henry David Thoreau

Henry David Thoreau / *Walden* and *Civil Disobedience* / Copyright © 1960 / by Houghton Mifflin Company.

Consider the above statement. Then, write a well-organized essay in which you explore the meaning of Thoreau's statement using examples from your reading, experience, studies and/or observation to illustrate your interpretation.

Scoring Rubric for Free-Response Question Two: Thoreau's "Goodness Tainted"

9   Essays earning a score of 9 meet all the criteria for 8 papers and in addition are especially thorough in their analysis or demonstrate a particularly impressive control of style.

8   Essays earning a score of 8 identify a work of literature, a historical incident, epoch or personage, or a personal instance that accurately reflects Thoreau's observation about "goodness tainted." They present a carefully organized response which eloquently interprets and convincingly illustrates the point made by the citation. Their prose demonstrates an impressive control of the elements of effective writing, though it is not flawless.

7   Essays earning a score of 7 fit the description of 6 essays but feature either a more thorough discussion or a greater command of prose style.

6   Essays scoring 6 identify a work of literature, a historical incident, epoch or personage, or a personal instance that reasonably demonstrates Thoreau's observation about "goodness tainted." These responses, while adequately supported and generally sound in nature, are nevertheless not as persuasive as papers earning scores of 7 or better due to their being less developed or less cogent. Though these papers may occasionally lapse in organization, diction or syntax, they are generally clear and effective.

5   Essays scoring 5 generally understand the task but are either limited in scope or insufficiently developed. Though they may be marked by shortcomings in organization, syntax or diction, they nevertheless reflect a certain level of competence.

4   Essays scoring 4 respond inadequately to the question's task, often misunderstanding, misinterpreting, or oversimplifying the task laid out by the prompt. Though the prose is often adequate enough to convey the writer's points, it generally suggests a limited control over organization, diction and syntax.

3   Essays earning a score of 3 meet the criteria for a score of 4 but are either less thorough in responding to the task, or display a more limited control over the elements of effective composition.

2   Essays scoring 2 achieve little success in understanding the concept of "goodness tainted" or in illustrating it through reference to a work of literature, a historical incident, epoch or personage, or a personal anecdote. They may on occasion misunderstand the citation, fail to choose an appropriate example, fail to develop their argument to any significant degree, or display significant weaknesses in organization, clarity, fluency or mechanics.

1   Essays earning a score of 1 meet the criteria for a score of 2 but are either overly simplistic or marred by severe deficiencies in the elements of composition.

0   Essays scoring 0 offer an off-topic response that receives no credit, or a mere repetition of the prompt.

—   Indicates a blank or completely off-topic response.

Sample Student Essay One

Henry David Thoreau once wrote "there is no odor so bad as that which arises from goodness tainted," meaning that although obvious evil is disgusting and repulsive in its own right, what is even worse is that which is thought to be good turning out to in fact be tainted, imperfect, and sometimes even evil itself. Few events in history portray this statement as accurately as the Holocaust, perpetrated by Hitler and his Nazi regime during World War II, during which eleven thousand innocent civilians were killed in a genocide of race and religion. No matter how horrible and insane the incident was, that Hitler was a fanatic madman can at least be understood. What cannot be understood (and is therefore even more horrifying) is the reaction of the German people and other civilians of occupied lands, the subsequent actions of certain prisoners in the camps, and the actions of the world community. These were groups that were thought to be good and pure, but when put to the test could not fully withstand outside influences and to a certain extent succumbed to the evil around them, providing an even greater horror then the ravings of a lunatic Hitler.

Few Jews of Germany even considered leaving their country when news of the Nazis' rise to power permeated their press. Most were on very good terms with their neighbors, such as the family of Anika in her memoir, <u>Upon the Head of a Goat</u>. She was best friends with her gentile neighbor and, upon being actually forced to leave her house gave her radio to her young friend for safe keeping. Germany was considered among the most civilized of nations and a center of European Jewry. Even with Nazism beginning to spread out and conquer, the idea that such an incredible tragedy could be perpetrated by such a civilized nation was too ridiculous to be believed. In <u>To Life</u>, the mother of the author, Riva, explains in a flashback that it never occurred to any of them that the Germans would harm a young widow with several young children. Her elder daughters and son she sent away to avoid them being put in forced labor, but death camps? The idea was preposterous. Even if a madman had taken over, how could their fellow citizens allow it? And that was the catastrophe–not Hitler, but the responses of the ordinary civilians. Even after the war, after every citizen knew the reality of what their neighbors had been subjected to, Riva went knocking from house to house without any reply. And that is what almost broke her. Not the murders of her family and the loss of her innocence through the Gestapo and the concentration camps, but the apathy of ordinary, good people, who really were not so good.

Perhaps it was that the horror of the concentration camps was too much for the mind to bear, but similar experiences strongly figure in Elie Wiesel's war memoir, <u>Night</u>. Yes, the concentration camps were awful, and he almost cracked at the murder of so many innocents, such as a young boy with the face of an angel, but one of the most telling moments in his experience was the reality that many of the Jews themselves could not handle the experience without cracking. Elie watched a man so hungry that he tore a piece of bread from his own father, and there was something in that moment that disgusted and repulsed him. Some of the most awful Holocaust stories are not those of the Germans, but of Jews that would charge their fellow Jews their last pieces of bread to share privileged items, such as a solitary tallis (prayer shawl). Or of Jews chosen by the Germans to act as Kapos, and enact cruel punishment and such on their co-religionists. The horrors perpetrated by the Germans, if not understood, were at least accepted based on a long history of prosecution. But the reaction of fellow Jews, always considered to be the good guys, was so surprising that it was somehow even worse.

Similar betrayal was felt by the actions of the United States and other free countries. That the United States could limit its Jewish immigration at such a crucial time, and then turn away boatloads of innocent refugees, sending them back to almost certain death in Europe, is almost preposterous to those of the modern world. But it happened, and it was not the only case. The English severely limited Jewish immigration to Palestine as well as to their home country, and Sweden only accepted Denmark's Jews after being forced to by world renowned scientist Niels Bohr. None of these countries were dictatorships such as Germany had become. Rather, they were democracies, full of their own self-righteousness. Which made their actions all the worse in the context of world events.

It is obvious from the events of the Holocaust that Thoreau was justified in his claim that "there is no odor so bad as that which arises from goodness tainted." No matter how awful the events begun by the Nazi regime of Hitler were, it is a fact that not enough good people stepped in to stop them, a failure that allowed such a systematic genocide to continue for 6 years. And that apathy and the active evil of such supposedly good people is the truest tragedy of the Holocaust.

You Rate It!

1. How thorough a job did the writer do in terms of <u>explaining the concept</u> of "goodness tainted" and in <u>selecting an appropriate example</u> to illustrate it?

_____

_____

_____

_____

2. To what degree did the writer provide <u>specific details</u> about the book, historical incident, etc. that made his/her argument persuasive?

_____

_____

_____

3. How effective was the writer's plan of organization? The fluency of his/her writing? The overall correctness of the paper?

_____

_____

_____

_____

4. On a 0-9 scale, how would you rate this response? Explain why.

_____

_____

_____

_____

Sample Student Essay Two

Malice, ill will, and corruption: the most horrendous aspects of human nature. It becomes apparent through observation that the most atrocious parts of life are those that are consumed by these factors, making bad habits or occurrences with good intentions acceptable, but corruption simply an abomination. To reach this conclusion, Martin Luther King, Jr. and a peer's personal experience must be considered.

Martin Luther King, Jr. creates a standard in which ill will is seen as far from satisfactory. Acceptable standards of his time, according to Plessy v. Ferguson, considered separate but equal facilities legitimate. Soon, however, the black population became desperate for equality and unable to reach this in even the smallest of quantities. It became apparent over time that the white population was not treating each race respectfully and, for the most part, was completely out of line. Though there were blacks who spoke out against inequality before King's time, by his generation the black population could not continue life without a definite leader because their treatments by the white community were atrocious. If blacks simply had economic trouble because they were not natives, this would have been more understandable, and blacks would have realized they needed to work efficiently and build up their status in the new country. However, these people could not stand idly by and watch the corrupted white population continue in their ways. Blacks were hung and kicked out of houses and their houses were destroyed. The need to fix this malevolence gave birth to King's leadership, and he soon preached the end to inequality and injustice towards blacks. King became so popular in his reform movement because he brought a light to the dark world and showed the victims that whites were acting with the most horrendous aspect of human nature.

A situation I witnessed between a peer and his significant other proved that corruption and deliberate cruelty are completely inexcusable and the poorest qualities in a person, thus making unintentional mishaps acceptable. This friend of mine planned a lunch as a conciliatory gesture for his love, Dorothy, but the date ended in disaster. Primarily, he fabricated a story about his plans for the day for he was using that time to arrange a picnic for her. Unfortunately, a friend of Dorothy's saw him when he claimed he was elsewhere, and when Dorothy found out, she was furious. Still not understanding where he had been that day, he tried to convince her to come with him to a mysterious place where he intended to give her this surprise, but he almost got into a car accident by doing so. At this point, she felt he was filled with complete malevolence and a lack of respect for her life or feelings and therefore stormed off before being able to see the surprise he had in store for her. After a week without speaking, Dorothy became increasingly infuriated for she felt that the worst trait of a person is that which is filled with malice. This silence, along with my friend's lack of knowledge as to why Dorothy was mad, made it quite difficult for my friend to mend their relationship. Finally, he gathered enough courage to overcome his timidity and explained to her the date he had planned. In an instant, Dorothy's facial expression changed from complete disgust to acceptance. She explained that his lies made him appear fraudulent and evil, but the situation was only a misunderstanding. Now that she realized his intentions were benevolent, she had no reason to be upset with him. After all, the most inexcusable events come from ill will and corruption, and Dorothy would have had every reason to be upset if this had been the case.

After considering Martin Luther King, Jr. and my peer's incident with Dorothy, it has become evident that there is no characteristic worse than malevolence. It therefore becomes necessary to watch our every move and insure that there is no confusion when we intend the best for others.

You Rate It!

1. How thorough a job did the writer do in terms of <u>explaining the concept</u> of "goodness tainted" and in <u>selecting an appropriate example</u> to illustrate it?

_____

_____

_____

_____

2. To what degree did the writer provide <u>specific details</u> about the book, historical incident, etc. that made his/her argument persuasive?

_____

_____

_____

_____

3. How effective was the writer's plan of organization? The fluency of his/her writing? The overall correctness of the paper?

_____

_____

_____

_____

4. On a 0-9 scale, how would you rate this response? Explain why.

_____

_____

_____

_____

Sample Student Essay Three

As one goes through life, one encounters many loves along the way—whether they come in the form of friends, family, hobbies, or dreams for the future. One of the worst experiences, however, is to find that something loved has gone awry, or that something treasured has been lost. Although one may lose much throughout one's life, nothing is more disappointing or disheartening than the ruin of something treasured. This is especially true among the relationships of people, friends and lovers alike.

A true friend is a concept that is varying in definition from person to person. Characteristics, such as loyalty, caring, humor, honesty, etc., all make up those friends whom we truly care about and love. As relationships develop, memories grow and burrow their way into our hearts to create little niches that become a part of who we are. However, just because one may have all the childhood memories in the world, does not necessarily mean that one has a "friend forever." Throughout adolescence especially, people change and mold into new people, even more than once along the way. Different paths may point friends in different directions, and even after a whole childhood history together, two people may end up in two completely different worlds, oftentimes without each other. This separation, whether determined by school, peers, or family, can be an incredibly frustrating and painful experience. Oftentimes, it's easy to take note of a friend who is drifting away, but it is far more difficult to either catch up with them or pull them back. It's hard to face the fact that, although one can hold on to past times, there may not be any future times. A good friendship proves to be far more valuable than a material loss, and if it somehow becomes tainted, one is faced with a most trying and difficult loss.

The loss of love is another example of a potentially excruciating experience. The most painful thing is the ruin of something once so treasured. F. Scott Fitzgerald tells a story of great sadness in his novel, <u>The Great Gatsby</u>, which involves a nasty love geometry that only results in sadness. One situation in particular involves the relationship between Gatsby and his lady fair, Daisy. All of his life, Gatsby has dreamed of a future with Daisy. He has worked hard to become one of the self-made men of the 1920's, even involving himself with suspicious businessmen and thieves. All he ever wanted was to win Daisy over, and he believes that he must impress her with a vast display of wealth. Truly, he is not even interested in becoming rich, only in her love. Once he finally meets up with her, their romance can only last a short while, as Daisy quickly leaves him to return to the economic and social stability that comes with her husband, Tom Buchanan.

How must Gatsby feel about all this? He worked is entire adult life for the sake of acquiring enough wealth to impress his beloved, and after teasing him with a brief romance, she runs off and abandons him. His love for her has gone to ruin and all his life-long plans have gone awry. Gatsby stands outside watching through a window in the moonlight as Daisy and Tom are deep in discussion. Her clear disregard for him is obviously a foil of his love for her. Gatsby even takes the blame for her car accident, which eventually resolves in his murder. It is clear that the loss of his dream of Daisy was extremely difficult for Gatsby. He'd been through a fairly poor childhood, fought through a war, built himself up in society, and yet none of this affected him in such a way as the loss of one whom he truly loved. Fitzgerald plainly shows the importance of love and the immense impact it can have on a person once it is ruined.

There is nothing as bad as the ruin of something treasured. Whether this ruin comes in the form of a lost friendship, or whether it takes the form a of a tainted love, hardships that develop because of the spoiling of something valued can be the most painful and hardest to bear of them all.

You Rate It!

1. How thorough a job did the writer do in terms of <u>explaining the concept</u> of "goodness tainted" and in <u>selecting an appropriate example</u> to illustrate it?

_____

_____

_____

2. To what degree did the writer provide <u>specific details</u> about the book, historical incident, etc. that made his/her argument persuasive?

_____

_____

_____

_____

3. How effective was the writer's plan of organization? The fluency of his/her writing? The overall correctness of the paper?

_____

_____

_____

4. On a 0-9 scale, how would you rate this response? Explain why.

_____

_____

_____

_____

Author's Response to Sample Student Essays on Thoreau's "Goodness Tainted"

Sample Student Essay One:

The writer of this essay, while clearly knowledgeable and capable of articulating and developing a topic, perceives "goodness tainted" not so much as corruption than as a stain or stigma. The discussion of people and governments that failed to respond to the plight of Jews in Nazi Germany, while depicting an acknowledged moral shortcoming, is a bit uneven, hindered ironically by the writer's desire to incorporate literary *and* historical examples. The second paragraph, which cites two Holocaust memoirs, drifts into a discussion about how unsuspecting European Jewry was to the horrifying events to come. The third paragraph experiences similar difficulties since the reference to Elie Wiesel's *Night* seems more an illustration of the horrors of the Holocaust than of "goodness tainted."

The essay begins to get back on track with the references to Jews who exploit their fellow prisoners or who collaborated with the Nazis as *kapos*. The references to countries that turned away Jews seeking asylum also seem more appropriate, as does the essay's conclusion which clarifies the author's intention of indicting those who remained apathetic as the individuals whose goodness was "tainted."

Generally free of compositional errors, the essay is only marred by an occasional fragment or malapropism ("prosecution" for "persecution"), and its only major shortcoming is this uneven presentation which does not stay sufficiently zeroed in on the topic to achieve a greater level of effectiveness.

Author's Score: 6

Sample Student Essay Two:

While the writer of this essay gives it the "old college try," this response fails to achieve its end in several significant ways. Though having a dual focus does not necessarily deter a paper's success, having one as disparate as this certainly does not help. The marriage of Martin Luther King's struggle for human rights and a romantic surprise gone awry simply is not a congruent one, and reading the essay makes the reader feel like he has read two separate essays rather than one coherent one. The writer also does not sufficiently understand the concept of "goodness tainted." While there is certainly a measure of interpretive latitude in any essay question, this student seems to equate Thoreau's observation with malevolence, violence, or, in the second instance, mere petulance. The result is a condemnation of racial prejudice and the evil it often spawns paired with an anecdotal account of a girlfriend's pique at her beau's supposed unfaithfulness. While the writer's compositional skills, other then some patches of rough syntax, are satisfactory, this response missed the bull's eye by too wide a margin to place in the upper-half.

Author's Score: 4

Sample Student Essay Three:

Much like the preceding essay, this student's paper has a dual focus, albeit a slightly more successful one. The student merges a general commentary on the loss of friendship with a discussion of F. Scott Fitzgerald's *The Great Gatsby*. While not a perfect match, the idea of relationship in each segment helps give this paper a greater sense of unity than the second sample essay. The student's clear introductory statement, "Although one may lose much throughout one's life, nothing is more disappointing or disheartening then the ruin of something treasured," is also much closer in spirit to the intent of the question, and her organizational plan also has some merit. The major shortcoming of this paper lies in the insufficiently defined focus of both parts. In the first half of the paper the student notes how "Different paths may point friends in different directions, and even after a whole childhood history together, two people may end up in two completely different worlds, oftentimes without each other." This statement, while true enough, has nothing to do with "goodness tainted" but with the caprices of career choice. Though the last sentence of the first body paragraph—"A good friendship proves to be far more valuable than a material loss, and if it somehow becomes tainted, one is faced with a most trying and difficult loss"–attempts to make this connection, it is simply unclear what circumstances have caused this tainting, and the attempt is ineffectual.

The second half of the student's paper achieves at least a partial degree of success in its discussion of Jay Gatsby's involvement in bootlegging and racketeering, an affiliation which can at least be inferentially read as tainting the purity of his love for Daisy. As those familiar with Chaucer's Pardoner know, "Avarice is the root of all evil;" hence, the student's inference that Gatsby's material drive has corrupted him has merit. The paper, however, soon shifts to a hasty kaleidoscope of the novel's plot, none of which is sufficiently developed to further this idea effectively. In fact, the essay tends to drift away from Gatsby and toward Daisy, suggesting that it is she who leaves Gatsby for the security of Tom's money. The writer's closing affirmation that "Fitzgerald plainly shows the importance of love and the immense impact it can have on a person once it is ruined," cannot sufficiently rescue the paragraph that precedes it, nor can the short but well-intentioned conclusion.

All told, this paper has all the characteristics of a mid-range essay: a partially successful argument, adequate compositional skills (the perplexing "nasty love geometry" aside) that do not hinder understanding, but enough inconsistencies to keep it out of the upper half.

Author's Score: 5

Explication of Free-Response Question Three: "Should New Orleans be Rebuilt?"

The third question required students to consider six diverse sources—passages from four newspaper articles and one book, and a cartoon—on the situation in hurricane-ravaged New Orleans. After examining them, students were asked to integrate at least three of them in an essay that defended, challenged, or qualified the claim that "the unique history of the city of New Orleans demands that it be returned to its former grandeur."

The sources selected provided passionate historical and cultural arguments for preserving the iconic Mississippi Delta city and equally ardent topographical and social arguments for not doing so. Document A, from William Alexander Percy's 1941 autobiography *Lanterns on the Levee*, depicts the Mississippi River as an implacable force that continues to defy any man-made efforts to check its natural flow and direction. Document B, from Tom Piazza's recent book *Why New Orleans Matters*, discusses the rich historical and cultural heritage of the fabled city. Document C, part of an article in the *Des Moines Register*, expresses confidence that the city will indeed be rebuilt, but wonders whether the plans to resurrect the city will sufficiently protect it against a similar catastrophe. Document D, a cartoon called by Jeff Koterba captioned "Eye to Eye," depicts the human spirit, personified as an old sage in a toga, staring defiantly into the vortex of an approaching storm. Document E, from an online article by Thomas J. Campanella, author of *The Resilient City*, suggests little doubt that the popular French Quarter and Garden District will return to form, but wonders whether sufficient resources will be devoted to the devastated low-income neighborhoods of the Ninth Ward whose residents comprise most of the service industry that is the foundation of New Orleans' restaurants, hotels and clubs. Document F, a scathing online article by Jack Shafter, offers the strongest case for not rebuilding—namely, the oppressive poverty, dismally failing schools and pervasive police corruption that have made New Orleans a woefully "dysfunctional" city in his eyes.

This rich diversity allowed students to examine an issue of controversy from multiple sides—to weigh the sentimental vs. the pragmatic; the expeditious vs. the utilitarian; the aesthetic vs. the economic. By doing so, they were afforded a limited but valuable exposure to the multiplicity of issues that a catastrophe of this scale generates on the local and national levels, issues that far exceed the physical destruction wreaked by the storm.

This question has been reprinted for your convenience.

<u>Question Three</u>

Directions:

The following prompt is based on the accompanying six sources.

This question requires you to integrate a variety of sources into a coherent, well-written essay. *Refer to the sources to support your position; avoid paraphrase or summary. Your argument should be central; the sources should support this argument.*

Remember to attribute both direct and indirect citations.

Introduction:

The summer of 2005 saw widespread devastation wreaked on the city of New Orleans by Hurricane Katrina. The colorful, Mississippi Delta city, home to world-renowned restaurants, jazz and blues' clubs, and universities, saw many of its neighborhoods inundated, even washed away by flood waters that breached the barrier of its levees. The extent of this calamity has triggered fierce debate over how the city should be rebuilt in light of its population displacement, economic crisis, and continued below sea-level vulnerability. In fact, there are some who think that the potential for a similar disaster in the future begs the question whether the city should be rebuilt at all.

Assignment:

Peruse the following sources (including any introductory information) carefully. **Then, in an essay that synthesizes at least three of the sources for support, take a position that defends, challenges or qualifies the claim that the unique history of the city of New Orleans demands that it be returned to its former grandeur.**

(It is recommended that you spend 15-20 minutes of the allotted time examining the sources and devote the remaining time to writing your essay.)

Scoring Rubric for Free-Response Question Three: "Should New Orleans be Rebuilt?"

9   Essays earning a score of 9 meet all the criteria for 8 papers and in addition are especially thorough in their analysis or demonstrate a particularly impressive control of style.

8   Essays earning a score of 8 take a position that defends, challenges, or qualifies the claim that "the unique history of the city of New Orleans demands that it be returned to its former grandeur." They present a carefully organized response which persuasively involves three of the sources that discuss the case for and against rebuilding the city. Their prose demonstrates an impressive control of the elements of effective writing, though it is not flawless.

7   Essays earning a score of 7 fit the description of 6 essays but feature either a more expansive discussion of the topic, or a greater command of prose style.

6   Essays scoring 6 take a position that defends, challenges, or qualifies the claim that "the unique history of the city of New Orleans demands that it be returned to its former grandeur." These responses, while adequately supported and generally sound in nature, are nevertheless not as persuasive as papers earning scores of 7 or better due to their being less developed or less cogent. Though these papers may occasionally lapse in organization, diction or syntax, they are generally clear and effective.

5   Essays scoring 5 generally understand the task but are either limited in scope or insufficiently developed. Though they may be marked by shortcomings in organization, syntax or diction, they nevertheless reflect a certain level of competence.

4   Essays scoring 4 respond inadequately to the question's task, often offering unpersuasive arguments for whether or not New Orleans should be rebuilt, or failing to involve the sources to a sufficiently effective extent. Though the prose is often adequate enough to convey the writer's points, it generally suggests a limited control over organization, diction and syntax.

3   Essays earning a score of 3 meet the criteria for a score of 4 but are either less thorough in documenting the problems in building New Orleans, or display a more limited control over the elements of effective composition.

2   Essays scoring 2 achieve little success in making the case for or against New Orleans being rebuilt. They may on occasion misunderstand a source, fail to develop their argument to any significant degree, paraphrase rather than analyze a source, or display significant weaknesses in organization, clarity, fluency or mechanics.

1   Essays earning a score of 1 meet the criteria for a score of 2 but are either overly simplistic or marred by severe deficiencies in the elements of composition.

0   Essays scoring 0 offer an off-topic response that receives no credit, or a mere repetition of the prompt.

—   Indicates a blank or completely off-topic response.

Sample Student Response One

New Orleans is a city whose past is more often ugly than it is rich. For every Tennessee Williams or Louis Armstrong there are probably a dozen people who live their entire lives in poverty. There are those who say that it is the unique history of the city that makes its reconstruction so important, but these people are misinformed and naïve. There are others who say that history repeats itself, that it would be foolish to rebuild a city below sea level. These people are cursed with ignorance and pessimism. The city of New Orleans needs to be rebuilt because of the people who lived in its 9th Ward and other neighborhoods like it, not for the people who visit the French Quarter during Mardi Gras or attend championships at the Superdome. America owes it to these people, who it forgot and betrayed, to rebuild their homes and their lives for the better.

There are many tangible reasons to avoid rebuilding New Orleans. Source F, a Jack Shafter article literally entitled "The Case Against Rebuilding the Sunken City [. . .]" lists a number of them. The article mentions that neighborhoods like the 9th Ward and Bywater were centers of crime and poverty, where a population without hope or trust failed to report 700 gunshots fired by the police during an afternoon experiment in early 2005. Shafter also indirectly makes reference to the rampant racism and de facto segregation in the city before Hurricane Katrina struck, pointing to the completely inept public schools and the wildly disproportionate number of Blacks with no other options in education. Indeed, Shafter notes that 25% of pre-Katrina New Orleans adults had no high school diploma. Without realizing it, however, the author makes a compelling argument for why New Orleans should be brought back to life. All of these numbers speak to a multitude of issues that plagued the historic city before the hurricane ever struck. In the old city, an entire race of people was held down by another through neglect in the school system and the corruption of the police department. Shafter seems to think of these people as uneducated criminals whose concentration in one center was a crime against humanity that rivaled any other. There may be some merit to his argument (the system of projects, which once promised so much hope, proved to be a failure in every city in America), but Shafter makes no mention of where these people are supposed to go. As of right now, many are grouped in new masses in other cities across the nation, and what little success they may have had has been stripped from them by a combination of racism and Mother Nature.

The American government has a moral obligation to these people, the poor blacks of New Orleans, to rebuild their homes and give them new lives with greater hope than ever before. Thomas Campanella says this much in his article entitled "Recovering New Orleans." He refers to two separate and distinct cities within the municipality that was New Orleans. The first was the city that so many tourists came to know and love, that of flowing liquor and elegant mansions and Super Bowls and Mardi Gras. As Campanella points out, that city's neighborhoods were not as badly flooded, its buildings were not as badly damaged, and the American people have a vested interest in seeing it returned to its former splendor as the party capital of the South. The second city, however, was quite different. Its people were poorer, darker, and less edified, and its buildings were smaller, older, and less valuable. The majority of Americans view this city's destruction as a godsend, even if there was an unfortunate loss of life. These people, however, were generally not put into this suffering because of an inherent laziness or some other flaw of their own. Rather, they were born into these neighborhoods, cursed with an existence where only the very brightest or the most athletic had any prayer at all of getting out. Yet as much as many would like to see these people stay away from the new city forever, New Orleans cannot live without them. They are the people who unload the boats at the port, they are the people who fill the service jobs the tourism industry desperately needs, and they are the people whose tortured history helped give the old city its signature character. If they never come back, then both cities will die.

Jeff Koterba's cartoon, "Eye to Eye," speaks volumes about the symbolic importance of bringing back New Orleans. The picture shows the human spirit, represented by an Olympus-style God, staring down the eye of a hurricane. It is easy to abandon New Orleans, to let the waters of Lake Pontchartrain overflow the levees and take their natural place. It is also easy to rebuild the city solely for tourists and rich people, to leave the large yet vibrant lower class to find their own way. Human history, however, is filled with bold nations that have avoided the easy way out. It would have been easy for the first Americans to stay in Asia, to never travel north and then east across the Bering Land Bridge and into the virgin continent. It would have been easy to leave the capital city in Philadelphia or New York City instead of draining seemingly worthless swampland and renaming it the District of Columbia. It would have been easy for the Airborne to surrender to the Germans during the Battle of the Bulge and wait out the rest of the war in POW camps. The human spirit, however, is a powerful thing, and it enables people and nations to overcome the dreariest odds and triumph over the impossible.

The easy decision is not often the right one. If New Orleans is not rebuilt, or if it is without its lower class, our descendents will look back on the whole debacle with nothing but shame, rather than feel pride over our ability to rebuild a once-flawed city into one of the world's finest. People who say there are no jobs for the lower class to come back to are lying. There is no shortage of jobs for people who need to rebuild their own homes. We can pay them to do it and give them temporary housing, while the federal level works on rebuilding the levees. We can send them to school and attract businesses to the area once they are residing there. We can do all these things, but only if America as a nation, and Louisiana as a state, overcome their racism and start to think about building people's lives for the first time instead of rebuilding the world's largest fraternity house.

You Rate It!

1. How thorough a job did the writer do in terms of <u>defending, challenging or qualifying the claim</u> that "the unique history of the city of New Orleans demands that it be returned to its former grandeur?"

_____

_____

_____

_____

2. To what degree of success did the writer <u>integrate at least three of the six sources</u> to support his/her argument for or against rebuilding the city?

_____

_____

_____

_____

3. How effective was the writer's plan of organization? The fluency of his/her writing? The overall correctness of the paper?

_____

_____

_____

_____

4. On a 0-9 scale, how would you rate this response? Explain why.

_____

_____

_____

_____

Sample Student Response Two

The city of New Orleans has always been an icon of many aspects of American culture. It represents the life of the American South, holds the roots of American jazz, and has the best party in the country. However, due to the destruction of Hurricane Katrina, New Orleans has been devastated and needs to be rebuilt. In the recent past, New Orleans has been a city with two sides: the historical side that tourists see and the impoverished side which they avoid. Reconstructing the city would not only be a chance to restore the historical district to its former grandeur, it would be a chance for the entire city to start fresh and improve upon itself.

Many people argue that New Orleans' location makes it vulnerable to future natural disasters. It is below sea level and right on the temperamental Mississippi River delta. Throughout history, citizens of New Orleans have been trying to prevent these disasters. As technology improves, so does protection of the city. According to Source A, settlers first used small dikes, which were ineffective. Next, they tried levee districts, which have been improved over time. The levees can be improved to withstand more pressure, and will be four to five feet taller than the ones that collapsed during Hurricane Katrina. Innovations in technology will help to prevent future disasters and keep the new New Orleans safe.

One of the most obvious reasons for rebuilding New Orleans is that it is rich in culture and history. More American culture comes from New Orleans than any other city in the country. Every aspect of culture can be found in the city, from jazz to architecture to literature, cooking, and history. Fortunately, the tourist circuit was relatively undamaged and can be rebuilt rather easily and reopened. The tourism will bring in money that can act as an economic base for the city's redevelopment. The author of Source E hopes that sympathy tourism will have the same effect on post-hurricane New Orleans as it did on post-9/11 New York and financially boost the area.

Because the French Quarter will not be hard to rebuild, there will be a lot of money left over to redevelop and improve upon the poorer areas of the city. Many critics of rebuilding New Orleans argue that the city's statistics are far from impressive. They say that poverty, education, and crime were at dismal levels right before the hurricane and that rebuilding would only encourage more of the same. However, not rebuilding may actually make matters worse. The area may again be re-inhabited, only to sink further below the poverty line, further into academic unacceptability, and further into high crime rates. Rebuilding the city, on the other hand, would give officials the chance to solve these problems by starting over. Previously bad statistics are a reason to rebuild the city, not let it sink.

New Orleans has always been an American icon. It is a rich gumbo of music, food, religion, history, literature, language, and architecture. It is important to every American and despite the disappointing statistics before the hurricane and the dangers of future hurricane damage, it is home to 484,000 Americans, to whom it is the most important.

You Rate It!

1. How thorough a job did the writer do in terms of <u>defending, challenging or qualifying the claim</u> that "the unique history of the city of New Orleans demands that it be returned to its former grandeur'?"

_____

_____

_____

_____

2. To what degree of success did the writer <u>integrate at least three of the six sources</u> to support his/her argument for or against rebuilding the city?

_____

_____

_____

_____

3. How effective was the writer's plan of organization? The fluency of his/her writing? The overall correctness of the paper?

_____

_____

_____

4. On a 0-9 scale, how would you rate this response? Explain why.

_____

_____

_____

_____

Sample Student Response Three

Hurricane Katrina was just another of the tremendously destructive hurricanes that the city of New Orleans has been subject to over the years. While some might suggest rebuilding this city immediately, others, if they stop to think, might begin to wonder if rebuilding a city so prone to devastation by hurricane and so inclined to crime and lack of education is such an uncomplicated idea. Taking these factors into account, New Orleans should not be rebuilt because no amount of money or technology can protect the city from future hurricanes and, furthermore, it could never return to the supposed "glory" it once maintained.

Louisiana has never had the greatest track record for safety from flooding. Even in 1941 residents had to concern themselves with the cost of dikes and levees that protected the production of their plantations as well as the likelihood of storms occurring again. At this point, they did not realize the futility of their efforts, besides which the country was recovering from the Depression, so any way to create jobs was eagerly taken on [Source A]. Now, people in the area have learned from the past and want guaranteed protection against Category 5 Hurricanes. History shows that Category 5 hurricanes can and will happen again, and technology dictates that there can be no protection against such a storm. It is absurd to put so many lives in danger when the future can be foreseen so easily.

When people think of what made the city of New Orleans so great, they think of tourist and entertainment sites. Yes, Jackson Square and the Vieux Carré are certainly enjoyable spots. These and other places in the tourist area, however, made it through Hurricane Katrina relatively undamaged and could be rejuvenated quickly, easily, and without much thought [Source E]. The areas that were truly devastated, the areas that were flooded beyond recognition, were not the sites people go for vacations. The locations with the most damage were places with 27 percent of the population living below the poverty line, with 47 percent of the schools deemed "Academically Unacceptable" and 25 percent of adults lacking high school diplomas; where the homicide rate is ten times the national average [Source F]. People forget this when they speak of the "glory" of the city. To insist upon the rebuilding of this part of New Orleans and the continuation of its former way of life is to ignore the truth of its corruption and destitution and to advocate the promotion of these immense problems.

New Orleans may be home to this or that famous author or jazz musician, but it is also home to many more imperative, looming problems. The probability of another devastating hurricane is likely too absolute and the protection that technology can currently handle is insufficient. In addition, the real New Orleans is where poverty, lack of education, and crime are rampant. More important than to let prosper the food that the city is famous for is to protect lives and to improve the quality of life, so New Orleans should not be rebuilt.

You Rate It!

1. How thorough a job did the writer do in terms of <u>defending, challenging or qualifying the claim</u> that "the unique history of the city of New Orleans demands that it be returned to its former grandeur?"

_____

_____

_____

_____

2. To what degree of success did the writer <u>integrate at least three of the six sources</u> to support his/her argument for or against rebuilding the city?

_____

_____

_____

_____

3. How effective was the writer's plan of organization? The fluency of his/her writing? The overall correctness of the paper?

_____

_____

_____

_____

4. On a 0-9 scale, how would you rate this response? Explain why.

_____

_____

_____

_____

_____

Author's Response to Sample Student Essays on "Should New Orleans Be Rebuilt?"

Sample Student Essay One:

This superb essay has so much obvious merit that a defense of its quality seems almost superfluous. For one, the student's essay features an extraordinary amount of development for the time allotted. However, what distinguishes this essay is its passionate sense of social concern, of "moral obligation" to cite the student, a stalwart position that generates the essay's impressive conviction. The essay is also characterized by equally impressive rhetoric, parallel constructions that have a Thomas Paine-like quality to them. For example, consider this nicely balanced pairing in the opening paragraph that indicts the shortcomings of two different camps:

> There are those who say that it is the unique history of the city that makes its reconstruction so important, but these people are misinformed and naïve. There are others who say that history repeats itself, that it would be foolish to rebuild the city below sea level. These people are cursed with ignorance and pessimism

Or the wonderful trinity that catalogs the impoverished residents whose lives were most negatively affected by the storm:

> They are the people who unload the boats at the port, they are the people who fill the service jobs the tourism industry desperately needs, and they are the people whose tortured history helped give the old city its signature character.

Or, for example, the use of the collective "we" to suggest not only our choices but our *responsibility*, as well as the concluding Swiftian sarcasm:

> We can pay them to do it and give them temporary housing, while the federal level works on rebuilding the levees. We can send them to school and attract businesses to the area once they are residing there. We can do all these things, but only if America as a nation, and Louisiana as a state, overcome their racism and start to think about building people's lives for the first time instead of rebuilding the world's largest fraternity house.

This wonderful essay not only involves three sources in detailed fashion, it alludes to things as diverse as the Bering Land Bridge and the siege of Bastogne. This potent combination of a firmly established stance and the "touch of the poet" makes this a truly exceptional paper.

Author's Score: 9

Sample Student Essay Two

Though not nearly as expansive as the first sample essay, student response two is also a very creditable response. The author has a very easy prose style, which makes reading the essay a pleasurable experience. The writing style is marked by compression, and the author integrates sources so glibly and unobtrusively that at first glance the paper may appear under-cited. This, I think, would do the essay an injustice since the writer takes a clear stand that the city needs to be rebuilt; summarizes a variety of issues, including the duality of culture and poverty that defines the city, the flawed levee system that underscores any rebuilding effort, and the long-term tragedies that might result from any decision not to rebuild; and conveys all of this is in a clear and fluent prose style. The writer's final paragraph metaphor, of New Orleans being "a rich gumbo of music, food, religion, history, literature, language, and architecture," is a clever closing touch. Though the writer could have perhaps expanded upon the content of the sources, his paper is, nevertheless, an admirable one.

Author's Score: 7, rising

Sample Student Essay Three:

Student response three offers an interesting bookend for the previous paper. It is of similar length, it takes an equally firm position (in this case, against rebuilding the city), and it cites the passage with a similarly light touch. The writer of this paper is more than competent, identifying New Orleans poor "track record" when it comes to safety from flooding, and suggesting that the areas that suffered the most damage are areas that are not worth being resuscitated: "To insist upon the rebuilding of this part of New Orleans and the continuation of its former way of life is to ignore the truth of its corruption and destitution and to advocate the promotion of these immense problems." Yet somehow this response lacks some of the completeness and fluency of the previous one. It cites material from the sources that is reasonable and effective in making a case for not rebuilding the city, but only the most obvious ones. The writer, while certainly competent, lacks the refinement of the author of the previous passage. This essay ekes into the upper-half but not by much.

Author's Score: 6

Sample Examination II

Questions 1-13. Refer to the following passage.

The following is excerpted from author Gene Smith's 1964 reflections upon revisiting World War I battle sites fifty years later.

O Verdun![1] All along the dull road up from Bar-de-Luc there are concrete posts with concrete helmets on top and raised lettering saying this is *La Voie*
(5) *Sacree*[2], the Sacred Road. At Souilly, Pétain's[3] headquarters is unchanged from the way it looks in the pictures that show him standing on the steps to watch the youth of a nation go northward to its fate.
(10) Seventy percent of the French army went up this road. Night and day the trucks went grinding by; battalions of men stood and flung crushed rock under the tires so that they would not sink into the mud.
(15) Today it is strangely silent, however one much strains to hear the sounds of motors and sloshing boots and the mumbled throbbing of the distant places where for months on end the guns were
(20) never quiet. But the visible signs of battle are still present. Here are the long trenches, twelve feet deep then, six feet now that nature has half filled them up; here are the craters with cows scrambling up their sides;
(25) here is the metal plate used for protection against the shells and now used to roof sheds and support garden walls. In these fields it is impossible to walk for long without seeing rusted metal protruding up
(30) through the wet moss; here if you leave the road and go past the signs warning of *Danger de Mort* —Danger of Death!— you will soon lose yourself in the scrub pine planted in the thirties when
(35) experts finally decided that the soil was too gas-and-shell-corrupted to reclaim it for agriculture. Under trees or in stream beds are rusted grenades or shells, as terrifying as coiled snakes. Dig and you will find
(40) bullets, shell fragments, broken rifles, sardine tins, decayed canteens, unidentifiable bits of metal. It requires but a few minutes of work to hold in your hand what was last seen two generations ago by a boy
(45) in field grey or horizon blue. Now he is an old man in Leipzig or Nancy or, more likely, he is known as the grandfather or great-uncle who perished at Verdun.
The name on the signpost, seen
(50) from a moving car, catches the eye and holds it as the car sweeps past. Verdun. In the city itself, in one of the long, deep galleries of the citadel where the French troops found rest during their infrequent
(55) respites from the ever-wet trenches (it always rains here), there is a one-eyed veteran. His glass eye never moves. He gives foreigners a piece of paper typed in their language which asks that they not
(60) forget to tip him. Inside the gallery there are eight coffins covered with oilcloth flags.[4] (No cotton or silk would last long in this dank, wet place.) On the wall there is a great sign, "They Shall Not Pass".[5]
(65) Past the terrible sign is a great cemetery. On a hill facing the graves is the *ossuaire*. In the rear are scores of windows at waist level. One must bend and shade the eyes to see what is there. Bones are
(70) there—the bones of 150,000 unidentified men of both sides. Here is a window: See the neat piles of leg bones. Another: arms. Another: skulls. Look at the hole in this one. See the spider weaving his web
(75) between the eye sockets. Through other windows in the ossuary one sees bones piled in unsorted confusion. This collection is ever-growing; often a wild boar rooting in the earth will show where more bones
(80) lie. Or during a forest fire a 75-mm. shell will blow up, fifty years late, and uncover more Unknown Soldiers.
All this happened at Verdun. And yet no drums beat and there are no bugles.
(85) Concentrating and looking back past the France and Germany that followed Verdun, past sick France sliding downhill and sick Germany with its monocled politicians in high stiff collars and their leather-booted
(90) prostitutes, you must say to yourself, Here

76

under my feet and within the space I see,
hundreds of thousands of men died, here
the entire world turned over.

---

[1] site of a crucial battle in the First World War
[2] the only safe supply line to Verdun
[3] Henri Phillipe Pétain, French officer appointed to oversee the
defense of Verdun
[4] remains of unidentified French soldiers
[5] *Ils ne passeront pas* (Fr): Pétain's pledge to thwart the German
advance

Mr. Gene Smith is the author of
"Still Quiet on the Western Front Fifty Years Later",
Until the Last Trumpets Sound", "Leon Grant",
"When the Cheering Stopped"
and other famous works.

1. The author develops his essay around which of
the following contrasts?

(A) reality and romance
(B) past and present
(C) victory and defeat
(D) youth and age
(E) courage and cowardice

2. The author's primary purpose in the passage is to

(A) pay homage to the fortitude of the
combatants
(B) lament the tremendous sacrifice demanded
by combat
(C) criticize the strategy of a military
commander
(D) salute the efforts of archaeologists in
recreating an important battle
(E) delineate the effects of time and weather on
historical sites

3. The exclamation, "Oh, Verdun!" (line 1), is likely
an expression of

(A) recognition
(B) frustration
(C) surprise
(D) mourning
(E) nostalgia

4. In recreating the world of Verdun, the author
relies upon all of the following EXCEPT

(A) onomatopoeic diction that conveys the
weather-induced struggles of men and
transport
(B) personal reminiscences of surviving veterans
(C) topographical landmarks that men and nature
have since altered
(D) uncovered relics of the fierce conflict
(E) parenthetical comments that describe the
sodden weather

5. Which of the following is NOT characteristic of
the style of the long second paragraph?

(A) the use of inversion to delineate still-visible
scars from the decisive battle
(B) a subtle shift to second person which
intensifies the immediacy of the experience
for the reader
(C) a preponderance of visual images which
contrasts the ubiquitous silence
(D) trenches that symbolize mass graves
(E) a somber and ominous tone

6. The effectiveness of lines 37-39, "Under trees or
in stream beds are rusted grenades or shells, as
terrifying as coiled snakes," is abetted by which
of the following?

I. The innocuous connotation of the word
"rusted."
II. A comparison that suggests latent and
imminent danger.
III. The disarming nature of the pastoral locale.

(A) II only
(B) III only
(C) I and II
(D) II and III
(E) I, II and III

7. Which BEST represents the arrangement of the
objects listed in lines 40-42?

(A) military to civilian
(B) archaic to contemporary
(C) whole to splintered
(D) extraneous to pragmatic
(E) large to small

8. The author likely includes the detail of the one-eyed veteran (lines 51-60) as a(n)

   (A) haunting image of the terrible carnage
   (B) stark reminder of the impoverished and dependent lot of many older vets
   (C) visible sign of the veneration afforded the Verdun dead
   (D) permanent tribute to the unyielding defense of the fortification
   (E) telling symbol of the political blindness that sparks such awful conflicts

9. The BEST equivalent of the word "terrible" in line 65 would be

   (A) terrifying
   (B) offensive
   (C) discomfiting
   (D) macabre
   (E) garish

10. Lines 83-84, "All this happened at Verdun. And yet no drums beat and there are no bugles," suggest that

   (A) the heroic dead have been grossly dishonored
   (B) there is no real victory at such a calamitous sacrifice
   (C) the Verdun countryside no longer resonates with war
   (D) present villagers have tried to forget the war
   (E) the military preparedness of France is again lax

11. Which of the following pairs of adjectives BEST captures the author's attitude toward the events at Verdun as expressed in the final paragraph?

   (A) heroic and lionized
   (B) unappreciated and wasted
   (C) costly and cataclysmic
   (D) unforeseen and embarrassing
   (E) momentary and forgotten

12. The third and fifth footnotes, and the initial description of Pétain in lines 7-9, suggest that he

   (A) took great pride in his French forces
   (B) was eager for promotion
   (C) was willing to absorb great casualties to hold the position
   (D) was more boastful than determined
   (E) kept himself out of harm's way

13. In light of the passage as a whole, the phrase "They Shall Not Pass" and its explanatory footnote do which of the following?

   I.   Account for the extreme number of unidentified remains in the *ossuaire*.
   II. Question grimly the sense of such adamancy.
   III. Epitomize the concept of "Pyrrhic victory"

   (A) I only
   (B) III only
   (C) I and II
   (D) II and III
   (E) I, II and III

Questions 14-26. Refer to the following passage.

Dear Child,—You have given me a great deal of satisfaction by your account of your eldest daughter. I am particularly pleased to hear she is a good arithmetician;
(5) it is the best proof of understanding: the knowledge of numbers is one of the chief distinctions between us and the brutes. If there is anything in blood, you may reasonably expect your children should be
(10) endowed with an uncommon share of good sense. Mr. Wortley's family and mine have both produced some of the greatest men that have been born in England [. . . .].

I will therefore speak to you as
(15) supposing Lady Mary not only capable, but desirous of learning: in that case by all means let her be indulged in it. You will tell me I did not make it a part of your education: your prospect was very different
(20) from hers. As you had no defect either in mind or person to hinder, and much in your circumstances to attract, the highest offers, it seemed your business to learn how to live in the world, as it is hers to learn how to be
(25) easy out of it. It is the common error of builders and parents to follow some plan they think beautiful (and perhaps is so) without considering that nothing is beautiful that is misplaced. Hence we see so
(30) many edifices raised that the raisers can never inhabit, being too large for their fortunes. Vistas are laid open over barren heaths, and apartments contrived for a coolness very agreeable in Italy, but killing
(35) in the north of Britain: thus every woman endeavours to breed her daughter a fine lady, qualifying her for a station in which she will never appear, and at the same time incapacitating her for that retirement to
(40) which she is destined. Learning, if she has a real taste for it, will not only make her contented, but happy in it. No entertainment is so cheap as reading, nor any pleasure so lasting. She will not want new fashions, nor
(45) regret the loss of expensive diversions, or variety of company, if she can be amused with an author in her closet [. . . .]; she cannot advance herself in any profession, and has therefore more hours to spare [. . . .].
(50) There are two cautions to be given on this subject: first, not to think herself learned when she can read Latin, or even Greek [. . . .]. True knowledge consists of knowing things, not words. I would wish her
(55) no further a linguist than to enable her to read books in their originals that are often corrupted, and always injured by translations. Two hours' application every morning will bring this about much sooner
(60) than you can imagine and she will have leisure enough besides to run over the English poetry, which is a more important part of a woman's education than it is generally supposed. Many a young damsel
(65) has been ruined by a fine copy of verses, which she would have laughed at if she had known it had been stolen from Mr. Waller. I remember when I was a girl, I saved one of my companions from destruction who
(70) communicated to me an epistle she was quite charmed with. As she had a natural good taste, she observed the lines were not so smooth as Prior's or Pope's but had more thought and spirit than any of theirs.
(75) She was wonderfully delighted with such a demonstration of her lover's sense and passion, and not a little pleased with her own charms, that had force enough to inspire such elegancies. In the midst of this
(80) triumph I showed her that they were taken from Randolph's poems and the unfortunate transcriber was dismissed with the scorn he deserved. To say truth, the poor plagiary was very unlucky to fall into
(85) my hands; that author being no longer in fashion, would have escaped any one of less universal reading than myself [. . . .].

The second caution to be given her (and which is the most absolutely
(90) necessary) is to conceal whatever learning she attains, with as much solicitude as she would hide crookedness or lameness; the parade of it can only serve to draw on her the envy, and consequently the most
(95) inveterate hatred, of all he and she fools, which will certainly be at least three parts in four of all her acquaintance [. . . .].

14. The most important revelation of the opening paragraph concerns the

    (A) precocious intelligence of the granddaughter
    (B) unquestioning subservience of the daughter
    (C) accuracy of the daughter's account of her children
    (D) characteristic conceit of the mother
    (E) the accomplishments of the extended family

15. Which of the following does NOT help to establish Lady Montagu's sense of social superiority?

    (A) "account" (line 2)
    (B) "distinctions" (line 7)
    (C) "blood" (line 8)
    (D) "endowed" (line 10)
    (E) "uncommon" (line 10)

16. Throughout her letter to her daughter, the mother's tone is

    (A) scornful and dismissive
    (B) contrary and argumentative
    (C) apologetic and conciliatory
    (D) sentimental and nostalgic
    (E) haughty and didactic

17. In the second paragraph the mother uses generalization to convey the desire of all mothers to see their daughters

    (A) secure the house of their dreams
    (B) earn an academic degree
    (C) improve their social lot
    (D) abandon an exclusively maternal focus
    (E) become fluent in Greek and Latin

18. The transitional sentence that opens paragraph two is intended to expose the mother's

    (A) ironclad confidence in her granddaughter's intelligence
    (B) pompous concession that her granddaughter should be educated
    (C) admirable confidence in her daughter's capabilities as a mother
    (D) offensive meddling in her daughter's affairs
    (E) stoic acceptance of her granddaughter's limitations

19. Lines 19-20, "your prospect was very different from hers," introduce information that confirms the mother's belief that her granddaughter is inferior to her own daughter in terms of

    (A) intelligence
    (B) physical beauty
    (C) potential for dowry
    (D) temperament
    (E) social refinement

20. The mother reinforces the difference between daughter and granddaughter through

    (A) extended metaphor
    (B) rhetorical questions
    (C) personal anecdote
    (D) comparison/contrast
    (E) hyperbolic characterization

21. In lines 25-40, the mother figuratively hints at her granddaughter's "unsuitability" through all of the following EXCEPT

    (A) the wrong-headedness of the builders' floor plan
    (B) the supercilious tone of the word "misplaced"
    (C) an intimation of financial inadequacy
    (D) a blanket condemnation of the architectural appeal of the edifice
    (E) the impracticality of the building's locale

22. The most disturbing nature of the mother's comments in lines 40-49 is her

    (A) observation that reading is "cheap"
    (B) suggestion that her granddaughter will not be distracted by vanities
    (C) intimation that the only value of literature is amusement
    (D) agreement that the prospect of girls should be limited by their gender
    (E) argument that girls have "more hours to spare"

23. In her anecdote in lines 64-87, the mother dramatizes the egregious nature of her childhood friend's literary *faux pas* through all of the following EXCEPT

    (A) employing hyperbolic diction that likens it to a loss of virginity
    (B) mocking the ineptitude of the deceitful attempt
    (C) celebrating her efforts as a sleuth and a savior
    (D) characterizing the letter's author as an incorrigible blackguard
    (E) linking her near "destruction" to the fates of other damsels

24. The mother implies that her young friend was primarily duped by which of the following?

    I. The seemingly original nature of the verse.
    II. The passionate appeal of her lover in the letter.
    III. A concession to her own vanity.

    (A) I only
    (B) III only
    (C) I and II
    (D) II and III
    (E) I, II and III

25. The concluding paragraph of the mother's letter seems to contradict which of the following characteristics of the mother?

    (A) her instructive bent
    (B) her supercilious attitude
    (C) her belief in the social limitations of her granddaughter
    (D) her belief in the importance of literacy
    (E) her surety in manners of social decorum

26. Overall, the letter unintentionally satirizes the mother's feelings about social

    (A) consciousness
    (B) activism
    (C) Darwinism
    (D) justice
    (E) mobility

Questions 27-38. Refer to the following passage.

The men of Troy fought often and with the immense generosity that only the Irish bring to brawling. They held back from each other nothing of their arms, their (5) backs, and their long bellies. Walk in Troy in the evening, and you come upon a place of special stillness. There is a ring of quiet men. Only grunts and the thud of unseen blows, the scrabbling of shoes on the (10) cobblestones suggests the business within the ring. Nudge between the circled watchers, and you will see them. Punch. Duck. Punch. Duck. All at once, one of the two is knocked off balance. He begins to (15) fall, but he knows he must not go down without pulling the other after him. Now they are rolling in bloody confabulation upon the cobblestones. These men are not ashamed to show their devotion to each (20) other's flesh. All at once, a sigh comes from the little crowd which had hitherto been silent. It is not a sigh of sorrow or satisfaction, but rather like a mark of punctuation, a semi-colon. It means that a (25) certain point has been reached. With a single punch or kick, one of the men has gained irreversible ascendancy over the other. When you hear that sigh, you can tell who is going to win.

(30) An hour later, you pass the tavern. You look in and see the two men toasting each other with beer. This time they will sing. Outside, a woman comes with a pail and a brush. She scours the place where the (35) cobblestones are stained with blood; then, she swings her pail to the gutter. A pink twine of scrub water races for the river.

There came the day when it was my turn. I enjoyed no great-muscled youth, (40) but was of that frail and pallid look that is often deceptive in that it may be coincident with true good health. Barry McKenna was bigger than I by half, and with a face so handsome it seemed to have been chipped (45) out with a clever Irish axe. He had curly lion-colored hair and green eyes. We were fourteen and in the eighth grade. The schoolyard had become a fascist pen of cement where no citizen was safe. For a (50) long moment, we faced each other while the ring of classmates formed and clanged shut about us. There was no escape.

"I'm going to kill you," Barry said, and smiled with immense charm.

(55) Then we closed, or rather, he bore down upon me. I raised my hands in a facsimile of boxing, holding them together lest my arms fly apart and I embrace my tragic destiny. His first punch hit me on the (60) ear, stung, then scattered. The second punch landed on my shoulder. Minutes went by. Barry punched. He danced away. I swung. It was my obligation to do so. I missed. And so it went. At last I slipped, (65) groped for him, and we were down. I no longer had to stand and face him. He sat astride, steadying me with his thighs and belling like a white stag. Just beyond one massy shoulder, something wild and gold (70) hovered, then broke in the air. Straining, I listened for the sigh of the crowd. When it came, I welcomed it as a Bedouin in the desert welcomes the flies that are the herald of an oasis. I had only to wait a little longer.

(75) "Aw, let him go, Barry." It was a voice from the ring.

"Come on, let the faggot go."

Above me, Barry hesitated, weighing, I suppose, the pros and cons of (80) the suggestion. But the words of that spectator had done what none of Barry's punches could. And from the ground, I drew my fist and threw it upward. It hit him in the Adam's apple. With the other fist, I (85) hit him in the chest over the breastbone. Barry paused, as though listening to a sound far-off, barely audible. And raising one terrible fist above my face, he brought it down [. . .] to his own chest, pressing. Then (90) he coughed, and blood ran from his mouth, dripping from his chin. Again he coughed, and I was splashed with his blood. Awkwardly, like a fat cow, he disengaged himself from my body and struggled to his (95) feet.

Again and again he coughed, each time raising new and meatier gobs of blood. I thought of Miss Cleary's cranberry conserve with which she paid father for her (100) bee-venom treatments. For a long moment, Barry and I stared at each other. Then, pale and sweating, he backed away from where I lay like a small creature that has been ripped and clenched, and dropped in midair. (105) The ring of faces opened, and he was gone.

"You won," Billy said later. "You made him bleed."

"No," I said. "I didn't win."

Confessions Of A Knife by Richard Selzer. Copyright © 1979 by David Goldman and Janet Selzer (New York: William Morrow). Reprinted by permission of Georges Borchardt, Inc. on behalf of the author.

27. In this excerpt the author seems most concerned with depicting the

    (A) characteristic pugnacity of an ethnic group
    (B) menial chores performed by peasant women
    (C) sickness which plagued his early years
    (D) unwillingness of bystanders to intercede
    (E) events which forged his own character

28. The author characterizes the ritualistic brawling depicted in the passage as all of the following EXCEPT

    (A) an unavoidable rite-of-passage
    (B) a pugilistic *danse macabre*
    (C) an ironically intimate bonding
    (D) a defense against bigotry
    (E) a mesmerizing and arresting spectacle

29. Which of the following elements is NOT used by the author in the first paragraph to capture the intensity of the public combat?

    (A) physical actions
    (B) a sequence of monosyllabic verbs
    (C) elongated sentences that mirror the duration of the battle
    (D) the counterpoint of the crowd's silence
    (E) onomatopoeic diction

30. The anonymity of the combatants in the opening paragraph is intended to imply the

    (A) ubiquitous animosity directed by the men of Troy at strangers
    (B) regular incidence of inebriated public confrontation
    (C) desire of the pugilists to avoid potential arrest
    (D) ignominious consequence of losing the battle
    (E) lack of a clear-cut victor

31. The primary purpose of the second paragraph is to illustrate which aspect of the combatants?

    (A) their ironic and incongruous bond
    (B) their minimal injury
    (C) their continued profession of hostility
    (D) their shameful drunkenness
    (E) their characteristic misogyny

32. Of the following phrases, which does LEAST to augment the fatalistic nature of the impending encounter?

    (A) "There came the day when it was my turn." (lines 38-39)
    (B) "The schoolyard had become a fascist pen of cement where no citizen was safe." (lines 47-49)
    (C) "[. . .] the ring of classmates formed and clanged shut about us." (lines 51-52)
    (D) "tragic destiny" (line 59)
    (E) "It was my obligation to do so." (line 63)

33. The overall description of the speaker's opponent, Barry McKenna, is BEST labeled

    (A) brutish
    (B) anomalous
    (C) leonine
    (D) corpulent
    (E) self-engrossed

34. The speaker develops the characterization of Barry McKenna via all of the following EXCEPT

    (A) comparisons to various animals
    (B) a physical handsomeness that belies his violent nature
    (C) a comment that captures his boastful confidence
    (D) a chorus of supporters that enthusiastically eggs him on
    (E) a wordless retreat that conveys his surprise at the speaker's resistance

35. The simile contained in lines 72-74—"I welcomed it [. . .] the herald of an oasis"—may be seen as reflecting which of the following?

    I. The speaker's bitter chagrin at being soundly beaten.
    II. The speaker's sense of relief that his ordeal is almost done.
    III. The speaker's stoic resignation to a massive concluding blow.

    (A) I only
    (B) II only
    (C) I and III
    (D) II and III
    (E) I, II and III

36. The import of the speaker's observation—"But the words of that spectator had done what none of Barry's punches could" (lines 80-82)—is BEST interpreted as meaning

    (A) bouy his spirits
    (B) provoke his manhood
    (C) exacerbate his fears
    (D) quicken his submission
    (E) injure his feelings

37. The speaker most likely utters the closing line of the passage because he

    (A) believes he won by default
    (B) has himself suffered a terrible beating
    (C) is too modest to boast about his victory
    (D) is troubled by his own capacity for violence
    (E) fears that McKenna will seek future reprisal

38. Ultimately, the speaker's account of his experience in the schoolyard also confirms which of the following?

    (A) his admirable boxing prowess
    (B) his cowardice in refusing to fight
    (C) Barry McKenna's empathy for his weaker opponent
    (D) the ineffectiveness of school officials in deterring such conflict
    (E) the impressionable nature of the schoolboys

Questions 39-51. Refer to the following passage.

In our time it is broadly true that political writing is bad writing. Where it is not true, it will generally be found that the writer is some kind of rebel, expressing his
(5) private opinions and not a "party line." Orthodoxy, of whatever color, seems to demand a lifeless, imitative style. The political dialects to be found in pamphlets, leading articles, manifestoes, White Papers[1]
(10) and the speeches of under-secretaries do, of course, vary from party to party, but they are all alike in that one almost never finds in them a fresh, vivid, home-made turn of speech. When one watches some tired hack
(15) on the platform mechanically repeating the familiar phrases—*bestial atrocities, iron heel, bloodstained tyranny, free peoples of the world, stand shoulder to shoulder*—one often has a curious feeling that one is not
(20) watching a live human being but some kind of dummy; a feeling that suddenly becomes stronger at moments when the light catches the speaker's spectacles and turns them into blank discs which seem to have no eyes
(25) behind them. And this is not altogether fanciful. A speaker who uses that kind of phraseology has gone some distance towards turning himself into a machine [. . . .]. If the speech he is making is one he is
(30) accustomed to make over and over again, he may be almost unconscious of what he is saying, as one is when one utters the responses in church [. . . .].

In our time, political speech writing
(35) is largely the defense of the indefensible. Things like the continuance of British rule in India, the Russian purges and deportations, the dropping of the atom bombs on Japan, can indeed be defended,
(40) but only by arguments which are too brutal for most people to face, and which do not square with the professed aims of political parties. Thus political language has to consist largely of euphemism, question-
(45) begging and sheer cloudy vagueness. Defenseless villages are bombarded from the air, the inhabitants driven into the countryside, the cattle machine-gunned, the huts set on fire with incendiary bullets: this
(50) is called *pacification*. Millions of peasants are robbed of their farms and sent trudging along the roads with no more than they can carry: this is called *transfer of population*

or *rectification of frontiers*. People are
(55) imprisoned for years without trial, or shot in the back of the neck or sent to die in Arctic lumber camps: this is called *elimination of unreliable elements*. Such phraseology is needed if one wants to name
(60) things without calling up mental pictures of them. Consider for instance some comfort-able English professor defending Russian totalitarianism. He cannot say outright, "I believe in killing off your opponents when
(65) you can get good results by doing so." Probably, therefore, he will say something like this:

> While freely conceding that the
> Soviet regime exhibits certain
(70) > features which the humanitarian
> way may be inclined to deplore, we
> must, I think, agree that a certain
> curtailment of the right to political
> opposition is an unavoidable
(75) > concomitant of transitional periods,
> and that the rigors which the
> Russian people have been called
> upon to undergo have been amply
> justified in the sphere of concrete
(80) > achievement.

The inflated style itself is a kind of euphemism. A mass of Latin words falls upon the facts like soft snow, blurring the outlines and covering up all the details. The
(85) great enemy of clear language is insincerity. When there is a gap between one's real and one's declared aims, one turns, as it were instinctively, to long words and exhausted idioms, like a cuttlefish
(90) squirting out ink.[2] In our age there is no such thing as "keeping out of politics." All issues are political issues, and politics itself is a mass of lies, evasions, folly, hatred and schizophrenia [. . . .].

---

[1] governmental policy papers that take a position or offer a solution to a particular problem

[2] small squid-like ocean-dweller that squirts ink as a defense

39. The author's central concern in the passage is

    (A) improving the quality of political writing
    (B) criticizing the poor delivery of political speech-makers
    (C) deploring the use of language to downplay or conceal true intent
    (D) defending freedom of speech in academic institutions
    (E) arguing passionately for world peace

40. The "color" to which the author refers in line 6 is BEST interpreted as meaning

    (A) race
    (B) genre
    (C) religion
    (D) manifestation
    (E) epoch

41. Which of the following does NOT contribute to framing the author's attitude toward political writing in general?

    (A) "lifeless" (line 7)
    (B) "imitative" (line 7)
    (C) "home-made" (line 13)
    (D) "mechanically" (line 15)
    (E) "familiar" (line 16)

42. The description of the "tired hack" in lines 14-33 does all of the following EXCEPT

    (A) illustrate the depersonalization effected by political rhetoric
    (B) intimate that the repetition of such epithets can result in a kind of brainwashing
    (C) present a frightening symbol of blind conformity
    (D) insinuate that religious institutions plant the initial seeds of conformity
    (E) imply that he exemplifies the "lifeless, imitative style" of political orthodoxy

43. Lines 34-35 exemplify which of the following?

    (A) understatement
    (B) paradox
    (C) metaphor
    (D) hyperbole
    (E) allusion

44. Which of the following is NOT mentioned by the author as a possible motivation for political speakers' use of "*pacification*" (line 50), "*transfer of population*" (line 53) and similar euphemistic phraseology?

    (A) a desire to rationalize largely irrational actions
    (B) a need to shroud the horrid realities of modern warfare
    (C) a wish to match political arguments with the professed aims of a party
    (D) an attempt by some speakers to protect themselves from a potentially unpopular backlash
    (E) a clear willingness to avoid sincerity

45. The primary effect that the English professor's commentary in lines 68-80 has upon the reader (and likely upon an audience) is one of

    (A) obfuscation
    (B) exhilaration
    (C) provocation
    (D) clarification
    (E) indignation

46. The author's choice of the adjective "comfortable" (lines 61-62) to describe the professor is likely intended to mock mildly his

    (A) economic security
    (B) political knowledge
    (C) rhetorical ability
    (D) academic freedom
    (E) quaint lodgings

47. In supporting his claim that "Such phraseology is needed if one wants to name things without calling up mental pictures of them" (lines 58-61), the author could NOT include which of the English professor's phrases?

    (A) "certain features" (lines 69-70)
    (B) "certain curtailment" (lines 72-73)
    (C) "transitional periods" (line 75)
    (D) "rigors" (line 76)
    (E) "concrete achievement" (lines 79-80)

48. Lines 82-84, "A mass of Latin words falls upon the facts like soft snow, blurring the outlines and covering up all the details," provide a contrasting image of

    (A) preponderancy and delicacy
    (B) clarity and confusion
    (C) specificity and ambiguity
    (D) darkness and illumination
    (E) descent and elevation

49. The author likely employs the simile "like soft snow" (line 83) in order to convey which of the following?

    I. The euphemistic nature of the rhetoric itself.
    II. The subtlety by which such rhetoric can evade the truth.
    III. The totality with which such rhetoric masks unpleasant realities.

    (A) II only
    (B) III only
    (C) I and II
    (D) I and III
    (E) I, II and III

50. In highlighting the euphemistic rhetoric of politicians in the passage, the author makes the most extensive use of

    (A) the simile comparing such speeches to responses made in church (lines 32-33)
    (B) blunt diction and images of violence (lines 46-61)
    (C) the paraphrase of the English professor (lines 68-80)
    (D) the declaration that "The great enemy of clear language is insincerity." (lines 84-86)
    (E) the simile of the ink-spouting cuttlefish (lines 89-90)

51. In the course of his argument, the author does all of the following EXCEPT

    (A) compare a political speaker to a mannequin
    (B) allude to episodes of imperialist and militaristic action
    (C) provide a catalog of diverse political writing
    (D) deride the platform of a specific political party
    (E) satirize politicians' tendency to euphemize the unpleasant

Question One

(Suggested time—40 minutes. This question counts as one-third of the total essay section score.)

Read the following passage carefully. Then, in a well-organized essay, discuss what the author implies about the role of art and the artist in depicting scenes of war, and show how she uses elements of language to convey it.

Central to modern expectations, and modern ethical feeling, is the conviction that war is an aberration, if an unstoppable one. That peace is the norm, if an unattainable one. This, of course, is not the way war has been regarded throughout history. War has been the norm and peace the exception.

(5)   The description of the exact fashion in which bodies are injured or killed is a recurring climax in the stories told in the *Iliad*. War is seen as something men do inveterately, undeterred by the accumulation of the suffering it inflicts; and to represent war in words or in pictures requires a keen, unflinching detachment. When Leonardo DaVinci gives instructions for a battle painting, he insists that artists have the courage and the imagination to show war in all its

(10)   ghastliness:

> Make the conquered and beaten pale, with brows raised
> and knit, and the skin above their brows furrowed with
> pain…and the teeth apart as with crying out in lamen-
> tation…Make the dead partly or entirely covered with
> (15)   dust…and let the blood be seen by its color flowing in
> a sinuous stream from the corpse to the dust. Others in
> the death agony grinding their teeth, rolling their eyes,
> with their fists clenched against their bodies, and the legs
> distorted [. . . .].

(20)   The concern is that the images to be devised won't be sufficiently upsetting: not concrete, not detailed enough. Pity can entail a moral judgment if, as Aristotle maintains, pity is considered to be the emotion that we owe only to those enduring undeserved misfortune. But pity, far from being the natural twin of fear in the dramas of catastrophic misfortune, seems diluted—distracted—by fear, while fear (dread, terror) usually manages to swamp pity. Leonardo is suggesting that

(25)   the artist's gaze be, literally, pitiless. The image should appall, and in that *terribilita* lies a challenging kind of beauty.

That a gory battlescape could be beautiful—in the sublime or awesome or tragic register of the beautiful—is a commonplace about images of war made by artists. The idea does not sit well when applied to images taken by cameras: to find beauty in war photographs seem heartless.

(30)   But the landscape of devastation is still a landscape. There is beauty in ruins. To acknowledge the beauty of photographs of the World Trade Center ruins in the months following the attack seemed frivolous, sacrilegious. The most people dared to say was that the photographs were "surreal," a euphemism behind which the disgraced notion of beauty cowered. But they *were* beautiful, many of them—by veteran photographers such as Gilles Peress, Susan Meiselas, and Joel Meyerowitz,

(35)   among others. The site itself, the mass graveyard that had received the name "Ground Zero," was of course anything but beautiful. Photographs tend to transform, whatever their subject; and as an image something may be beautiful—or terrifying, or unbearable, or quite bearable—as it is not in real life.

Transforming is what art does, but photography that bears witness to the calamitous and

(40)   reprehensible is much criticized if it seems "aesthetic"; that is, too much like art [. . . .].

Excerpt from REGARDING THE PAIN OF OTHERS by Susan Sontag. Copyright (c) 2003 by Susan Sontag

Question Two

(Suggested time—40 minutes. This question counts as one-third of the total essay section score.)

The following passage, from American historian C. Vann Woodward's *The Burden of Southern History* (1960), makes the following observation about the American people:

> The painful truth that Americans were so frantically fleeing
> was that history had at last caught up with them. It was no
> longer "something unpleasant that happens to other people,"
> for it was happening to them too in their own part of the world.
> Neither their fabulous wealth nor their unequaled power, their
> superb technology nor their legendary "know-how," nor all
> those endowments combined assured them of success in solving
> their most pressing problems. On both the foreign front and the
> domestic front they had at last encountered problems that defied
> solutions of the traditional short-term sort and mocked their
> religion of optimism [. . . .].

Reprinted by permission of Louisiana State University Press from *The Burden Of Southern History* by C. Vann Woodward. Copyright © 1969 by Louisiana State University Press.

Take a moment to reflect upon the preceding comment. Then, write a well-organized essay in which you explore the validity of Woodward's assertion, either in Woodward's era or in some other time period, using examples from your reading, observation, studies or experience to develop your position.

<u>Question Three</u>

(Suggested time—55 minutes. This question counts as one-third of the total essay section score.)

Directions:

The following prompt is based on the accompanying six sources.

This question requires you to integrate a variety of sources into a coherent, well-written essay. *Refer to the sources to support your position; avoid paraphrase or summary. Your argument should be central; the sources should support this argument.*

Remember to attribute both direct and indirect citations.

Introduction:

An association between corporate and educational institutions could have many benefits, from technological improvements in the classroom to needed upgrades in athletic facilities. Such assistance could be especially beneficial to districts with limited economic means which otherwise might not be able to effect such improvements. But will the benefits that come from such association outweigh the drawbacks, such as schools exposing their students to a morally questionable sales pitch?

Assignment:

Peruse the following sources (including any introductory information) carefully. **Then, in an essay that synthesizes at least three of the sources for support, take a position that defends, challenges or qualifies the claim that corporate sponsorship could have a positive effect in American high schools by providing resources that schools otherwise might not be able to afford.**

(It is recommended that you spend 15-20 minutes of the allotted time examining the sources and devote the remaining time to writing your essay.)

Document A

Farahmandpur, Ramin and Peter McLaren. "Corporate Sponsorship Threatens Quality of Education." *Daily Bruin Online*. http://www.dailybruin.ucla.edu /db/issues /00/ 04.19/view.farahmandpur.html.

The growing privatization and corporatization of public education come at a time when the welfare state and civil society are increasingly under attack by the private sector, and when class polarization is widening. Public schools and universities across the nation are in desperate need of financial assistance, particularly those schools serving working-class and minority students.

Many are turning to corporate philanthropists such as Bill Gates for financial help. Gates has offered $1 billion in scholarship funds to economically disenfranchised students of color [. . . .].

The corporate-sponsored curriculum is finding its way into schools that are willing to sacrifice critical citizenship for the creation of consumer identities. Corporate lessons-in-a-box and free technology seem to be an appropriate reward for transforming school premises into a youth-oriented Times Square [. . . .].

The Center for Commercial-Free Public Education reports that public schools are signing contracts that allow corporate sponsors like Burger King and Sprite to place advertisements on school buses. In New York City, the board of education recently signed a nine-year, $53 million contract with an advertising agency that allows it to advertise on the district's buses. But considering the school district's annual $8 billion budget, the estimated $5.9 million a year the district receives seems rather trivial.

In another case, Exxon provides free educational videos to classroom teachers in a concerted effort to restore its much tainted public image after the Valdez oil spill in Alaska. Exxon's propaganda depicts the company as an environmentally-friendly organization helping to protect the wildlife in Alaska.

The Hershey corporation teaches the nutritional values of its chocolate candies to students and suggests how it can be an integral part of a balanced daily diet. Finally, Nike provides teachers with "sneaker-making kits" that teach students how Nike shoes are assembled as part of a classroom lesson that focuses on protecting the environment [. . . .].

The Daily Bruin, UCLA

Document B

Manning, Steven. "Students for Sale." *The Nation*. 27 Sept 1999. Online
http://www.thenation.com/doc/19990927/manning.

[. . . .] Nowhere is the convergence of schoolhouse need and corporate greed more apparent than in Colorado Springs High School. At Palmer High School, students walk through hallways dotted with signs for national brands and local companies, eat in a snack bar sporting brand-new vending machines, use computers with ad-bearing mouse pads and play basketball in a gym decorated with banners of corporate sponsors.

"This was the first school district in the nation to offer advertising opportunities, and the results have been great for our students," says Kenneth Burnley, superintendent of Colorado Springs School District 11. Burnley dreamed up the district's advertising and corporate-sponsorship program in 1993, after years of coping with harsh budget cuts. When Burley took over in 1989, the school district was $12 million in the red. Although Colorado Springs, located about sixty miles south of Denver, is best known for its beautiful weather and tourist attractions like Pike's Peak, it's also the state's second largest city, and its schools suffer from ills common to urban school districts: overcrowded classes, lack of extracurricular programs and crumbling school buildings. There's also the problem that until 1996, city voters had not approved a tax increase for education in more than two decades. (In a 1999 survey by *Education Week*, Colorado was ranked forty-ninth in the nation in the adequacy of resources devoted to education.)

"Our taxpayers have challenged us to be more creative and businesslike in how we finance the schools, so we decided to take a page out of a business's book," says Burnley. "I realized we could sell for cash something we always had, but never knew we had"—access to students. So far, some fifty companies have signed up as corporate partners, at a cost ranging from $1,500 to $12,000. Top dollar buys advertising rights on school buses, in all schools and four public-address announcements at every basketball and football game, among other benefits. A $1,500 check buys a 2 feet x 5 feet sign in one school and tickets to attend school athletic events. District 11 officials say the advertising packages bring in about $100,000 in revenue annually [. . . .].

Document C

"Channel One in a Nutshell." Online http://www.obligation.org/ch1.html.

[. . . .] The Channel One deal is this: School boards would be loaned a TV network for each 6-12th grade schools if the board agreed to show the 12-13-minute in-school TV show called "Channel One News" at least 90% of all school days in, at least, 80% of all classrooms and when they did show the program the school agreed to show the program in its entirety [. . . .].

Each school is loaned a satellite dish (that can only pick up Channel One's signals), two VCRs, and a 19" TV set for each room. They receive, via satellite the daily "news" show and also can receive several hours of documentaries that contain no commercials. This is called the Classroom Channel.

The TV show starts out with a piece of art that a student has sent in. Each artwork must contain the Channel One logo somewhere in the picture. (This makes children into unpaid graphic artists for Channel One's advertising department.) Then several one sentence headlines are flashed on the screen. Then a quote for the day, usually tied into a story on the show. The anchors introduce themselves. Then a MTV-styled introductory segment with music and graphics. The top story is read. Maybe another one and then the first batch of commercials, usually one minute and either two or three commercials. Another story, not necessarily hard news, but a teen feature. One minute of commercials followed by a "Pop Quiz" that may have nothing to do with the stories reported on. The anchors sign off and the program appears to come to an end, but usually one or two more commercials are featured after the "end" of the show. Total time is usually 13 minutes.

School boards have to sign a contract before they receive Channel One. The contract is for three years and renews automatically. Schools can end the contract at any time without any extra penalty being incurred.

Document D

"Captive Kids: A Report on Commercial Pressures on Kids At School." Online
http://www.consumersunion.org/other/captivekids/evaluations.htm

Group	Position:In-School Commercialism		Position:SEMs	Position:Ad-Bearing Materials	Comments
American Federation of Teachers (AFT)	Has no formal position.	Is opposed to television commercials in the classroom and districts being forced to obtain equipment "with...learning time."	Has no formal position but as a general philosophy does not endorse for classroom use.	Has no formal position but is not inclined toward it.	Many AFT locals have been vigorous opponents of *Channel One*. AFT does not endorse sponsored educational materials for use in the classroom considering the implicit, and often explicit, commercial and political targeting of children involved. AFT resolved at its 1990 convention that it "opposes television commercials in the classroom and condemns the lack of economic resources that puts school districts in the position of buying television and other electronic equipment with the valuable learning time of children. AFT understands the decisions regarding such arrangements some locals might nevertheless make out of a pragmatic need for television and other electronic equipment." It endorses the guidelines developed at the Milwaukee Conference in 1990.
National Association of Secondary School Principals (NASSP)	Has no "broad" formal position on in-school commercialism.	Opposes *Channel One*, specifically the idea of forcing students to watch commercials.	Has no formal position. Advises teachers and principals to review SEMs on a case-by-case basis.	Has no formal position.	Dr. Tom Koerner, Deputy Executive Director, states that NAASP's criteria for opposing *Channel One* is that "it forces students to watch commercials" as opposed to ad-bearing materials, which are more passive. "Scoreboards, billboards...no one is forcing students to view these." Regarding SEMs, it is NASSP's position that while there are some good and many poor ones, they are best handled by a teacher and principal on a case-by-case basis.
National Parent Teacher Association (National PTA)	Strongly opposes required viewing/ usage of commercial materials; will seek and support legislation to protect children from required usage.	Is opposed and would support government limitations; opposes "any provision which requires children to watch TV commercials as a condition of their instruction."	Has no specific position on classroom materials outside of its general position on commercialism.	Is opposed to the concept of requiring students to "read advertising as a condition of corporate donations to schools."	Opposes "any provision which requires children to watch TV commercials as a condition of their instruction." Suggests that corporations with the same concern for enhancing the education of children as PTA has could serve students better if they'd "provide technology and high quality programs without demanding direct commercial return on the investment" and that "as a marketplace for ideas, the school should offer a balance...of views, not free access for those who pay entrance." It endorses the guidelines developed at the 1990 Milwaukee Conference.

Document E

"Cash-strapped schools look for sponsors." CNN.com/Education. 15 Aug 2002.
http://cnnstudentnews.cnn.com/2002/fyi/teachers.ednews/08/15/school.sponsors.ap/.

At Vernon Hills High School, the new football stadium will bear the name of a paint maker and the $80,000 scoreboard will be sponsored by a computer company.

In Naperville, an announcement will be made each game naming equipment manufacturer Under Armour as the official sponsor of the hometown Redhawks—in case fans missed the company's two banners hanging in the high school stadium.

Commercialism in sports is hardly new, even at the prep level, but it's a route cash-strapped schools are taking with greater frequency to pay for new athletic facilities [. . . .].

Marty Hickman, executive director of the Illinois High School Association, said he knew of no other high school district in Illinois to make a naming rights deal. He said he doubts this will be the last.

"I think part of it reflects the kind of economic situation we're in," he said. "People are looking for creative ways to fund programs, and this is certainly a creative way to do that."

Vernon Hills athletic booster Richard Friedenberg, who helped secure several corporate donations for the school, said it had no other option, other than asking voters to approve a tax increase to pay for the construction costs.

"We worked very hard to make sure we weren't exploiting these kids," he said. "They probably won't sell one more can of paint because of this, because if I didn't tell you where (the stadium) is you couldn't find it. There is no intrinsic value to them other than giving back to the school."

Document F

Anderson, Kirk. "Corporate Sponsorship Invades Educational System." Online
http://zone.artizans.com/product.htm?pid=281567. 23 Dec 2003.

Sample Examination Two: Explications and Answers

Explication of Passage One: From Gene Smith's "Still Quiet on the Western Front"

The initial passage in this exam reflects upon arguably the most crucial and costly battle of the First World War, Verdun, in which the German commander, Erich von Falkenhayn, besieged the French fortifications of the city in an attempt to inflict insurmountable casualties on the French army. Under the leadership of General Pétain, however, who organized a series of counter-offensives, the French army denied the German advance until Allied troops diverted the German focus on Verdun with an attack along the Somme River. All told, the price of upholding Pétain's defiant claim, *Il ne passeront pas*! ("They shall not pass!), was approximately 400,000 French fatalities, with a similar number suffered by the German attackers.

Smith's account of the battle of Verdun is not a vivid description such as one finds in the poetry of Wilfred Owen or Siegfried Sassoon, but an account of a visit years after the conflict. The narrator functions as somewhat of a tour guide, but one who is respectful of the great sacrifice that was made here. The description of Verdun is a mix of present and past, a catalog of the scars and relics that yet survive occasionally interspersed with imagined scenes of the actual battle.

The author begins with a mournful exclamation, "O Verdun!," as if this were "too bloody a spectacle" to conceive. The initial details noted are commemorative, "concrete posts with concrete helmets on top and raised lettering saying this is *La Voie Sacree*, the "Sacred Road" (lines 2-5). Though the derivation of the road's nickname was its status as the sole supply road to the besieged city, its bloody toll, exacted by the fierce fighting, calls to mind that other road of suffering, the *via dolorosa*, the bloody path of Christ's journey to Golgotha and the crucifixion. Here the author first mentions Pétain (noting how his headquarters remain nearly unchanged) as well as the endless progression of men and equipment that slugged its way through the mud under his approving glance.

In the second paragraph the author notes the eerie silence, that ethereal sense of reverential calm that pervades Normandy, Gettysburg and all the sites of great human sacrifice. He also observes the "visible signs of battle" (line 20) that still remain to the present day: trenches in which men desperately fought, armor now scavenged and used to roof rustic sheds. Indeed the remnants of war are so omnipresent, notes the author, that signs still warn of the potential for death if one wanders too far into the gas-and-shell corrupted wasteland. He notes how just a little bit of excavation can yield everything from undetonated shells to rusted canteens, ironic reminders of the death and life of the combatants.

The third and fourth paragraphs shift to indoor scenes. The first is a commemorative museum in which a one-eyed veteran, a contemporary Tiresias, maintains a solemn guardian presence over eight coffins containing the unidentified remains of fallen soldiers that rest under a great sign repeating Pétain's adamant vow. The second is a more gothic edifice, an *ossuaire*, in which mingle the bones of 150,000 fatalities—neatly divided in some cases into classifications of legs, arms, and skulls; randomly juxtaposed in others in a confused collage of bone. While these two edifices remind visitors of the awful price of Verdun (and war, in general), the author's remark that "This collection is ever-growing; often a wild boar rooting in the earth will show where more bones lie. Or during a forest fire a 75-mm. Shell will blow up, fifty years late, and uncover more Unknown Soldiers" (lines 77-82), suggests that the toll of Verdun is never-ending; that the innocent web being woven by the spider in an unsuspecting skull is the fatal web of war in which humanity seems endlessly entrapped.

The simplicity of the opening two lines of the concluding paragraph—"All this happened at Verdun. And yet no drums beat and there are no bugles" (lines 83-84)—suggests that there is no reason for the proud defiance of martial tunes. Here "the ceremony of innocence [was] drowned," as Yeats would have it, and the nature of the world was forever altered. Smith's haunting, elegiac piece offers a solemn reminder of war's awful capacity for destructiveness, leaving the reader with little to offer but the feeble commiserating phrase, "Oh Verdun!"

1. The author develops his essay around which of the following contrasts? **(B) past and present**.

   The first paragraph of the passage is devoted to flashbacks of the actual Verdun siege: portraits of the French army mucking its way up *La Voie Sacree* under the gaze of their stalwart leader, Pétain. The poet uses onomatopoeia to capture the trucks' struggle through the mud as they pressed to deliver supplies to the front. The third paragraph also flashes back to troops in the "long, deep galleries of the citadel" and the "ever-wet trenches" (lines 52-55). The remainder of the passage examines a more contemporary Verdun, one in which the visitor must "[strain] to hear the sounds of motors and sloshing boots and the mumbled throbbing of the distant places where for months on end the guns were never quiet" (lines 16-20). Here the scars of war are partly obscured by nature as in the "craters with cows scrambling up their sides" (line 24), or lurking seditiously to still mar the unsuspecting visitor, as in the "rusted grenades or shells, as terrifying as coiled snakes" (lines 38-39). The contrast is decidedly past vs. present.

2. The author's primary purpose in the passage is to **(B) lament the tremendous sacrifice demanded by combat**.

   Choice B garners its support from a variety of places: lines 8-9, in which Pétain watches "the youth of a nation go northward to its fate;" the reference in lines 45-48 to grandfathers or great-uncles who perished in the battle; the haunting, Gothic-like partial remains of the 150,000 unidentified dead from either side piled neatly in the *ossuaire*; (lines 67-71) and the passage's closing paragraph, in which the author suggests all visitors must say to themselves "Here under my feet and within the space I see, hundreds of thousands of men died, here the entire world turned over" (lines 90-93).

3. The exclamation, "Oh, Verdun!" (line 1), is likely an expression of **(D) mourning**.

   This choice of D is based upon the overall elegiac tone of the passage, which mourns the tremendous loss of life in this pivotal battle. The great sign on the wall that recounts Pétain's stalwart oath, "They Shall Not Pass" (lines 63-64), subtly implies the enormous sacrifices made for a principle.

4. In recreating the world of Verdun, the author relies upon all of the following EXCEPT **(B) personal reminiscences of surviving veterans**.

   Onomatopoeic diction is evident in "grinding" (line 12) and "sloshing" (line 17), as well as in "mumbled throbbing" (line 18). The altered topography may be seen in the "craters with cows scrambling up their sides; here is the metal plate used for protection against the shells and now used to roof sheds and support garden walls" (lines 24-27). The uncovered relics of the fierce conflict are visible in lines 37-42, "Under trees or in stream beds are rusted grenades or shells, as terrifying as coiled snakes. Dig and you will find bullets, shell fragments, broken rifles, sardine tins, decayed canteens, unidentifiable bits of metal." The parenthetical comments that describe the sodden weather are visible in lines 55-56 "trenches (it always rains here)," and in lines 62-63, "(No cotton or silk would last long in this dank, wet place.)" This confirms choices A, C, D and E, leaving B as the exception.

5. Which of the following is NOT characteristic of the style of the long second paragraph? **(D) trenches that symbolize mass graves**.

Inversion is evident in "Here are the long trenches, twelve feet deep then, six feet now that nature has half filled them up; here are the craters with cows scrambling up their sides" (lines 21-24), the use of second person in lines 30-37, "here if you leave the road and go past the signs warning of *Danger de Mort*—'Danger of Death'—you will soon lose yourself in the scrub pine planted in the thirties when experts finally decided that the soil was too gas-and-shell-corrupted to reclaim it for agriculture," and in other places. Choice C gains credibility from the contrast between the paragraph's opening statement, "Today it is strangely silent [. . .]" (line 15), and the visual reminders of the war recounted earlier in this paragraph. Choice E is supported by the sign warning of potential hazards, the "rusted metal protruding up through the wet moss" (lines 29-30), and the simile of the "coiled snakes" (line 39). There is nothing to suggest that the trenches are symbolic however tempting their six-foot depth may be.

6. The effectiveness of lines 37-39, "Under trees or in stream beds are rusted grenades or shells, as terrifying as coiled snakes," is abetted by which of the following?

   I. The innocuous connotation of the word "rusted."
   II. A comparison that suggests latent and imminent danger.
   III. The disarming nature of the pastoral locale.

(E) I, II and III.

Though the word "rusted" suggests something that is no longer extant, it also connotes potential danger. The simile "as coiled snakes" suggests something waiting to spring, while the setting of stream and tree beds suggests something idyllic, not directly threatening. The danger here is a subtle, not blatant one.

7. Which BEST represents the arrangement of the objects listed in lines 40-42?
(C) whole to splintered.

The arrangement of the objects moves from the intact (bullets) to the broken (rifles, shells and canteens) to the shattered (the "unidentifiable bits of metal").

8. The author likely includes the detail of the one-eyed veteran (lines 51-60) as a(n) **(A) haunting image of the terrible carnage**.

Like a character out of Greek tragedy or the mariner of Coleridge's famous "Rime," the spectral presence of the silent, one-eyed veteran provides a haunting reminder of the Verdun carnage. Though he says nothing, only offering a card to visitors that reminds them not to forget to tip him, he is reminiscent of Ishmael in *Moby Dick* or the character in MacLeish's *J.B.* who utters the refrain "I alone have survived to tell thee."

9. The BEST equivalent of the word "terrible" in line 65 would be **(C) discomfiting**.

In context, the word "terrible" means upsetting, disconcerting. Of the choices, C is most suitable.

10. Lines 83-84, "All this happened at Verdun. And yet no drums beat and there are no bugles," suggest that **(B) there is no real victory at such a calamitous sacrifice**.

Drums and bugles are associated with martial music, with proud parades of military might. The battlefield of Verdun is marked by an eerie but reverential silence. These details, when linked with the hundreds of thousands of fatalities and the pyrrhic rhetoric of Pétain's oath, lead to choice B as the best answer.

11. Which of the following pairs of adjectives BEST captures the author's attitude toward the events at Verdun as expressed in the final paragraph? **(C) costly and cataclysmic**.

The allusion to "sick France sliding downhill" (line 87) and to the sexual decadence of post-World War One Germany suggests both political and moral decline. The final sentence suggests the terrible cost in human life. This is best conveyed by choice C.

12. The third and fifth footnotes, and the initial description of Pétain in lines 7-9, suggest that he **(C) was willing to absorb great casualties to hold the position**.

In the initial description of Pétain, he is seen overseeing the fatal progress of over seventy percent of the French army. Pétain's defiant boast, coupled with the enormous number of fatalities, confirms C as the best choice.

13. In light of the passage as a whole, the phrase "They Shall Not Pass" and its explanatory footnote do which of the following?

   I. Account for the extreme number of unidentified remains in the *ossuaire*.
  II. Question grimly the sense of such adamancy.
  III. Epitomize the concept of "Pyrrhic victory"

(E) I, II and III

Pétain's determination to hold Verdun despite the awful toll that such a decision demanded certainly accounts for the 150,000 skeletal fragments that are neatly stacked in the *ossuaire*. It calls to mind the senselessness of such chauvinistic rhetoric in light of the enormous human toll, while at the same time epitomizing the infamous "Pyrrhic victory," in which the price of victory severely outweighs the triumph. While one may perhaps argue that the battle of Verdun turned the tide of the war, the enormous casualties, like those suffered by each side at Gettysburg, make it hard for anyone to call this a triumph.

Explication of Passage Two: From Lady Mary Wortley Montagu's "Letter to Countess Bute, Her Daughter [On her Granddaughter]"

Composed on January 28, 1753, Lady Ashley Montagu's letter to her daughter provides great insight into her nature as well as into the nature of the privileged society to which she belonged. Her mother's having died when she was but five, Lady Ashley initiated her education in her father's library, becoming in time an impressive woman of letters who counted in her literary circle noted writers such as her cousin Henry Fielding, the satirists Addison and Steele, and Alexander Pope. Somewhat unconventional, she eloped against her family's wishes, traveled with her husband to Constantinople, and upon her return championed the smallpox inoculation of children. Even so, she was no stranger to the finer things and, as this letter suggests, retained the tastes and prejudices of her class.

In her letter to her daughter, Lady Montagu first expresses her satisfaction in her granddaughter's mathematical skill, calling it "the best proof of understanding" (line 5). This seemingly sincere compliment, however, is quickly amended by Lady Montagu's observation that "the knowledge of numbers is one of the chief distinctions between us and the brutes" (lines 5-7). The condescending word "brutes" and her assurance to her daughter that the superior Montagu "blood" will undoubtedly endow her children with "an uncommon share of good sense" (lines 10-11) clearly reveal Lady Montagu's conviction that she and her peers belong to a higher caste.

After an approving nod towards her granddaughter's learning, Lady Montagu draws a distinction between her own daughter's education and that of her granddaughter, saying "[her daughter's] prospect was very different" (line 19). By this she clearly means her daughter's chances of a suitable marriage were superior because she was more intelligent and more attractive: "As you had no defect either in mind or person to hinder, and much in your circumstances to attract, the highest offers, it seemed your business to learn how to live in the world, as it is hers to learn how to be easy but of it" (lines 20-25). Lady Montagu then employs an extended metaphor drawn from architecture in which she laments those "builders and parents [who] follow some plan they think beautiful (and perhaps is so) without considering that nothing is beautiful that is misplaced" (lines 26-29). The final word of the sentence, "misplaced," reveals her clear conviction that individuals must not attempt to elevate themselves beyond the caste that suits them. This "common error" (line 25) of endeavoring to rise above one's station is confirmed more concretely by lines 35-40, "thus every woman endeavours to breed her daughter a fine lady, qualifying her for a station in which she will never appear, and at the same time incapacitating her for that retirement to which she is destined." Thus, Lady Montagu feels her granddaughter should be "contented" and "happy" but no more than that: "She will not want new fashions, nor regret the loss of expensive diversions, or variety of company, if she can be amused with an author in her closet [. . . .]" (lines 44-47).

The remainder of her letter is devoted to supervising the nature of her granddaughter's learning, a limited knowledge of Latin and Greek. As Lady Montagu affirms, "I would wish her no further a linguist than to enable her to read books in their originals that are often corrupted, and always injured by translations" (lines 54-58). She also advocates a familiarity with English poetry, enough at least to save her from "destruction" (line 69). Lady Montagu then relates an anecdote in which a companion of her youth receives romantic verses from a suitor whose poetry is "not so smooth as Prior's or Pope's but [which] had more thought and spirit than any of theirs" (lines 72-74). Though her companion is predictably delighted by their wit and sentiment, Lady Montagu explodes them as a plagiary of another, and "the unfortunate transcriber [is] dismissed with the scorn he deserved" (lines 81-83). The anecdote reveals the preoccupation of the gentry with appearance, suggesting that any suitor engendering such a fraud must be summarily and soundly rejected. The final caution given by Lady Montagu to her daughter is, somewhat ironically, that her granddaughter should "conceal whatever learning she attains, with as much solicitude as she would hide crookedness or lameness [. . .]" (lines 90-92) since it will only provoke hatred and envy from the lesser fools around her. All told, Lady Montagu's letter reveals her to be eloquent and literate but equally supercilious and condescending. It would, in the hands of a dramatist like Goldsmith or a novelist like Austen, offer fertile ground for satire.

14. The most important revelation of the opening paragraph concerns the **(D) characteristic conceit of the mother**.

Though Lady Montagu's initial comments about her granddaughter's skill in arithmetic seem to be the innocuous utterance of a proud grandparent, lines 5-7, "the knowledge of numbers is one of the chief distinctions between us and the brutes," reflect the supercilious attitude that is her defining trait. The word "brutes," in particular, suggests a disdain of the lower classes and is the antithesis of "blood" or refinement. Her subsequent observation that, "If there is anything in blood, you may reasonably expect your children should be endowed with an uncommon share of good sense" (lines 7-11), suggests her conviction that the progeny of the upper class naturally inherits their defining traits: namely, culture, refinement, economic success, etc. This conceit is crowned by her concluding boast that "Mr. Wortley's family and mine have both produced some of the greatest men that have been born in England [. . . .]" (lines 11-13).

15. Which of the following words does NOT help to establish Lady Montagu's sense of social superiority? **(A) "account" (line 2)**.

Choices B, C, D and E all contain words that connote social distinction. The word "account," in this context, has nothing to do with financial status, but with a revelation or a story.

16. Throughout her letter to her daughter, the mother's tone is **(E) haughty and didactic**.

The first half of the correct answer is amply explicated in the answer to question #14 although it is prevalent throughout the passage. The second half is apparent in phrases such as "I will therefore speak to you as [. . .]" (line 14), "It is the common error [. . .]" (line 25), and "There are two cautions to be given [. . .]" (line 50), in addition to mild imperatives such as "let her be indulged in it" (line 17). Additional support is provided by the mother's short moralizations on breeding, reading, fashion, and socialization.

17. In the second paragraph the mother uses generalization to convey the desire of all mothers to see their daughters **(C) improve their social lot**.

This is derived directly from her observation that "every woman endeavours to breed her daughter a fine lady, qualifying her for a station in which she will never appear, and at the same time incapacitating her for that retirement to which she is destined" (lines 35-40).

18. The transitional sentence that opens paragraph two is intended to expose the mother's **(B) pompous concession that her granddaughter should be educated**.

Lines 14-17, "I will therefore speak to you as supposing Lady Mary not only capable, but desirous of learning: in that case by all means let her be indulged in it," contain two key words: "supposing," which concedes the possibility that her granddaughter may be intelligent; and "indulged," which suggests a concession that learning something "can't do her any harm."

19. Lines 19-20, "your prospect was very different from hers," introduce information that confirms the mother's belief that her granddaughter is inferior to her own daughter in terms of **(C) potential for dowry**.

Lady Montagu's observation that she did not stress education for her own daughter in the same way as she is doing so for her granddaughter is clarified by her subsequent comment that "your prospect was very different from hers. As you had no defect either in mind or person to hinder, and much in your circumstances to attract, the highest offers, it seemed your business to learn how to live in the world, as it is hers to learn how to be easy but of it" (lines 19-25). Here the key phrase is "highest offers," which connotes the negotiation of an acceptable dowry. Clearly she perceives her own daughter as having had much more going for her (in terms of virtues that would attract suitors) than her granddaughter.

20. The mother reinforces the difference between daughter and granddaughter through **(A) extended metaphor**.

The choice of A as the most appropriate answer is based on the lengthy comparison that begins on line 25 and continues until line 35. This metaphor uses architecture and architectural planning to convey how certain people have unrealistic aspirations for their children. In the comparison parents are compared to builders who pursue a beautiful plan without stopping to consider that "nothing is beautiful that is misplaced" (lines 28-29). Lady Montagu notes how edifices are constructed that the builder cannot financially sustain, how rooms with the best view are often directed at "barren heaths" (lines 32-33) or apartments designed with a ventilation inappropriate for that cold a climate. In each case, the same theme is reinforced: that everything has its place, and that the place for a young lady with some talent but limited attractiveness is a low one.

21. In lines 25-40, the mother figuratively hints at her granddaughter's "unsuitability" through all of the following EXCEPT **(D) a blanket condemnation of the architectural appeal of the edifice**.

The intimation that "It is the common error of builders and parents to follow some plan they think beautiful (and perhaps is so) without considering that nothing is beautiful that is misplaced" (lines 25-29) supports A, and also B since the mother clearly views her granddaughter as inferior to her own progeny. The suggestion that there are "so many edifices raised that the raisers can never inhabit, being too large for their fortunes" (lines 29-32) provides a defense for C, while her observation that "Vistas are laid open over barren heaths, and apartments contrived for a coolness very agreeable in Italy, but killing in the north of Britain" (lines 32-35) confirms E. The phrase "blanket condemnation" makes choice D untenable.

22. The most disturbing nature of the mother's comments in lines 40-49 is her **(D) agreement that the prospect of girls should be limited by their gender**.

The mother's attitude towards a woman's place in society suggests that there is clearly a ways to go before we reach Mary Wollstonecraft Shelley. The intimation in these lines is that learning for most girls will bring them contentment: "She will not want new fashions, nor regret the loss of expensive diversions, or variety of company, if she can be amused with an author in her closet [. . . .]." (lines 44-47); in short, a little education will make up for all the things she cannot achieve in her station. Perhaps the more damning concession is that "she cannot advance herself in any profession, and has therefore more hours to spare [. . . .]" (lines 47-49), which suggests that young girls should concede their futureless lot and curl up with a good book. Somewhere between the Wife of Bath and Edna Pontellier, Lady Montagu took a wrong turn.

23. In her anecdote in lines 64-87, the mother dramatizes the egregious nature of her childhood friend's literary *faux pas* through all of the following EXCEPT **(D) characterizing the letter's author as an incorrigible blackguard**.

Lines 64-65, "Many a young damsel has been ruined by a fine copy of verses," confirm the validity of A, while calling the author's work a "poor plagiary" (line 84) supports B. Lady Montagu's claims that she "saved one of [her] companions from destruction [. . .]" (lines 68-69) and that she "showed her that they were taken from Randolph's poems [. . .]" (lines 80-81) prove the presence of C, while lines 64-65, "Many a young damsel has been ruined by a fine copy of verses," validate E. Though the author is dismissed as a "poor plagiary," there is no moral attack upon his character.

24. The mother implies that her young friend was primarily duped by which of the following?

    I. The seemingly original nature of the verse.
    II. The passionate appeal of her lover in the letter.
    III. A concession to her own vanity.

(E) I, II and III

Lady Montagu celebrates her careful eye, recounting how she "showed her that they were taken from Randolph's poems and the unfortunate transcriber was dismissed with the scorn he deserved" (lines 80-83). She prefaces this by saying that even though "the lines were not so smooth as Prior's or Pope's" her young friend was "wonderfully delighted with such a demonstration of her lover's sense and passion" (lines 72-77), implying that the counterfeit verse and the sentiment it expressed were good enough to fool a less practiced eye (I and II). Her additional observation, that her young friend was "not a little pleased with her own charms, that had force enough to inspire such elegancies" (lines 77-79), provides a defense for III as well.

25. The concluding paragraph of the mother's letter seems to contradict which of the following characteristics of the mother? **(D) her belief in the importance of literacy**.

The mother's advice that her granddaughter should "conceal whatever learning she attains, with as much solicitude as she would hide crookedness or lameness [. . .]" (lines 90-92) does not seem to correspond with her earlier suggestion to permit her to indulge in learning.

26. Overall, the letter unintentionally satirizes the mother's feelings about social **(E) mobility**.

Though Lady Montagu herself is undoubtedly quite sincere in her belief that every woman has her assigned place in society, her letter unintentionally makes a clarion cry for social change that subsequent female writers will turn into an anthem. Though the author of this passage is obviously a product of her time and social caste, the heroines of future novels will reject the passive acceptance of social place, clamoring for the vote, independence, and a room of their own.

Explication of Passage Three: From Richard Selzer's "Confessions of a Knife"

Richard Selzer's childhood memoir merges the traditional rite-of-passage story with a social commentary on the ritualistic brawling of Irish immigrants in Troy. The opening paragraph both recollects and satirizes the bloody street donnybrooks in which these proud warriors mimic the epic and sanguinary confrontations of their Trojan counterparts. The author's opening declaration—in particular the subtly sardonic phrase "immense generosity" (line 2)—establishes the paradoxical nature of the ritual, in which pairs of men square off in a no-holds-barred combat in which they generously exchange a rain of violent blows. The place of combat has the stillness of a sanctuary, and the ritualistic nature of the combat is reflected in the author's observation that "These men [were] not ashamed to show their devotion to each other's flesh" (lines 18-20). The ballet of the combat, mirrored by the sequence of simplistic one-line verbs—"Punch. Duck. Punch. Duck." (lines 12-13)—mesmerizes so long as neither combatant has achieved dominance. Once one does, there is an audible sigh from the circle of observers that "means that a certain point has been reached. With a single punch or kick, one of the men has gained irreversible ascendancy over the other. When you hear that sigh, you can tell who is going to win" (lines 24-29). The ensuing scene, in which the combatants are later seen toasting each other with a beer as a scrubwoman scours the bloodied pavement, highlights the senselessness of the combat.

With the third paragraph the memoir shifts from a general childhood remembrance of fighting to a more personal one. The curt transitional sentence, "There came the day when it was my turn" (lines 38-39), comes across with the finality of a hard swallow. Despite their identical age and grade, there is little similarity in size between the author and his imposing foe, Barry McKenna, who assumes the role of Goliath to the author's David, outsizing him by a half. Despite the disparity of the combatants, there is no escaping the conflict, the schoolyard having become "a fascist pen of cement where no citizen was safe" (lines 48-49). Even the crowd of classmates that encircles the pair is said to have "clanged shut" (lines 51-52) about them, reinforcing the sense of inevitability and entrapment. The amiable description of Barry McKenna—handsome and winsome to a fault—is made uncomfortably sinister by his confident and smiling declaration, "I'm going to kill you" (line 53), to the effete and puny author.

When the combat (if it can be called that) first commences, the author is more target than foe, raising his hands in a "facsimile of boxing," resigned to embracing his "tragic destiny" (lines 57-59). One punch connects with his ear, another with his shoulder while the author makes an infrequent cosmetic attempt at a reply. This almost choreographed encounter proceeds until the author predictably winds up on the ground, straddled by his physically superior foe and awaiting his imminent demise much "as a Bedouin in the desert welcomes the flies that are the herald of an oasis" (lines 72-74). The author's antithetical simile captures the ironic duality of the moment: the sense of Damaclean suffering tempered by the feeling of euthanasia, of being released from all pain.

Surprisingly, it is a plea for mercy from one of the observers—"Aw, let him go, Barry [. . .] Come on, let the faggot go" (lines 75-77)—which provides the author's slingshot moment as, stung by the demeaning epithet, he summons the nerve to punch his opponent forcefully in the throat and breastbone. When, surprised by the author's unforeseen retaliation and spitting up blood from some internal injury, Barry McKenna staggers to his feet and stumbles off, the author is hailed as the victor and the crowd disappointedly disperses.

It is, however, the author's one line answer, "No, I didn't win" (line 108), that provides the passage's more subtle epiphany and that elevates the story from a clichéd tale of underdog triumph to something more significant. This compact admission reveals the author's understanding that in this dire moment of self-preservation he has become what he detests: a brute just like Barry McKenna. This is symbolically buttressed by the baptism of blood that the author receives from the coughing figure above him. The pale, sweating figure that retreats from the circle in lines 101-102 bears a striking resemblance to the author's self-description in line 40, and it is clear that the roles of the combatants have been reversed. For the author, however, there is no joy in his victory, only the Swiftian knowledge that the capacity for "man's inhumanity to man" lies in all of us.

27. In this excerpt the author seems most concerned with depicting the **(E) events which forged his own character**.

   Though there is some defense for A in the colorful brawling of the Irish which has even spawned the nickname for one of the most renowned college sports' teams in America, the central focus of the episode is the character-building events that the author experiences as a youth: the rite-of-passage confrontation with Barry McKenna in which he defines his manhood by defeating a schoolyard bully. Though a hero in the eyes of a fellow classmate, the author himself senses the true hollowness of his victory, knowing that in order to triumph he had descended to the same level of brutality as his opponent.

28. The author characterizes the ritualistic brawling depicted in the passage as all of the following EXCEPT **(D) a defense against bigotry**.

   The author's observation in lines 38-39, "There came the day when it was my turn," confirms the presence of A, while the choreography of "Punch. Duck. Punch. Duck" (lines 12-13) and their subsequent pugilistic embrace support B. Lines 18-20, "These men are not ashamed to show their devotion to each other's flesh," validate C, while the "special stillness" of the "ring of quiet men" (lines 7-8) supports E. Since the fight involves two Irishmen, choice D has no credibility.

29. Which of the following elements is NOT used by the author in the first paragraph to capture the intensity of the public combat? **(C) elongated sentences that mirror the duration of the battle**.

   The "thud of unseen blows" (lines 8-9), the "scrabbling of shoes" (line 9), the punching, ducking, and "rolling in bloody confabulation upon the cobblestones" (lines 17-18) provide definitive support for the presence of A in the passage. Lines 12-13, "Punch. Duck. Punch. Duck," support B, while the "special stillness" of the "ring of quiet men" (lines 7-8) supports D. Onomatopoeic words such as "grunts" (line 8), "thud" (line 8), "scrabbling" (line 9), and "sigh" (line 22) confirm E. There is insufficient evidence to make a case for choice C in the paragraph.

30. The anonymity of the combatants in the opening paragraph is intended to imply the **(B) regular incidence of inebriated public confrontation**.

   This inference is drawn from the opening lines of the paragraph which suggest that "The men of Troy fought often" and "held back from each other nothing of their arms, their backs, and their long bellies" (lines 1-5). The description, which delineates little about the combatants apart from their nationality and the size of their stomachs, gives them a certain interchangeable quality, and the author's subsequent observation, "Walk in Troy in the evening, and you come upon a place of special stillness" (lines 5-7), implies that such combat is an every night occurrence.

31. The primary purpose of the second paragraph is to illustrate which aspect of the combatants? **(A) their ironic and incongruous bond**.

This is derived primarily from lines 30-33, "An hour later, you pass the tavern. You look in and see the two men toasting each other with beer. This time they will sing," which imply that a mere hour after beating each others' brains in, these men are acting like the best of friends.

32. Of the following phrases, which does LEAST to augment the fatalistic nature of the impending encounter? **(E) "It was my obligation to do so." (line 63)**.

Choice A suggests the inevitability of the author's turn in the ring, choice B—in particular the phrase "Fascist pen"—suggests his inability to escape. Choice C, in the onomatopoeic "clanged shut," connotes the finality of a closing door, while the phrase "tragic destiny" in choice D likens the author's plight to the deterministic lot of a tragic hero. Choice E, on the other hand, does less to portend the event than it does to acknowledge that the author could not elect to take a dive or a passive beating but had to offer at least a token measure of resistance.

33. The overall description of the speaker's opponent, Barry McKenna, is BEST labeled **(B) anomalous**.

Despite his imposing size and clear status as a bully, Barry McKenna is described in rather attractive terms. His face is said to be "so handsome it seemed to have been chipped out with a clever Irish axe" (lines 43-45) and to be graced by "curly lion-colored hair and green eyes" (lines 45-46). Even his ominous to threat to kill the author is delivered with a smile and "immense charm" (line 54).

34. The speaker develops the characterization of Barry McKenna via all of the following EXCEPT **(D) a chorus of supporters that enthusiastically eggs him on**.

Barry McKenna is described as "belling like a white stag" (line 68) and having "lion-colored hair" (line 46). Later, after he has been debilitated by the author's punches to his chest and throat, he stumbles away "like a fat cow" (line 93). As has been sufficiently delineated in the explication of question #33, he has extremely handsome features which belie his sense of cruelty. He boasts to the fallen author in line 53, "I'm going to kill you," and, after being struck in the Adam's apple, staggers off, coughing but saying nothing. This information corroborates choices A, B, C and E. Though there is a crowd about the combatants, they maintain a church-like silence, their only sounds being a sigh of disappointment at the fight's imminent end and the merciful but demeaning implorations, "'Aw, let him go, Barry [. . .]. Come on, let the faggot go'" (lines 75-77).

35. The simile contained in lines 72-74—"I welcomed it [. . .] the herald of an oasis"—may be seen as reflecting which of the following?

    I. The speaker's bitter chagrin at being soundly beaten.
    II. The speaker's sense of relief that his ordeal is almost done.
    III. The speaker's stoic resignation to a massive concluding blow.

(D) II and III.

The comparison to how "a Bedouin in the desert welcomes the flies that are the herald of an oasis" suggests that the author perceives the final descending blow as a tolerable prelude to imminent relief. To the thirsty, dehydrating man the annoyance of the flies is vitiated by the awareness that the succor of the oasis is near. To the author, a final punch that will render him unconscious seems but a small pain to endure if it will end a greater suffering. The fact that he "welcomes" the blow and remarks "I had only to wait a little longer" (line 74) buttresses this sense of relief. This provides evidence for II and III. If there is any sense of chagrin, it does not become apparent until after someone in the crowd demeaningly refers to him as "a faggot" (line 77).

36. The import of the speaker's observation—"But the words of that spectator had done what none of Barry's punches could" (lines 80-82)—is BEST interpreted as meaning **(B) provoke his manhood**.

Clearly, until this comment is made the author is willing to take his beating passively to "get it over with." He barely offers resistance, his most effective action being his pulling Barry McKenna down to the ground with him when he falls. These words, however, provoke him to summon whatever latent fury he possesses and to strike his opponent in the throat and chest, incapacitating him and forcing him to disengage.

37. The speaker most likely utters the closing line of the passage because he **(D) is troubled by his own capacity for violence**.

As has been suggested in the explication of the passage as a whole, the author's final comment, "'No' [. . .] 'I didn't win,'" reveals his understanding that by this desperate retaliation he has become what he detests: a brute just like Barry McKenna. As those familiar with *Lord of the Flies* will undoubtedly recognize, in killing the beast one often becomes the beast, and though the author's friend is impressed by his triumph, the author himself knows there are no winners in such a barbaric action.

38. Ultimately, the speaker's account of his experience in the schoolyard also confirms which of the following? **(E) the impressionable nature of the schoolboys**.

Like their masculine elders, who celebrate the "fight club" culture on the streets of Troy, so their male progeny mirror this pugilism in the "fascist pen" of the schoolyard. The passage offers a powerful commentary on the deleterious impact that the thoughtless actions of adults can have upon impressionable children.

Explication of Passage Four: From George Orwell's "Politics and the English Language"

George Orwell's essay, "Politics and the English Language," deplores the degeneration of the spoken and the written word due, in his eyes, to the decadence of civilization. Orwell claims that our language has become "ugly and inaccurate" due to the foolish nature of our thought, but also that the carelessness of our language paradoxically encourages such foolishness. In his essay Orwell not only provides examples of prose that has been marred by what he refers to as "mental vices," but also classifies these writing flaws. Though Orwell's commentary is fairly derisive, he observes that this corruption of language is "not irreversible," and in the tradition of the best satirists works to redress it.

In this passage, from the latter part of the essay, Orwell turns his satirical lens on political writing, immediately averring that most of it is "bad writing" (line 2). The primary reason for this is captured in lines 6-7, in which Orwell observes that "Orthodoxy, of whatever color seems to demand a lifeless, imitative style." Offering a catalog of traditional political writing, Orwell notes that "they are all alike in that one almost never finds in them a fresh, vivid, home-made turn of speech" (lines 12-14). Citing the familiar language of the 1940s, the "familiar phrases" directed against the swelling threat of ruthless dictatorship—*bestial atrocities, iron heel, bloodstained tyranny, free peoples of the world, stand shoulder to shoulder*" (lines 16-18), Orwell notes how they seem to come out of the mouths of a ventriloquist's dummy, someone manipulated into voicing them in a programmed, robotic fashion. The image chosen by Orwell, of the light catching a speaker's spectacles and turning them into "blank discs which seem to have no eyes behind them" (lines 24-25), suggests a dehumanization that is further supported by his assertion that "A speaker who uses that kind of phraseology has gone some distance towards turning himself into a machine [. . . .]" (lines 26-28). The inference being made is that the repetition of such dogma destroys individual human consciousness (and conscience?) until language is reduced to words with no personal meaning, like "when one utters the responses in church [. . . .]" (lines 32-33): in short, the iterance of the stereotypical 'party line.'

The transitional sentence that opens the second paragraph—"In our time, political speech writing is largely the defense of the indefensible" (lines 34-35)—is a paradox: not some airy by-product of the wit of Gilbert and Sullivan, but a deliberate deceit concocted by politicians to euphemize violent and immoral actions. Citing British imperialism, Russian purges, and the nuclear bombings of Hiroshima and Nagasaki as examples of events which "can indeed be defended, but only by arguments which are too brutal for most people to face, and which do not square with the professed aims of political parties" (lines 39-43), Orwell implies that humans have had to invent nebulous and misleading terms to conceal the brutality of their actions:

> Defenseless villages are bombarded from the air, the inhabitants driven into the countryside, the cattle machine-gunned, the huts set on fire with incendiary bullets: this is called *pacification*. Millions of peasants are robbed of their farms and sent trudging along the roads with no more than they can carry: this is called *transfer of population or rectification of frontiers*. People are imprisoned for years without trial, or shot in the back of the neck or sent to die in Arctic lumber camps: this is called *elimination of unreliable elements* (lines 46-58).

The subsequent description of the defense of Russian totalitarianism by the "comfortable English professor" (lines 61-80) further illustrates what Orwell perceives as the modern tendency to coat unpleasant, even brutal, realities with a mask of "euphemism, question-begging and sheer cloudy vagueness" (lines 44-45). His simple declarative sentence, "The great enemy of clear language is insincerity" (lines 84-86), captures the essence of his argument—that our language has been sold into its own form of enslavement, forcibly impressed into a servitude of disinformation and deceit. The similes of the "soft snow" (line 83) and the "cuttlefish squirting out ink" (lines 89-90) offer two strikingly different images of obfuscation, suggesting perhaps the diverse means by which language can conceal the truth—by blanketing it under a soft dusting of innocuous lies, or by blurring it in a benighted cloud of pernicious propaganda.

39. The author's central concern in the passage is **(C) deploring the use of language to downplay or conceal true intent**.

Though the author opens the first paragraph by lamenting the tired rhetoric of political speech makers, his true intent emerges in the topic sentence of paragraph two which asserts that "In our time, political speech writing is largely the defense of the indefensible" (lines 34-35). The subsequent lines illustrate how political speakers employ language that consists primarily of "euphemism, question-begging and sheer cloudy vagueness" (lines 44-45) to cloak or ameliorate the "gap between [their] real and [their] declared aims [. . .]" (lines 86-87). In short, the language they employ makes these awful actions seem innocuous. The author categorically concludes that "All issues are political issues, and politics itself is a mass of lies, evasions, folly, hatred and schizophrenia [. . . .]" (lines 91-94).

40. The "color" to which the author refers in line 6 is BEST interpreted as meaning **(D) manifestation**.

The "Orthodoxy" referred to in line 6 is directly connected to the "party line," or the agenda that a particular group or organization wishes to promote. Since the context is largely political, the word "color" refers to whatever organizational orthodoxy is being demonstrated. Choice D fits this best.

41. Which of the following does NOT contribute to framing the author's attitude toward political writing in general? **(C) "home-made" (line 13)**.

Choices A, B, D and E all reflect the repetitious, hackneyed, and all-too-familiar nature of most political rhetoric. Choice C actually presents the opposite.

42. The description of the "tired hack" in lines 14-33 does all of the following EXCEPT **(D) insinuate that religious institutions plant the initial seeds of conformity**.

The "tired hack" has only become one by "mechanically repeating the familiar phrases" (lines 15-16). This supports both A and E. The description of the speaker's spectacles as "blank discs which seem to have no eyes behind them" (lines 24-25) confirms C, while the author's assertion that "If the speech he is making is one he is accustomed to make over and over again, he may be almost unconscious of what he is saying [. . .]" (lines 28-32) and the accompanying claim that by using "that kind of phraseology [the speaker] has gone some distance towards turning himself into a machine [. . .]" (lines 26-28) validates B. Though there is a reference to responses uttered in church (lines 31-33), there is no intimation that religion is the source of such conformity.

43. Lines 34-35 exemplify which of the following? **(B) paradox**.

The phrase "the defense of the indefensible" exemplifies an apparent contradiction, or paradox.

44. Which of the following is NOT mentioned by the author as a possible motivation for political speakers' use of "*pacification*" (line 50), "*transfer of population*" (line 53) and similar euphemistic phraseology? **(D) an attempt by some speakers to protect themselves from a potentially unpopular backlash.**

The author's indication that, "Things like the continuance of British rule in India, the Russian purges and deportations, the dropping of the atom bombs on Japan, can indeed be defended, but only by arguments which are too brutal for most people to face [. . .]" (lines 36-41), supports A, while his claim that "Thus political language has to consist largely of euphemism, question-begging and sheer cloudy vagueness" (lines 43-45) buttresses B. His assertion that these acts of violence "do not square with the professed aims of political parties" (lines 41-43) defends C, while his observation that "The great enemy of clear language is insincerity" (lines 84-86) validates E. Choice D garners no support from the passage.

45. The primary effect that the English professor's commentary in lines 68-80 has upon the reader (and likely upon an audience) is one of **(A) obfuscation.**

The author indicates that the English professor's words "[fall] upon the facts like soft snow, blurring the outlines and covering up all the details" (lines 82-84). This is best conveyed by choice A.

46. The author's choice of the adjective "comfortable" (lines 61-62) to describe the professor is likely intended to mock mildly his **(D) academic freedom.**

The professor exists in *academia*, a land of freely-spoken ideas. He does not suffer the privations of those living in a totalitarian state; thus, it is easy for him to discuss an economic and political system without repercussions. Choice D best reflects this "comfortable" position.

47. In supporting his claim that "Such phraseology is needed if one wants to name things without calling up mental pictures of them" (lines 58-61), the author could NOT include which of the English professor's phrases? **(E) "concrete achievement" (lines 79-80)**

Each of the other four phrases is either ambiguous ("certain features," "certain curtailment") or euphemistic ("transitional periods," "rigors"). Choice E does not function in this manner.

48. Lines 82-84, "A mass of Latin words falls upon the facts like soft snow, blurring the outlines and covering up all the details," provide a contrasting image of **(A) preponderancy and delicacy.**

Choice A is derived from the contrast of the words "mass" (suggesting great bulk or weight) and "soft snow" (suggesting lightness and delicacy).

49. The author likely employs the simile "like soft snow" (line 83) in order to convey which of the following?

     I. The euphemistic nature of the rhetoric itself.
     II. The subtlety by which such rhetoric can evade the truth.
     III. The totality with which such rhetoric masks unpleasant realities.

(E) I, II and III.

The phrase "like soft snow" exemplifies the euphemistic language that the speaker employs: for example, calling periods of rebellion, "transitional periods." The speaker's observation that this mass of words is "blurring the outlines and covering up all the details" (lines 83-84) suggests a deliberate attempt to conceal or evade the truth, as well as conveying, through a visual image, a blanket that obscures all truth; thus, the selection of E as the answer.

50. In highlighting the euphemistic rhetoric of politicians in the passage, the author makes the MOST extensive use of **(B) blunt diction and images of violence (lines 46-61)**.

Though a reasonable case can be made for choices C and E, the catalog of euphemisms, used to illustrate politicians' ability to mask unpleasant, even immoral action (lines 46-61), is clearly the most extensive. In addition, choice C can be eliminated because it is the language of a professor, not that of a politician.

51. In the course of his argument, the author does all of the following EXCEPT **(D) deride the platform of a specific political party**.

In the opening paragraph a political speaker is said to be like "some kind of dummy" (lines 20-21). Lines 36-39 allude to British imperialism, Stalinist purges, and the U.S. dropping of the atomic bomb on Hiroshima. Lines 8-10, "pamphlets, leading articles, manifestoes, White Papers and the speeches of under-secretaries [. . .]," offer a catalog of political writings, while the italicized words in the second paragraph provide examples that ridicule politicians' euphemizing the unpleasant. This supports choices A, B, C and E. Nowhere is a specific political party's platform mocked.

Explication of Free-Response Question One: Susan Sontag's *Regarding the Pain of Others*

The first passage in Sample Examination Two, from Susan Sontag's book *Regarding the Pain of Others*, examines the way in which war has been depicted in different artistic media. Looking at exclusively art and photography, Sontag seems to suggest that the chroniclers of war, from Homer to DaVinci to celebrated modern photographers, have all presented war in its unvarnished gruesomeness. Though the belief that viewing scenes of horror can be somehow cathartic has been around since it was first articulated by Aristotle in his *Poetics*, Sontag surprisingly suggests that artistic media can transform such scenes into a 'perilous beauty,' that even scenes as devastating as the smoldering ruins of the World Trading Center can, when captured by the practiced eye, contain an ironic but undeniable beauty.

Sontag begins her essay by noting humanity's inexplicably ironic conviction that "war is an aberration, if an unstoppable one. That peace is the norm, if an unattainable one" (lines 1-2). The graphic description of casualties, which Sontag notes has been in vogue since Homer's record of battlefield deaths on the plains of Troy, is almost as commonplace as war itself, "and to represent war in words or in pictures requires a keen, unflinching detachment" (lines 7-8). Sontag's allusion to Leonardo DaVinci's meticulous instructions to younger artists as to how best to present the "ghastliness" of war emphasizes facial and bodily manifestations of agony and lamentation, mingled with the lurid and eschatological symbols of blood and dust. Alluding to the Aristotelian *catharsis*, Sontag suggests that of the two emotions supposedly purged by tragedy, pity and fear, the former seems "diluted," easily swamped or overcome by the awful power of the latter. As she concludes in lines 24-25, "Leonardo is suggesting that the artist's gaze be, literally, pitiless. The image should appall [. . .]."

Sontag's closing thought in that sentence—the contention that "in that *terribilita* lies a challenging kind of beauty" (lines 25-26)—permits a transition into her final observation about the ability of photography also to transform devastation into something beautiful. Speaking of the oppressive concrete and steel mausoleum formed by the collapsed towers of the World Trade Center, Sontag defiantly claims "There is beauty in ruins" (line 30). Though "To acknowledge the beauty of photographs of the World Trade Center ruins in the months following the attack seemed frivolous, sacrilegious" (lines 30-32), Sontag draws a sharp distinction between the horror of the *actual site* and the *images* of that horror captured by veteran photographers. She sums up by noting how "Photographs tend to transform, whatever their subject; and as an image, something may be beautiful—or terrifying, or unbearable, or quite bearable—as it is not in real life" (lines 36-38).

The two-line concluding paragraph bookends the essay with another appropriate irony—the human belief that, though photography "bears witness to the calamitous and reprehensible," it comes under fire "if it seems 'aesthetic'; that is, too much like art [. . . .]" (lines 39-40). This suggests a seminal difference between photography and other forms of artistic expression: namely, that the former, which captures life *exactly as it is*, tends perhaps to upset more than other media which merely provide an *impression* or an *interpretation* that may distance the reader from the gruesomeness of the subject. For Sontag, however, "[a] landscape of devastation is still a landscape" (line 30), and her essay recalls the famous lines from Keats' "Ode on a Grecian Urn," " Beauty is truth, truth beauty—that is all / Ye know on earth, and all ye need to know."

Sontag's essay suggests that artists must portray war as it is—heartless, destructive and sanguinary; that great masters of the human form such as Leonardo DaVinci understood this well and gave elaborate instructions to their apprentices as to how to present human agony graphically; that artists must forsake pity and emotionally detach themselves from scenes of war, no matter how wrenching their subject; and that it is not irreverent to capture artistically a site of great death because such sites can, by the medium, be "transformed" into scenes of perilous beauty.

This question has been reprinted for your convenience.

<u>Question One</u>

Read the following passage carefully. Then, in a well-organized essay, discuss what the author implies about the role of art and the artist in depicting scenes of war, and show how she uses elements of language to convey it.

Central to modern expectations, and modern ethical feeling, is the conviction that war is an aberration, if an unstoppable one. That peace is the norm, if an unattainable one. This, of course, is not the way war has been regarded throughout history. War has been the norm and peace the exception.

(5)   The description of the exact fashion in which bodies are injured or killed is a recurring climax in the stories told in the *Iliad*. War is seen as something men do inveterately, undeterred by the accumulation of the suffering it inflicts; and to represent war in words or in pictures requires a keen, unflinching detachment. When Leonardo DaVinci gives instructions for a battle painting, he insists that artists have the courage and the imagination to show war in all its

(10)   ghastliness:

> Make the conquered and beaten pale, with brows raised
> and knit, and the skin above their brows furrowed with
> pain…and the teeth apart as with crying out in lamen-
> tation…Make the dead partly or entirely covered with
> *(15)*   dust…and let the blood be seen by its color flowing in
> a sinuous stream from the corpse to the dust. Others in
> the death agony grinding their teeth, rolling their eyes,
> with their fists clenched against their bodies, and the legs
> distorted [. . . .].

(20)   The concern is that the images to be devised won't be sufficiently upsetting: not concrete, not detailed enough. Pity can entail a moral judgment if, as Aristotle maintains, pity is considered to be the emotion that we owe only to those enduring undeserved misfortune. But pity, far from being the natural twin of fear in the dramas of catastrophic misfortune, seems diluted— distracted—by fear, while fear (dread, terror) usually manages to swamp pity. Leonardo is suggesting that

(25)   the artist's gaze be, literally, pitiless. The image should appall, and in that *terribilita* lies a challenging kind of beauty.

That a gory battlescape could be beautiful—in the sublime or awesome or tragic register of the beautiful—is a commonplace about images of war made by artists. The idea does not sit well when applied to images taken by cameras: to find beauty in war photographs seem heartless.

(30)   But the landscape of devastation is still a landscape. There is beauty in ruins. To acknowledge the beauty of photographs of the World Trade Center ruins in the months following the attack seemed frivolous, sacrilegious. The most people dared to say was that the photographs were "surreal," a euphemism behind which the disgraced notion of beauty cowered. But they *were* beautiful, many of them—by veteran photographers such as Gilles Peress, Susan Meiselas, and Joel Meyerowitz,

(35)   among others. The site itself, the mass graveyard that had received the name "Ground Zero," was of course anything but beautiful. Photographs tend to transform, whatever their subject; and as an image something may be beautiful—or terrifying, or unbearable, or quite bearable—as it is not in real life.

Transforming is what art does, but photography that bears witness to the calamitous and

(40)   reprehensible is much criticized if it seems "aesthetic"; that is, too much like art [. . . .].

Scoring Rubric for Free-Response Question One: From Susan Sontag's *Regarding the Pain of Others*

9   Essays earning a score of 9 meet all the criteria for 8 papers and in addition are especially thorough in their analysis or demonstrate a particularly impressive control of style.

8   Essays earning a score of 8 persuasively establish what the author implies about the role of art and the artist in depicting scenes of war. They present a carefully organized response that eloquently involves the diverse elements of language that the author uses to illustrate this role. Their prose demonstrates an impressive control of the elements of effective writing, though it is not flawless.

7   Essays earning a score of 7 fit the description of 6 essays but feature either a more thorough discussion or a greater command of prose style.

6   Essays scoring 6 reasonably establish what the author implies about the role of art and the artist in depicting scenes of war. These responses, while adequately supported and generally sound in nature, are nevertheless not as persuasive as papers earning scores of 7 or better due to their being less developed or less cogent. Though these papers may occasionally lapse in organization, diction or syntax, they are generally clear and effective.

5   Essays scoring 5 generally understand the task but are either limited in scope or insufficiently developed. Though they may be marked by shortcomings in organization, syntax or diction, they nevertheless reflect a certain level of competence.

4   Essays scoring 4 respond inadequately to the question's task, often misunderstanding, misinterpreting, or oversimplifying what the author implies about the role of art and the artist in depicting scenes of war, or providing insufficient evidence of the diverse elements of language that the author uses to convey this. Though the prose is often adequate enough to convey the writer's points, it generally suggests a limited control over organization, diction and syntax.

3   Essays earning a score of 3 meet the criteria for a score of 4 but are either less thorough, or display a more limited control over the elements of effective composition.

2   Essays scoring 2 achieve little success in identifying what the author implies about the role of art and the artist in depicting scenes of war, or in illustrating how the author uses elements of language to convey this. They may on occasion misread the passage, fail to develop their argument to any significant degree, summarize rather than analyze the passage, or display significant weaknesses in organization, clarity, fluency or mechanics.

1   Essays earning a score of 1 meet the criteria for a score of 2 but are either overly simplistic or marred by severe deficiencies in the elements of composition.

0   Essays scoring 0 offer an off-topic response that receives no credit, or a mere repetition of the prompt.

—   Indicates a blank or completely off-topic response.

Sample Student Essay One

The author of this passage establishes the relationship between art and war. Beauty and gruesome brutality seem to be on opposite ends of the spectrum, yet artists depicting war must find the intersection of the two. The author discusses the interpretative nature of art and its power to transform its subjects, making the artist sensitive to the victims of the misfortune and open to criticism when the art is overly aesthetic. She presents the difficult task of making art about war (as appalling beauty is the most difficult to achieve) and how it is necessary to be detached from an event. The author explores her topic with critical diction, examples from artists' past, and elements of vivid imagery.

The author opens her discussion by mentioning artists and works of art dealing with the grotesque subject of war and death. Homer, Leonardo DaVinci, and the photographers of Ground Zero all have examined, in great detail, the brutality of war. The author conveys that the pervasiveness of war has made it a timeless subject in literature, painting and photography. The Iliad *contains graphic scenes included to excite the reader; DaVinci desires to show the absolute horror of war in the most perfect detail possible. The author highlights her opinion with a quote providing detailed imagery of a battle scene subject. A key point the author makes is that while a subject itself may not be beautiful, its presentation as an image may be emotionally stirring and amazingly constructed.*

The author makes an important evaluation of the difference between pity and fear. She uses the most critical diction in this section of her passage, as she moves from expository speech to more debatable assertion and instruction. The author derides those who use pity as a means of conveying a war scene, saying pity creates a "moral judgment" and brings the focus to the individuals in the scene, those who suffered the "undeserved misfortune." She states that pity in a representation distracts from the raw fear and emotion of the scene. The author is of the belief that if the artist is to accurately portray all gruesome details in her piece of art, she is required to be detached and coldly objective. Man's appetite for hunger is insatiable, there are nearly always causalities in conflict, and the artist must be able to both cut ties with humanity and its predilection for battle as well as eliminate her pity for the victimized.

The general opinion of war art changes when the medium of paint is replaced with film. The capturing of images on film conveys a definite realism that is inescapable. The author gives the reader imagery of Ground Zero: architecturally amazing buildings reduced to mere rubble, absolute devastation. The author argues that despite the horrific nature of this landscape, it is no different from any lily pads painted by Monet. Emotions of sadness, anger and pity blind many art critics and the general public from seeing the artistic value in the photographs of the World Trade Center. Many believe that a photographer is irresponsible or irreverent to make art out of "the mass graveyard" of Ground Zero; that any who witness the atrocity, with or without the lens of a camera, should not find aestheticism in ruins. The author takes the side of the photographers, believing that their transformation in film is as much art as is DaVinci's attempt to "make the conquered and beaten pale and the teeth apart as with crying out in lamentation."

The author of the passage evaluates how artists have and can continue to interpret horrific scenes of war. She examines past evidence of war in art and discusses the modern conflict between artistic responsibility and human sensitivity. The author firmly believes that art about war or destruction must invoke deep emotional responses, and is no different from any other work of art in its potential to be stunningly beautiful. She conveys this criticism with careful diction, imagery of war, and support from historic examples of the genre.

You Rate It!

1. How thorough a job did the student do in terms of <u>identifying the implications</u> made by the author about the role of art and the artist in depicting scenes of war? List the ones the student identified:

_____

_____

_____

_____

2. What <u>elements of language</u> did the author employ to convey these implications?

_____

_____

_____

_____

3. How effective was the writer's plan of organization? The fluency of his/her writing? The overall correctness of the paper?

_____

_____

_____

_____

4. On a 0-9 scale, how would you rate this response? Explain why.

_____

_____

_____

_____

Sample Student Essay Two

The main thrust of the speaker's argument is that war, while atrocious and undoubtedly incredibly horrendous, is, in its very horror, somehow very human and even uniquely beautiful, and hence is a fit subject for the artist. In order to make an effective case for such a controversial argument, the speaker must take a number of pre-emptive steps before commencing her argument in earnest. First, she must attempt to remove the notions—ingrained in most readers—that war is an inappropriate subject for art and that to evoke pain and suffering in a painting is a despicable action. This is accomplished by demonstrating that this idea (of destruction and beauty as mutually exclusive ideas) was not always held true. After all, great artists such as Homer and Leonardo da Vinci utilized (if not glamorized) war in their respective writing and painting. Therefore, it may be that our inherent distrust of artistic depictions of war and violence in art (stemming perhaps, from a suspicion of exploitation or solely a visceral reaction to the brutal nature of the content) is perhaps misguided.

The speaker must first go through these steps in order to make the reader more amenable to the argument put forward in the following paragraph, that "a gory battlescape could be beautiful—in the sublime or awesome or tragic register of the beautiful." To make such an unpopular argument, the speaker employs one particular element of language, and this is particularly notable in the tone of the piece. The author uses a tone of impersonal detachment in setting forth her argument. The piece contains no heated argument, but is rather put forward in a very reasoned and objective way. The fact that the author relies so much on the examples of other artists—and even goes so far as to allow a quote from Leonardo to dominate the piece—demonstrates that she knows the case she is putting forth is a provocative one, and believes that the best way to not alienate the reader is to prove right away that she is not in favor of glamorizing war but merely recognizes the power of violent or tragic images.

Another element of language the author utilizes is perspective. She writes in the third person (and a rather impersonal third person at that) to distance herself from her case, thereby making the argument more effective. To state that an "image should appall, and in that terribilità lies a challenging kind of beauty" is to propose an unconventional perspective as to exactly what constitutes a work of beauty. Such an assertion must be grounded in calm and rational thought since, presented in any other way, it would appear as the claim of an irrational and imbalanced individual.

You Rate It!

1. How thorough a job did the student do in terms of <u>identifying the implications</u> made by the author about the role of art and the artist in depicting scenes of war? List the ones the student identified:

_____

_____

_____

_____

2. What <u>elements of language</u> did the author employ to convey these implications?

_____

_____

_____

3. How effective was the writer's plan of organization? The fluency of his/her writing? The overall correctness of the paper?

_____

_____

_____

_____

4. On a 0-9 scale, how would you rate this response? Explain why.

_____

_____

_____

_____

Sample Student Essay Three

Periods of peace are rare and difficult to sustain, and perhaps it is the frequency of war that stimulates artists to portray suffering and bloodshed in their images and fictions. However, the author of this passage maintains that it is most difficult to depict the horrors of war without sending an unintended message of approbation or evoking an unsuitable emotion of sublimity. The speaker's diction, tone, and use of contrast in her passage support her argument that it is the artist's duty to transform the merely shocking and macabre into a transcendent experience of beauty. However, while recognizing that the beauty in horrific images is difficult for both the artist and the viewer to take, the author implies that it is also the artist's duty to separate the work of art from the tangible, often ugly incident on which it is based.

The strong connection between art based on an event and the event itself is particularly problematic, especially in the case of photographs. The diction in the speaker's paragraph on photographs has a high level of clarity that aids the reader in understanding the audience's dilemma in realizing the beauty in photographs. She first explains that many people believe that finding beauty in war photographs is cruel. The speaker recognizes the opposing view before disputing it. She gives the example of the photographs of the World Trade Center ruins, and notes the belief of some that seeing beauty in them is "sacrilegious." Her choice of words perfectly conveys her intention. Although it seems inhumane, even immoral to find beauty in tragedy, one must realize that the art serves the function of disconnecting the horrible from an image of potential beauty; that photographs transform their subject; and that, for a moment, the representation of the foulness of war can be converted to a vision of beauty, a deviation from the normalcy of fear and dread.

The choice of words the speaker chooses sets an appropriate tone. She appears to be reassuring the reader that it is acceptable to believe war photographs to be beautiful. She maintains, "But they were beautiful, many of them—by veteran photographers." The speaker is defending the photographers, saying, that they were creating beautiful images despite the fact that the reality from which they sought their inspiration was horrifying. The tone the speaker uses is a serene one. She is calmly conveying what she believes to be true: that art transforms its subject, leaving the reality behind She is not trying to persuade the reader to view every photograph as beautiful; rather, she simply asks her audience to consider her theory, to not quickly dismiss a controversial image as heartless or sadistic.

The contrast the speaker uses to describe DaVinci's approach at representing war versus photographs of war shows the different attitudes artists possess when representing these images. The speaker cites DaVinci's instructions for the painting of a battle scene, noting that DaVinci wants his war scenes to be thoroughly realistic, wants his images to sicken their viewers, but maintain beneath the revolting layer an image of beauty. The speaker recognizes that beauty can be appreciated in a painting of war, but that for man, a war photograph holds no beauty. By describing a war photograph directly after a painting of war, the speaker is better able to support her declaration that a photograph of war can be valued for its beauty just like a painting. Her implication is that paintings and photographs, though both forms of art, capture war in two distinct ways—one, interpretive, the other factual—but that they both transform their subject.

It is clear that the speaker is bothered by the unwillingness of some to see beauty in war photographs. The speaker believes that art must be separated from the emotional attachment to the event. Photographs are condemned if they appear too much like art, as if they somehow offend the truth of the incident. The speaker seems to contend that it is the artist's role to reverse the notion that beauty can only be found in art that is not an actual reproduction of the occurrence. If people might recognize that photographs can also successfully transform their subjects, the speaker believes the beauty of war photographs might be more readily accepted.

You Rate It!

1. How thorough a job did the student do in terms of <u>identifying the implications</u> made by the author about the role of art and the artist in depicting scenes of war? List the ones the student identified:

_____

_____

_____

_____

2. What <u>elements of language</u> did the author employ to convey these implications?

_____

_____

_____

3. How effective was the writer's plan of organization? The fluency of his/her writing? The overall correctness of the paper?

_____

_____

_____

_____

4. On a 0-9 scale, how would you rate this response? Explain why.

_____

_____

_____

_____

Author's Response to Sample Student Essays on Susan Sontag's *Regarding the Pain of Others*

Sample Student Essay One:

The writer of this essay firmly establishes the role of art and the artist in presenting war. The second sentence of this paper indicates that though "Beauty and gruesome brutality seems to be on opposite ends of the spectrum, yet artists depicting war must find the intersection of the two." She notes that finding this intersection is a challenging task since the artist must delicately balance depicting the grisly reality that is war with a sensitivity to the feelings of those viewing it. She notes the author's belief that the artist needs a certain measure of detachment to present war effectively.

The writer also notes the author's preference for fear or pity, suggesting that "Pity creates a 'moral judgment' and brings the focus to the individuals in the scene, those who suffered the 'undeserved misfortune.'" She accurately understands that pity interferes with detachment since it implies an emotional connection to the scene being depicted. She also notes the irony that although painting and film are much different media, the devastating rubble of the World Trade Center site is "no different from any lily pads painted by Monet."

The writer of this paper concludes strongly "that art about war or destruction must invoke deep emotional responses, and is no different from any other work of art in its potential to be stunningly beautiful."

Though the writer of this essay is a writer of strong competence whose paper is certainly upper-half, her paper also has a lock-step feel to it and consists largely of a litany of what the writer does. Though the introduction makes reference to "critical diction, examples from artists past, and elements of vivid imagery," these are never really examined in anything but an oblique way. There are, to be fair, references to these elements, but the reader must infer in which place the writer is alluding to what specific technique. Overall, the essay seems formulaic, lacking the spark of the very best papers.

Author's Score: 7

Sample Student Essay Two:

The second sample essay creates some problems for the reader in that the writer never really articulates in any clear fashion what he perceives as the role of art and the artist in representing war Though the paper engaged the passage and is not without ideas, it lacks any focused thrust, forcing the reader to search for what point(s) the student wishes to make. The student does attempt to address the tone of the piece, labeling it one of "impersonal detachment," and suggests that the writer's reliance on the passage from Leonardo da Vinci is done to insure that her audience realizes that she is "not for glamorizing war but merely recognizes the power of violent or tragic images."

This student's inability to develop a clear thesis, the rather short development, and the somewhat *in medias res* introduction prevent it from moving into the upper-half though its general writing competence spares it from being demoted to the lower-half.

Author's Score: 5

Sample Student Essay Three:

The final essay has some good things going for it. Its opening paragraph, while perhaps lacking in some internal unity, does make a clear statement that it is "the artist's duty to transform the merely shocking and macabre into a transcendent experience of beauty" and that it is "the artist's duty to separate the work of art from the tangible, often ugly incident on which it is based." The author correctly notes the difference in how art and photography represent scenes of war and terrible violence, citing the contrast between da Vinci's extremely lurid directions and the more realistic and exact nature of photographs. In developing his case, the student also makes some reference to the passage's diction and tone.

Though not without some shortcomings—most notably, not maintaining a sufficient grip on the question's focus and lapsing a little into redundancy—the writer nevertheless develops his argument with greater success than that of the previous sample.

Author's Score: 6

Explication of Free-Response Question Two: From C. Vann Woodward's *The Burden of Southern History*

The second free-response question on this examination provided students with a passage from C. Vann Woodward's book, *The Burden of Southern History*. This particular selection made a less-regional, more national observation about America's frustration with seemingly insoluble problems, and the date of the book suggests that Woodward was likely referring to the quagmire of Vietnam or the tensions over civil-rights, the two dominant social issues of the day. Students were asked to "explore the validity of Woodward's assertion, either in Woodward's era or in some other time period, using examples from [their] reading, observation, studies or experience to develop [their] position."

Though students who have studied the controversies of the Sixties could easily draw upon material studied in their social studies' curriculum to address this question, a purely historical approach is not the only one. Very interesting essays could be rendered using novels such as Harper Lee's *To Kill A Mockingbird* or Tim O'Brien's *The Things They Carried*, both of which examine these two issues through a fictional lens. Students who desired to examine the problems of a different epoch could look at the effects of the Great Depression in novels such as John Steinbeck's *The Grapes of Wrath* or Thomas Wolfe's *You Can't Go Home Again*, or might consider more contemporary threats to the environment in a nonfictional work such as Rachel Carson's *Silent Spring*. Other students will likely consider the real and pressing problems of their own era including the AIDS epidemic, our messy involvement in the Middle East, global warming, the difficulties of securing our borders, invasion of privacy, unemployment, the failure of many of our nation's schools and a host of other possibilities.

Though most students will probably opt for agreeing with Woodward's assertion, there are some who may take issue with it and steadfastly defend America's ability to overcome all difficulties by employing its vast financial and technological resources. They could, for example, cite FDR's success in putting America back to work through the WPA projects, or cite the fact that it has been five years since a major terrorist attack has been carried out on American soil. These essays, while likely to comprise the minority, should be given the same consideration as those which support Woodward's assertion.

This question has been reprinted for your convenience.

Question Two

The following passage, from American historian C. Vann Woodward's *The Burden of Southern History* (1960), makes the following observation about the American people:

> The painful truth that Americans were so frantically fleeing
> was that history had at last caught up with them. It was no
> longer "something unpleasant that happens to other people."
> for it was happening to them too in their own part of the world.
> Neither their fabulous wealth nor their unequaled power, their
> superb technology nor their legendary "know-how," nor all
> these endowments combined assured them of success in solving
> their most pressing problems. On both the foreign front and the
> domestic front they had at last encountered problems that defied
> solutions of the traditional short-term sort and mocked their
> religion of optimism [. . . .].

Take a moment to reflect upon the preceding comment. Then, write a well-organized essay in which you explore the validity of Woodward's assertion, either in Woodward's era or in some other time period, using examples from your reading, observation, studies or experience to develop your position.

Scoring Rubric for Free-Response Question Two: From C. Vann Woodward's *The Burden of Southern History*

9 Essays earning a score of 9 meet all the criteria for 8 papers and in addition are especially thorough in their analysis or demonstrate a particularly impressive control of style.

8 Essays earning a score of 8 agree with, challenge, or qualify C. Vann Woodward's assertion that Americans finally encountered a pressing problem that stymied their wealth and power, and defied their "religion of optimism." They present a carefully organized response that is persuasively supported by a contemporary or past example that has been drawn from their reading, observation, studies or experience. Their prose demonstrates an impressive control of the elements of effective writing, though it is not flawless.

7 Essays earning a score of 7 fit the description of 6 essays but feature either a more thorough discussion or a greater command of prose style.

6 Essays scoring 6 also agree with, challenge, or qualify C. Vann Woodward's assertion These responses, while adequately supported and generally sound in nature, are nevertheless not as persuasive as papers earning scores of 7 or better due to their being less developed or less cogent. Though these papers may occasionally lapse in organization, diction or syntax, they are generally clear and effective.

5 Essays scoring 5 generally understand the task but are either limited in scope or insufficiently developed. Though they may be marked by shortcomings in organization, syntax or diction, they nevertheless reflect a certain level of competence.

4 Essays scoring 4 respond inadequately to the question's task, often misunderstanding, misinterpreting, or oversimplifying C. Vann Woodward's assertion. Though the prose is often adequate enough to convey the writer's points, it generally suggests a limited control over organization, diction and syntax.

3 Essays earning a score of 3 meet the criteria for a score of 4 but are either less thorough, or display a more limited control over the elements of effective composition.

2 Essays scoring 2 achieve little success in responding to C. Vann Woodward's assertion or in illustrating it through reference to a work of literature, a historical incident, epoch or personage, or a personal anecdote. They may on occasion misunderstand the citation, fail to choose an appropriate example, fail to develop their argument to any significant degree, or display significant weaknesses in organization, clarity, fluency or mechanics.

1 Essays earning a score of 1 meet the criteria for a score of 2 but are either overly simplistic or marred by severe deficiencies in the elements of composition.

0 Essays scoring 0 offer an off-topic response that receives no credit, or a mere repetition of the prompt.

— Indicates a blank or completely off-topic response.

Sample Student Essay One

Although articulated almost a half century ago, C. Vann Woodward was correct when he made the perpetually contemporary observation that the American people are encountering problems that challenge the nation's demonstrated ability to transcend the difficult issues that periodically plague all societies. As a world power, America has delivered its people affluence and the most advanced technology. But even its global dominance does not ensure an easy surmounting of all obstacles. Two current evils that threaten America's pride and reputation are the AIDS epidemic and the danger posed by nuclear power plants. The plight of AIDS and the quandary over the transportation of nuclear waste have prompted Americans into often harsh debates over how to develop new answers to the problems plaguing the modern world.

Since its appearance in the 1980s, AIDS has spread rapidly around the world. The Center for Disease Control in the United States has been unable to develop a cure for the disease. Millions of people are afflicted with the virus while researchers remain perplexed by the mystery illness. Beyond knowing that AIDS is transmitted sexually, cures have not been discovered because the virus is constantly mutating. The failure to find a cure has undermined American medicine's self-confidence and its standing in the world. As millions more become infected and die of AIDS, America's belief in its "legendary 'know how'" will most likely diminish.

In addition to protecting American health, safeguarding national security is vital to maintaining America's sense of exceptionalism. While nuclear power plants have been effective in supplying the country with the massive quantities of energy its expanding population requires, the dangers inherent in this technology haunt people who live within proximity of these plants as well as the governmental authorities that regulate them. Since nuclear power produces radioactive waste which is a danger to anyone exposed to it, where to store this waste has been the subject of heated debate. After much political wrangling, the decision has been made to store the waste produced by all the power plants in the United States in Yucca Mountain in Nevada. A related question, of course, is how the highly radioactive waste will be transported to Yucca Mountain. Even America's vaunted technological capabilities seem stymied by the seemingly unsolvable problem of transporting this material without subjecting a substantial portion of the American populace to unacceptable danger. How humbling for a nation of fabulous wealth" and "unequaled power" to be forced to consider the prospect of a "Chernobyl" on American soil.

No nation is exempt from the forces of history. Woodward's assessment in 1960 of history catching up with the American people seems fresh today. Although the problems confronting the nation may be different than those to which Woodward referred, and perhaps the American character has evolved in ways he did not foresee, history can be "unpleasant" to all civilizations and it is a useful exercise in humility for Americans to understand this fundamental truth.

You Rate It!

1. How effectively did the writer understand the assertion by C. Vann Woodward about the American people? Did the writer take a position on the validity of the assertion?

_____

_____

_____

_____

2. Did the writer support the position taken through a reference to an episode or event in American history taken from his/her reading, observation, studies or experience? To what degree did the writer provide <u>specific details</u> about the book, historical incident, etc. that made his/her argument persuasive?

_____

_____

_____

_____

3. How effective was the writer's plan of organization? The fluency of his/her writing? The overall correctness of the paper?

_____

_____

_____

_____

4. On a 0-9 scale, how would you rate this response? Explain why.

_____

_____

_____

_____

Sample Student Essay Two

C. Vann Woodward's statement from <u>The Burden of Southern History</u> provides a critical lens through which one can examine history and current events. He correctly alleges that Americans in 1960 were suddenly confronted with their past crimes and atrocities, unable to turn a blind eye to domestic inequity and heated Cold War-era foreign relations. Woodward's assertion was specifically directed towards the South, yet his categorization encompasses all of the American people, both in 1960 and 2004. Decades of optimism, of "Father Knows Best" assurance of the 1950s and dot-com hipsters of the 1990s left the American people unaware of impending contemporary crises. The Cold War of Woodward's time has been replaced with an interminable War on Terror, McCarthyism by the Patriot Act, and a battle for civil rights for African-Americans with a war for justice for African-Americans, immigrants, Hispanic-Americans, women and homosexuals. The severity of these problems cannot be hidden under America's affluence, military superiority, and "know-how."

The constant, historic abuses committed by the American majority and the American government have created a tangled web of complications and offenses. The belief in American superiority, economic priority, and inalienable rights has caused the country to alienate any who stand in the way of domination. American conviction that one way is the right way has caused slavery, near nuclear war, and now war with fundamentalist Muslims. The American cocktail of one part arrogance, one part decadence, and one part over-militarization (with a garnish of Republican leadership) creates a hangover of enemies, deficit spending and unwanted occupation. To borrow a phrase from Al Franken's <u>Lies and the Lying Liars who Tell Them</u>, the American people are more than ready to deploy "Operation Ignore" when it comes to foreign policy issues, and then have to deal with massive crises.

There is no short term solution to win the war on terror. There is no quick fix to disarm all of American enemies and create a peaceful, secure domestic home front. Yet, the American government is ready to create temporary methods of routing out terrorists and dissenters, usually employing fraudulent methods, in spite of the Constitution. The right to privacy is overhauled by the Patriot Act, in the most egregious display of infringement of rights since Joe McCarthy waved his fabricated list of Communist traitors. As Woodward's book picked apart the ignorance and close-mindedness of the South, Michael Moore is a vulture to the dead carcass of the Bush administration in his film <u>Fahrenheit 911</u>. The futile attempts of the government to find traitors include infiltration of a middle aged peace consciousness rap group, an elderly man working out at the gym, and a baby-toting single mother, as pointed out by Moore. Without a real plan for the future and feeding on traditional optimism that events will work out in American favor, our "pressing problems" go unsolved.

The American majority is unable to change or recognize their own stupidity until history has recorded it. While protests are held because of human rights violations in China, the U.S. Congress violates human rights every day that it debates whether gays are allowed to be married. American consciousness pities the victims of atrocities committed in lesser developed nations, but fails to see that race, sexual identity, socioeconomic background and religion change nothing about a person's undeniable rights. Tradition is more important than history as policy makers choose what marriage means, registrars disenfranchise black voters, and bureaucracy detains and tortures immigrants for having done nothing wrong. How, in a country that witnessed the death of men like Martin Luther King Jr., could the crucifixion of Matthew Shepard be seen as anything less than appalling? How could the Confederate flag still be a symbol of Southern pride yet so few people actually know what Lynard Syknyrd's "Sweet Home Alabama" represents? How is it that the grandchildren of Mexican immigrants and slaves still face similar prejudices their ancestors bore? Americans run away from their history rather than confront it, fating them to only repeat their own mistakes.

C. Vann Woodward declares that in 1960, the unrecognized domestic and foreign problems of America finally caught up with its people. America's refusal to accept its history, America's blindness because of its supposed affluence and superior technology, and weak government policy-making led to disastrous civil and global conflict. Woodward's statement is highly applicable to modern day and the "war on terror" as well as the domestic war on homosexuals and minorities. Our modern political and social calamities support every element of Woodward's observation.

You Rate It!

1. How effectively did the writer understand the assertion by C. Vann Woodward about the American people? Did the writer take a position on the validity of the assertion?

_____

_____

_____

_____

2. Did the writer support the position taken through a reference to an episode or event in American history taken from his/her reading, observation, studies or experience? To what degree did the writer provide <u>specific details</u> about the book, historical incident, etc. that made his/her argument persuasive?

_____

_____

_____

_____

3. How effective was the writer's plan of organization? The fluency of his/her writing? The overall correctness of the paper?

_____

_____

_____

_____

4. On a 0-9 scale, how would you rate this response? Explain why.

_____

_____

_____

_____

Sample Student Essay Three

I believe that Mr. Woodward's assessment of the American people and of America as a whole—is both a valid and interesting perspective on exactly what led to the great socio-political problems the country faced both in the Sixties and today.

In order to assess the validity of Mr. Woodward's observations, it is incumbent upon the reader to understand the context in which he was writing these words. As Woodward states: "On both the foreign front and the domestic front they had at last encountered problems that defied solutions of the traditional short-term sort and mocked their religion of optimism...". He is referring, of course, to what was our increasing involvement in Vietnam (to disastrous results) as well as the domestic turmoil brought about by the civil rights struggle.

The Vietnam War was the first major war in which the United States was not the victor since the War of 1812 (and even that could be considered almost a draw) and definitely the first non-civil conflict in which the country was not united in its resolve. What Woodward refers to in his book is the fact that no easy solution could be found to either win the war or to mend its divisive impact on the American people.

The Sixties were the first time that such issues of national unity came to the fore (leaving aside the Civil War as an atypical and irrelevant period). This type of problem was unique to the American public because neither presented an easy physical impediment to surmount. The struggle for civil rights best illustrates this point. Throughout the history of the United States, most national problems were at their heart logistical in nature and even those which were not could be surmounted by creativity, hard work and obstinacy. The Great Depression, for example, while an economic crisis, was solved in large part by putting Americans to work. This time, the physical manifestation of unrest (the marches and sit-ins) were emblematic of a long-held and not easily dispelled racism that was endemic in the psyche of much of the populace. Because of this, there were no easy solution to be set forth which would solve the problems causing the rift between the people of our nation.

It is the lack of an easy solution, or even an obvious solution, which Woodward hints at. As he so aptly puts it, the American people had, for the first time "encountered problems that defied solutions of the traditional short-term sort and mocked their religion of optimism." Sadly, it was not to be the last.

You Rate It!

1. How effectively did the writer understand the assertion by C. Vann Woodward about the American people? Did the writer take a position on the validity of the assertion?

   _____

   _____

   _____

   _____

2. Did the writer support the position taken through a reference to an episode or event in American history taken from his/her reading, observation, studies or experience? To what degree did the writer provide <u>specific details</u> about the book, historical incident, etc. that made his/her argument persuasive?

   _____

   _____

   _____

   _____

3. How effective was the writer's plan of organization? The fluency of his/her writing? The overall correctness of the paper?

   _____

   _____

   _____

   _____

4. On a 0-9 scale, how would you rate this response? Explain why.

   _____

   _____

   _____

   _____

Author's Response to Sample Student Essays on the Passage from
C. Vann Woodward's *The Burden of Southern History*

Sample Student Essay One:

This compact essay enjoys a solid measure of success in responding to the citation from C. Vann Woodward's book. The writer divides his essay into a consideration of how successful America has been in finding a cure for AIDS, and a consideration of how successful the country has been in ridding itself of the waste products of nuclear power plants. The essay has a clear introduction, body and conclusion, good fluency, and minimal compositional error. Its shortcoming is its lack of development, in particular the AIDS section, which consists of four, largely superficial sentences. The subsequent section on nuclear waste has more specifics and is more persuasive, particularly in its allusion to an American Chernobyl.

Splitting a focus always runs the danger of creating imbalance, either in the disparity of the topics or the development of them. This paper, while certainly an upper-half effort, falls prey to the latter.

Author's Score: 6 (but a strong one)

Sample Student Essay Two:

This very gifted writer lays into the topic with an approach that is almost too passionate. Clearly written by a very able student, the essay alludes not only to Woodward's text but to a book by Al Franken, to a song by an appropriately Southern band, Lynyrd Skynrd, and to a film (*Farenheit 451*) by Michael Moorer. Unlike the two-pronged focus of sample essay one, this paper is a guns-blazing attack on American policies toward counter-terror and a broad spectrum of human rights.

The author opens by contrasting problems of previous decades with those of today, suggesting that we have made little progress in solving them. The two sentences which conclude this writer's introduction—"The Cold War of Woodward's time has been replaced with an interminable War on Terror, McCarthyism by the Patriot Act, and a battle for civil rights for African-Americans with a war for justice for African-Americans, immigrants, Hispanic-Americans, women and homosexuals. The severity of these problems cannot be hidden under America's affluence, military superiority, and 'know-how'"—leave no doubt as to the student's passion or position. Of the three body paragraphs, which treat the three issues established in the introduction, the first is perhaps the weakest since the author's allusion to scenes in the Michael Moorer film is insufficiently clear to be effective.

The student has an impressive voice which manifests itself in effective rhetorical constructions such as "How, in a country that witnessed the death of men like Martin Luther King Jr., could the crucifixion of Matthew Shepard be seen as anything less than appalling? How could the Confederate flag still be a symbol of Southern pride yet so few people actually know what Lynard Syknrd's 'Sweet Home Alabama' represents? How is it that the grandchildren of Mexican immigrants and slaves still face similar prejudices their ancestors bore?" The parallel trinity of "How" clauses, the juxtaposition of historical allusions, and the tone of incredulity are the trademarks of a superior writer. So impressive is the scope of the student's knowledge that one can overlook the less than successful movie reference.

Author's Score: 9

Sample Student Essay Three:

The third and final sample for this question is representative of a writer who understands the task but who is not able to pull things together enough to generate an upper-half paper. The writer clearly states his agreement with C. Vann Woodward's observation and suggests the importance of considering their historical context, mentioning both the Vietnam conflict and the '60's struggle for civil rights. Both allusions, however, are not very developed, and the author briefly wanders off into comments on the Civil War and the Great Depression. Though the lapse into first-person is limited to the writer's opening sentence and the writer's sentences show no major flaws, the writing reflects deficiencies in both the organization of idea and the development of it. This is a fine example of a median paper.

Author's Score: 5

Explication of Free-Response Question Three: "Corporate Sponsorship & the American School"

The final question of Sample Examination Two required students to consider six diverse sources—passages from four articles, a cartoon, and a chart—on the controversy over corporate sponsorship in American high schools. After examining them, students were asked to integrate at least three of them in an essay that defended, challenged, or qualified the claim that "corporate sponsorship could have a positive effect in American high schools by providing resources that schools otherwise might not be able to afford."

The sources offered diverse perspectives and information on the topic. Document A. for example, took a somewhat neutral stance, merely providing examples of the types of companies that are trying to buy their way into schools (though a clear subtext of disapproval was apparent in the qualification "schools that are willing to sacrifice critical citizenship for the creation of consumer identities"). Document B chose to examine the marriage of greed and need in one Colorado school system, noting how "Top dollar buys advertising rights on school buses, in all schools and four public-address announcements at every basketball and football game, among other benefits." Document C discusses an 'educational' cable program called Channel One, subscription to which gets a school "a satellite dish (that can only pick up Channel One's signals), two VCRs, and a 19" TV set for each room." Though the source is largely impartial, the author does comment that the show's use of student art "makes children into unpaid graphic artists for Channel One's advertising department." Document D is a chart that provides the position taken by the American Federation of Teachers, the National Association of Secondary School Principals, and the National Parent Teacher Association on the aforementioned cable program, all of whom seem to some degree opposed to it, either formally or in principle. The final two documents—an article that justifies one high school's need for and benefit from such sponsorship, and a wry cartoon in which a teacher's economics' classroom is papered with corporate advertising—round out a potpourri of material upon which students may base their argument.

Much as in the New Orleans' question in Sample Examination One, students were provided with a controversial issue, but in this case one of financial and moral complexity and one that could very well be relevant in their own schools.

This question has been reprinted for your convenience.

<u>Question Three</u>

Directions:

The following prompt is based on the accompanying six sources.

This question requires you to integrate a variety of sources into a coherent, well-written essay. *Refer to the sources to support your position; avoid paraphrase or summary. Your argument should be central; the sources should support this argument.*

Remember to attribute both direct and indirect citations

Introduction:

An association between corporate and educational institutions could have many benefits, from technological improvements in the classroom to needed upgrades in athletic facilities. Such assistance could be especially beneficial to districts with limited economic means which otherwise might not be able to effect such improvements. But will the benefits that come from such association outweigh the drawbacks, such as schools exposing their students to a morally questionable sales pitch?

Assignment:

Peruse the following sources (including any introductory information) carefully. **Then, in an essay that synthesizes at least three of the sources for support, take a position that defends, challenges or qualifies the claim that corporate sponsorship could have a positive effect in American high schools by providing resources that schools otherwise might not be able to afford.**

(It is recommended that you spend 15-20 minutes of the allotted time examining the sources and devote the remaining time to writing your essay.)

Scoring Rubric for Free-Response Question Three:
"Corporate Sponsorship & the American School"

9   Essays earning a score of 9 meet all the criteria for 8 papers and in addition are especially thorough in their analysis or demonstrate a particularly impressive control of style.

8   Essays earning a score of 8 take a position that defends, challenges, or qualifies the claim that "corporate sponsorship could have a positive effect in American high schools by providing resources that schools otherwise might not be able to afford." They present a carefully organized response that persuasively involves at least three of the sources that discuss the case for and against corporate sponsorship. Their prose demonstrates an impressive control of the elements of effective writing, though it is not flawless.

7   Essays earning a score of 7 fit the description of 6 essays but feature either a more expansive discussion of the topic, or a greater command of prose style.

6   Essays scoring 6 take a position that defends, challenges, or qualifies the claim that "corporate sponsorship could have a positive effect in American high schools by providing resources that schools otherwise might not be able to afford." These responses, while adequately supported and generally sound in nature, are nevertheless not as persuasive as papers earning scores of 7 or better due to their being less developed or less cogent. Though these papers may occasionally lapse in organization, diction or syntax, they are generally clear and effective.

5   Essays scoring 5 generally understand the task but are either limited in scope or insufficiently developed. Though they may be marked by shortcomings in organization, syntax or diction, they nevertheless reflect a certain level of competence.

4   Essays scoring 4 respond inadequately to the question's task, often offering unpersuasive arguments for or against permitting corporate sponsorship in high schools, or failing to involve the sources to a sufficiently effective extent. Though the prose is often adequate enough to convey the writer's points, it generally suggests a limited control over organization, diction and syntax.

3   Essays earning a score of 3 meet the criteria for a score of 4 but are either less thorough in documenting the problems of corporate sponsorship, or display a more limited control over the elements of effective composition.

2   Essays scoring 2 achieve little success in making the case for or against corporate sponsorship in schools. They may on occasion misunderstand a source, fail to develop their argument to any significant degree, paraphrase rather than analyze a source, or display significant weaknesses in organization, clarity, fluency or mechanics.

1   Essays earning a score of 1 meet the criteria for a score of 2 but are either overly simplistic or marred by severe deficiencies in the elements of composition.

0   Essays scoring 0 offer an off-topic response that receives no credit, or a mere repetition of the prompt.

—   Indicates a blank or completely off-topic response.

Sample Student Essay One

Within the last fifteen years, there has been a dramatic increase in corporate sponsorship in schools. The advocates of these programs claim, with some merit, that the additional money that is brought in enables extra-curricular programs to survive and academic necessities to be purchased. Many districts, however, have mobilized themselves to fight an imagined war over their students' intellectual independence, and have thus prevented large amounts of money from flowing into the schools.

Those who fight the battle against corporate sponsorship in schools argue that such deals forfeit the consumer discretion of the students. These people, however, miss out on the fact that, above all, the advertising in schools is meant to benefit the children who roam the halls. In Colorado Springs, Colorado, for instance, an advertising campaign in the schools in the late nineties was bringing in over $100,000 a year (Document B). Money in those sums can pay for many things that schools vitally need: two more teachers, better and more extensive extra-curricular programs, more books than one could ask for, and/or computers for every classroom. These types of things can be the difference between a mediocre school and a great one.

The deals also benefit the businesses that pay to advertise in educational institutions, and perhaps this is the reason that so many people take issue with the practice. Anytime a big business benefits from something involving the nation's children, alarm bells are bound to go off, and rightfully so. That said, the people who advertise in schools are often making long-term investments, banking that an early relationship between a student and a product will result in high profits down the road. For this reason, many of the sponsors have a vested interest in making sure that the schools succeed, as this ultimately will give the students a better chance to earn more money to spend.

The benefits of in school advertising should not shield anyone from its dangers, however. There is a difference between the way Apple and other computer companies advertise (in which they sell large numbers of their products to a school at a discounted price in the hope of associating computer usage with their brand in the student's mind) and the way that fast food companies like Burger King advertise (Document A). Companies like Burger King, or Hershey, have little or no interest in the long-term success of a school. Rather, they make and sell products that are cheap enough for middle school and high school students to buy and enjoy. Along those lines, schools should not be blindly selling themselves to any company willing to buy. A line should be drawn when it comes to fast food companies, candy and soda companies, and pharmaceuticals (nobody wants to see painkiller advertisements around every corner of a school). When a company like Nike or Exxon advertises in a school, there is bound to be natural hesitation. The question that needs to be asked, however, is whether or not the students gain more from the sponsorship in the form of better facilities and teachers than they lose in the form of a wasted class period spewing propaganda for the company. In the case of computer companies and similar establishments, the students are indeed most likely receiving a net gain. In the case of candy and soda companies, however, much more discretion needs to be advised, especially because we are in the midst of an obesity epidemic that is slowly killing millions of Americans. Having these companies advertise on the sides of school buses is akin to advertising pet rats for sale in the midst of the Bubonic Plague.

Private sponsorship in schools holds great potential. A free market always operates more efficiently than a command economy, which is how American schools raise their money. That said, there are significant dangers in an unregulated free market, and that is why most modern markets are monitored by their governments. It certainly would be a shame if corporate sponsorship degenerated to the point that Victoria's Secret and Pfizer lied around every corner in American high schools. It would be just as big a shame, however, if millions of American students were denied access to better learning and extra-curricular activities by school boards and superintendents who were blind to the vast potential the premise holds.

You Rate It!

1. How thorough a job did the writer do in terms of defending, challenging or qualifying the claim that "corporate sponsorship could have a positive effect in American high schools by providing resources that schools otherwise might not be able to afford?"

_____

_____

_____

_____

2. To what degree of success did the writer integrate at least three of the six sources to support his/her argument for or against corporate sponsorship in schools?

_____

_____

_____

_____

3. How effective was the writer's plan of organization? The fluency of his/her writing? The overall correctness of the paper?

_____

_____

_____

_____

4. On a 0-9 scale, how would you rate this response? Explain why.

_____

_____

_____

_____

Sample Student Essay Two

The concept of creating associations between corporate and educational institutions is one that has been widely disputed. While allowing companies to sponsor schools and school-related programs such as sports teams can provide a variety of benefits for the school and students, it also exposes students to arguably unneeded commercialism.

Allowing a variety of corporations to sponsor schools can be extremely beneficial for students and faculty. Document B describes a situation with Palmer High School in Colorado. Palmer High School allows companies to sign on as corporate sponsors for varying increments of money, and the larger the dollar amount, the more advertising space the company receives. The superintendent of the school district believes that without the sponsors, the school system would have never improved from their previous lackluster state of crowded classes, lack of extracurricular programs, and poorly kept school buildings. With the corporate sponsors, the students now enjoy a variety of benefits which would have been completely unavailable before the advertising agreements.

Despite these benefits, there are a variety of counteracting arguments that demonstrate the down side of corporate sponsors. Document A believes that allowing companies to come into schools and plaster posters and advertisements within the educational atmosphere takes away from the learning experience for the students. The article discusses how schools that allow corporate sponsors are giving away their student's and school's identities in order to become a "youth-oriented Times Square". The cartoon illustrated in Source F demonstrates the extreme irony in a school environment that allows sponsorship in their schools. As shown in the cartoon, an economics lesson is taking place discussing credit card debt. Credit card debt is brought on by the excessive use of credit cards. However, Visa is the company sponsoring the lecture. Visa's sponsorship is promoting their own card, while at the same time discussing how credit cards are dangerous. Their sponsorship is adding to the problem of credit card debt because the students are exposed to their brand while the fact Visa is sponsoring the lesson degrades the entire lesson. These two documents pose valid arguments against corporate sponsors in the school environment because by allowing companies to invade schools, the schools are losing part of their individual identities and are succumbing to marketing techniques utilized by the companies.

The idea of allowing companies to create relationships with schools across the nation has been argued both as immoral, but also as beneficial. Many schools and individuals believe that the benefits that come from these associations overpower the tangible advertisements throughout the schools. However, other individuals believe allowing companies to invade educational environments takes away from the learning experience. A potential compromise for this argument is shown in Document C. Channel One, an educational news show, would allow companies to put commercials into the show, but students would also learn what is going on in the world through the educational news segments. In a way, this could be a "happy medium" because students would continue to learn through the show, and companies would be able to advertise without plastering posters and ads throughout the school. Because of the valid conflicting sides in this argument, the only way schools would be able to reach a final decision is if something similar to what is shown in Document C is derived.

You Rate It!

1. How thorough a job did the writer do in terms of defending, challenging or qualifying the claim that "corporate sponsorship could have a positive effect in American high schools by providing resources that schools otherwise might not be able to afford?"

_____

_____

_____

_____

2. To what degree of success did the writer integrate at least three of the six sources to support his/her argument for or against corporate sponsorship in schools?

_____

_____

_____

_____

3. How effective was the writer's plan of organization? The fluency of his/her writing? The overall correctness of the paper?

_____

_____

_____

_____

4. On a 0-9 scale, how would you rate this response? Explain why.

_____

_____

_____

_____

Sample Student Essay Three

Everywhere we look, there are advertisements to be found. But how harmful are these messages? While they may, of course, encourage us to buy a particular product, there are no obligations, and our actions are completely of our own accord. Even when advertisements are used in schools and money is given to improve educational facilities, students are by no means compelled to obey the signs and buy what is suggested. The only importance of these signs is that they allow the schools to expand and become more technologically advanced, two things that are incalculable for a school. American high schools should accept corporate sponsorships because they reap unprecedented benefits for the schools and put no pressure on the students to help the companies.

With advertisements come irreplaceable benefits for schools. Oftentimes, schools do not have the budgets to support modernizing their technology when they cannot even afford new, needed supplies. At Colorado Springs, for example, Manning explains that city voters did not allow a tax increase to support the school's funding for almost twenty years. This school, along with other city schools, has too many students and too few programs. Because the most important thing for growing children is having efficient schools and great opportunities, we should go to any measure to bring these to them. One possibility is the use of advertising in schools: "Top dollar buys advertising rights on school buses, in all schools and four public-address announcements at every basketball and football game" (Manning). The money earned from this can be used to obtain incredible items, such as the eighty thousand dollar scoreboard given to Vernon Hills High School ("Cash-strapped schools look for sponsors"). Items such as this one would never have been purchased without the help of a company, and it is impractical to believe that an old item can even be replaced as long as the current one is working and safe. Other benefits include free educational videos and televisions in classrooms, each of which would help to give teachers new means to educate students. These companies are saving schools and giving them incredible opportunities that would not have been possible without corporate money. Schools should be welcoming of this occasion and continue to do whatever possible to help the students learn and enjoy their education.

While some condemn corporate sponsoring of schools, after careful observation it becomes apparent that this opportunity is not only understandable but also more beneficial for the schools than the companies. Primarily, because schools are given so many wonderful advancements, it is only reasonable that the schools do something in return to help the companies and keep them in business. The most convenient way to do this is to use advertising, for it takes almost no energy for a school to put up a sign or make an announcement. In addition, no student is obligated to buy the products, and most likely will not be swayed drastically by them: "We worked very had to make sure we weren't exploiting the kids [. . .] [t]hey probably won't sell one more can of paint because of this" (Cash-strapped schools look for sponsors). In today's modern world, the streets and televisions are so packed with advertisements that if a person were to be swayed a significant amount by each sign, he would be completely overwhelmed. In fact, a school could just as easily put up a black sign rather than a sponsored one and the schools would be affect in the same way. To not use this limited effort to earn great amounts of money and new opportunities would be a foolish mistake for any school to make.

Because advertisements give money to improve schools and they have only positive effects on the students, corporate money is acceptable to help education systems. We head towards a world full of advertisements, but as long as they have good intentions for the younger generations there is no reason to be bothered by these various pictures and slogans.

You Rate It!

1. How thorough a job did the writer do in terms of defending, challenging or qualifying the claim that "corporate sponsorship could have a positive effect in American high schools by providing resources that schools otherwise might not be able to afford?"

_____

_____

_____

_____

2. To what degree of success did the writer integrate at least three of the six sources to support his/her argument for or against corporate sponsorship in schools?

_____

_____

_____

_____

3. How effective was the writer's plan of organization? The fluency of his/her writing? The overall correctness of the paper?

_____

_____

_____

_____

4. On a 0-9 scale, how would you rate this response? Explain why.

_____

_____

_____

_____

**Author's Response to Sample Student Essays on
"Should Corporate Sponsorship Be Permitted in American High Schools?"**

Sample Student Essay One:

This initial response to Question Three, on corporate sponsorship in the American high school, is really an exemplary paper. For one, it incorporates the source material judiciously and fluently, and the reader never feels bombarded by detail even though there are plenty of references to the sources. The writer presents a balanced perspective, summarizing the benefits and drawbacks of permitting corporate sponsorship in American high schools. He demonstrates the various uses to which $100,000 might be put in terms of equipment and personnel, but also considers the potential problems that might be caused by allowing fast food, candy or soda companies to advertise their products in a school setting. The writer expands this connection to a national problem—obesity—that is assuming epidemic proportions.

The writer's astute observation at the conclusion of the third paragraph, that "Ideally, a symbiotic relationship between the school and the sponsor forms for the benefit of both," implies that it is not only the corporation but the school that perceives the advantage of such a relationship. The final paragraph, which seemingly buttresses its argument with knowledge gleaned in an economics' elective, closes with a nice parallel construction: "It certainly would be a shame if corporate sponsorship degenerated to the point that Victoria's Secret and Pfizer lied [sic] around every corner in American high schools. It would be just as big a shame, however, if millions of American students were denied access to better learning and extra-curricular activities by school boards and superintendents who were blind to the vast potential the premise holds."

Though the writer chooses exclusively to paraphrase and never to cite directly, he nevertheless does so in a fluent and cogent fashion. Though the essay is not without peccadilloes, the overall synthesis of sources and the quality of the argument are impressive. This and droll but apropos observations, such as "Many districts, however, have mobilized themselves to fight an imagined war over their students' intellectual independence," or "Having these companies advertise on the sides of school buses is akin to advertising pet rats for sale in the midst of the Bubonic Plague," make this a superior essay.

Author's Score: 9

Sample Student Essay Two:

This student essay, while written quite fluently and involving to good effect five of the six sources, is not as persuasive as the previous paper primarily because its author never really takes a position. It does a very fine job of delineating the arguments for and against corporate involvement in the American high school, and is occasionally very insightful (of particular note is the student's discussion of the Visa advertisement in the economics' class in Source F). Though the student does suggest a "happy medium" in the final paragraph, this is less the student's idea as it is an idea expressed by the source itself. Still, the sound organizational plan and generally fluent writing makes this a good upper-half paper, but not one in the upper tier.

Author's Score: 7

Sample Student Essay Three:

The first positive about the third student sample is its clearly defined and unwavering perspective. The writer firmly indicates her support for corporate sponsorship in the high school in the concluding sentence of her introduction, cites several examples of the benefits such association has provided individual schools, and adamantly concludes that because students "head towards a world full of advertisements there is no reason to be bothered by these various pictures and slogans." Nevertheless, there are aspects of this paper which are inferior to the preceding student samples. For one, the student seems to involve only two, not three, of the six sources. The integration of the sources with the writer's text is also not optimal, and there are instances of ragged syntax. In addition, the writer pretty much chooses to ignore, rather than rebut, any material that might contradict her position. Though this essay certainly displays competence, a strong voice, and good organization, it is nevertheless less effective than the ones that precede it.

Author's Score: 6

Sample Examination III

Questions 1-12. Refer to the following passage.

Nothing but deep familiarity with his subject will protect the short-story writer from another danger: that of contenting himself with a
(5) mere sketch of the episode selected. The temptation to do so is all the greater because some critics, in their resentment of the dense and the prolix, have tended to overestimate the tenuous and the tight [. . . .]. It is easy to be brief and
(10) sharply outlined if one does away with one or more dimensions; the real achievement, as certain tales of Flaubert's and Turgenev's, of Stevenson's and Maupassant's show, is to suggest illimitable air within a narrow space [. . . .].
(15) The phrase "economy of material" suggests another danger to which the novelist and the writer of short stories are equally exposed. Such economy is, in both cases, nearly always to be advised in the multiplication of accidental
(20) happenings, minor episodes, surprises and contrarieties. Most beginners crowd into their work twice as much material of this sort as it needs. The reluctance to look deeply enough into a subject leads to the indolent habit of
(25) decorating its surface. I was once asked to read a manuscript on the eternal theme of a lovers' quarrel. The quarrelling pair made up, and the reasons for dispute and reconciliation were clearly inherent in their characters and situation;
(30) but the author, being new at the trade, felt obliged to cast about for an additional, a fortuitous, pretext for their reunion—so he sent them for a drive, made the horses run away, and caused the young man to save the young lady's
(35) life. This is a crude example of a frequent fault. Again and again the novelist passes by the real meaning of a situation simply for lack of letting it reveal all its potentialities instead of dashing this way and that in quest of fresh effects. If,
(40) when once drawn to a subject, he would let it grow slowly in his mind instead of hunting about for arbitrary combinations of circumstance, his tale would have the warm scent and flavour of a fruit ripened in the sun
(45) instead of the insipidity of one forced in a hot house.

There is a sense in which the writing of fiction may be compared to the administering of a fortune. Economy and expenditure must each bear a part in it, but they should never
(50) degenerate into parsimony or waste. True economy consists in the drawing out of one's subject every drop of significance it can give, true expenditure in devoting time, meditation, and patient labour to the process of
(55) extraction and representation.
It all comes back to a question of expense: expense of time, of patience, of study, of thought, of letting hundreds of stray experiences accumulate and group themselves
(60) in the memory, till suddenly one of the number emerges and throws its sharp light on the subject which solicits you. It has been often, and inaccurately, said that the mind of a creative artist is a mirror, and the work of art
(65) the reflection of life in it. The mirror, indeed, is the artist's mind, with all his experiences reflected in it; but the work of art, from the smallest to the greatest, should be something projected, not reflected, something on which
(70) his mirrored experiences, at the right conjunction of the stars, are to be turned for its full illumination.

1. The author's attitude toward the "economy" of prose includes all of the following EXCEPT

   (A) a reluctance to sacrifice artistic vision to please the critics
   (B) a concern that trimming a narrative may negatively impact its layers of complexity
   (C) a fear that such shortening may embarrassingly unmask an author's unfamiliarity with the subject matter
   (D) a desire to dissuade novice writers from marring their narratives with arbitrary and unnecessary plot twists
   (E) a conviction that a work of fiction grows at its own natural pace if a writer will be patient

2. The author likely includes commentary about the novice's manuscript (lines 24-34) in order to

   (A) advance the fortunes of an evolving literary talent
   (B) illustrate a potential compositional pitfall
   (C) acknowledge an enduring literary theme
   (D) lament the death of a young author
   (E) provide an example of effective literary economy

3. The author's comments about the manuscript of the young writer are BEST classified as

   (A) demeaning and derisive
   (B) callous and acerbic
   (C) analytical and objective
   (D) abashed and apologetic
   (E) detached and indifferent

4. The metaphor that concludes the second paragraph provides a(n)

   (A) admonition against the unnatural forcing of a narrative
   (B) argument for a greater use of description
   (C) paean to the heroic actions of the story's protagonist
   (D) concession that two different approaches may yield two equally successful results
   (E) an intimation that the road to literary success is a slow one

5. Of the following, which does LEAST to demonstrate the misguided bent of young writers, a flaw that the author clearly does not like?

   (A) "indolent habit of decorating its surface" (lines 23-24)
   (B) "cast about for an additional, a fortuitous, pretext for their reunion" (lines 30-31)
   (C) "crude example of a frequent fault" (line 34)
   (D) "dashing this way and that in quest of fresh effects" (lines 37-38)
   (E) "hunting about for arbitrary combinations of circumstance" (lines 40-42)

6. It may be inferred from the concluding paragraph that for the artist the act of creation ultimately remains

   (A) random and spontaneous
   (B) frustrating and enervating
   (C) costly and unattainable
   (D) exhilarating and gratifying
   (E) time-consuming and painstaking

7. In the final two paragraphs the author primarily relies upon

   (A) paradox
   (B) extended metaphor
   (C) simile
   (D) ironical understatement
   (E) allusion

8. The opening sentence of the final paragraph (lines 56-62) may be said to do which of the following?

   I. Mirror, through its syntax, the gradual manner in which literary ideas come to fruition.
   II. Convey the growing frustration of the struggling artist.
   III. Imply that the most significant inspirations occur spontaneously and of their own accord.

   (A) I only
   (B) II only
   (C) I and III
   (D) II and III
   (E) I, II and III

9. It may be inferred from the passage that a writer who "projects" would treat the details of his experience in which of the following manners?

    (A) meticulously cataloging them exactly as he remembers them
    (B) intentionally distorting them in a surrealistic manner
    (C) imaginatively channeling them into a unique artistic vision
    (D) recklessly utilizing them to form ungrounded predictions
    (E) brusquely rejecting them as unreliable reflections of society

10. In advancing her argument, the author employs all of the following contrasts EXCEPT

    (A) confinement and boundlessness
    (B) patience and haste
    (C) ripening and rotting
    (D) conserving and spending
    (E) ignorance and illumination

11. Which of the following would BEST qualify as a paradox?

    (A) "the real achievement [. . .] is to suggest illimitable air within a narrow space [. . . .]" (lines 10-13)
    (B) "Such economy is, in both cases, nearly always to be advised in the multiplication of accidental happenings, minor episodes, surprises and contrarieties." (lines 17-20)
    (C) "The reluctance to look deeply enough into a subject leads to the indolent habit of decorating its surface." (lines 22-24)
    (D) "True economy consists in [. . .] patient labour to the process of extraction and representation." (lines 50-55)
    (E) "The mirror, indeed, is the artist's mind, with all his experiences reflected in it [. . .]" (lines 65-67)

12. Of the following, which is NOT characteristic of the author's rhetoric?

    (A) the use of an analogous situation to express the attributes of good writers
    (B) allusions to several world-renowned writers
    (C) a predominantly objective perspective broken only by a relevant personal anecdote
    (D) the use of technical terms of writing to illustrate common compositional flaws
    (E) a mildly didactic tone

Questions 13-27. Refer to the following passage.

The following is a biographical snapshot of Oliver Cromwell.[1]

He was one of those men, *quos vituperare ne inimici quidum possunt nici ut simul laudent;*[2] for he could never have done half that mischief without great
(5) parts of courage and industry and judgement [. . . .] who, from a private and obscure birth—though of a good family—without interest of estate, alliance of friendship, could raise himself to such
(10) a height and compound and knead such opposite and contradictory tempers, humours and interests into a consistence that contributed to his designs, and to their own destruction [. . . .]. Without doubt,
(15) no man with more wickedness ever attempted anything or brought to pass what he desired more wickedly, more in the face and contempt of religion and moral honesty; yet wickedness as great as
(20) his could never have accomplished those designs without the assistance of a great spirit, an admirable circumspection and sagacity, and a most magnanimous resolution [. . . .].
(25)   After he was confirmed and invested Protector [. . .] he consulted with very few upon any action of importance, nor communicated any enterprise he resolved upon with more than those who
(30) were to have principal parts in the execution of it; nor to them sooner than it was absolutely necessary. What he once resolved in which he was not rash, he would not be dissuaded from, nor endure
(35) any contradiction of his power and authority, but extorted obedience from them who were not willing to yield it.
    When he had laid some very extraordinary tax upon the city, one
(40) Cony, an eminent fanatic, and one who had heretofore served him very notably, positively refused to pay his part, and loudly dissuaded others from submitting to it, as an imposition notoriously against
(45) the law and the propriety of the subject, which all honest men were bound to defend. Cromwell sent for him, and cajoled him with the memory of the old kindness and friendship that had been
(50) between them, and that of all men he did

not expect this opposition from him, in a matter that was so necessary for the good of the commonwealth [. . .] so this man remembered him how great an enemy he
(55) had expressed himself to such grievances, and declared that all who submitted to them and paid illegal taxes were more to blame, and greater enemies to their country, than they who imposed them,
(60) and that the tyranny of princes could never be grievous but by the tameness and stupidity of the people. When Cromwell saw that he could not convert him, he told him he had a will as stubborn
(65) as his [. . .] and thereupon, with some terms of reproach and contempt, he committed the man to prison [. . . .]. Maynard, who was counsel with the prisoner, demanded his liberty with great confidence, both upon
(70) the illegality of the commitment, and the illegality of the imposition, as being laid without any lawful authority. The judges could not maintain or defend either, but enough declared what their sentence
(75) would be; and therefore the Protector's Attorney required a farther day to answer what had been urged. Before that day, Maynard was committed to the Tower, for presuming to question or make doubt
(80) of his authority; and the judges were sent for, and severely reprehended for suffering that license; and when they with all humility mentioned the law and *Magna Charta*, Cromwell told them their
(85) *magna farta* should not control his actions, which he knew were for the safety of the commonwealth. He asked them who made them judges and therefore advised them to be more tender
(90) of that which could only preserve them [. . . .].

---

[1] Puritan leader who in 1653 assumed the position of Lord Protector of England after deposing King Charles I.

[2] (Lat) "With whom even his enemies could not find fault without also praising"

13. The passage is BEST described as a(n)

    (A) laudatory tribute to a master statesman
    (B) vituperative vilification of totalitarian rule
    (C) nostalgic flashback to a halcyon age
    (D) balanced delineation of a complex potentate
    (E) unabashed apology for political expediency

14. In light of the intentions of the author in the passage, footnote one may be said to provide information that

    (A) hints at a religious motive for Cromwell's actions
    (B) foreshadows Cromwell's willingness to use force
    (C) confirms Cromwell's traitorous nature
    (D) evinces Cromwell's reluctance to claim the title of monarch
    (E) establishes an important chronological touchstone

15. The second footnote, a paraphrase of the author's Latin comment, confirms which of the following about Cromwell?

    (A) his admirable industry
    (B) his intellectual capacity
    (C) his military prowess
    (D) his political ambition
    (E) his crafty statesmanship

16. The author's description of Cromwell depicts his rise to prominence as a consequence of

    (A) the preeminent social status of his family
    (B) a relentless work ethic that lifted him out of poverty
    (C) the economic advantages of property and finance that he enjoyed
    (D) a self-centered ambition aided by an acute intellect
    (E) his shameless bribery of influential statesmen

17. Which of the following does NOT contribute to the author's antithetical characterization of Cromwell?

    (A) the Latin expression in lines 1-3
    (B) the depiction of Cromwell's motive and character in lines 14-24
    (C) the level of confidence Cromwell displays in his subordinates in lines 25-32
    (D) the earlier position Cromwell took on tax levies in lines 53-62
    (E) the actions Cromwell takes toward Cony in lines 62-67

18. The primary purpose of the anecdote in paragraph three is expressed by which of the following?

    I. It delineates the many ways in which Cromwell exerted influence.
    II. It shows that Cromwell occasionally acted outside the law.
    III. It implies that power had changed Cromwell's nature.

    (A) I only
    (B) II only
    (C) I and III
    (D) II and III
    (E) I, II and III

19. The anecdote suggests that Cromwell endeavored to get his way by all of the following means EXCEPT

    (A) covert bribes
    (B) stern reprimand
    (C) unwarranted incarceration
    (D) judicial pressure
    (E) friendly persuasion

20. It may be inferred that the comments made by Cony about Cromwell's tax levy

    (A) infuriated Cromwell into taking impetuous action
    (B) bemused Cromwell since they were old friends
    (C) embarrassed Cromwell because they exposed the hypocrisy of his decision
    (D) baffled Cromwell because he could not understand such resistance
    (E) prompted Cromwell into rethinking the legitimacy of the tax levy

21. The sentence, "Maynard, who was counsel [. . . .] without any lawful authority" (lines 67-72), does which of the following?

    I. Exposes Cromwell's petulant response to being contradicted publicly by a subordinate.
    II. Belies Maynard's naïve belief that he could challenge Cromwell's authority and countermand his decision.
    III. Confirms Cromwell's penchant for sustaining personal vendettas until he could resolve them.

    (A) I only
    (B) III only
    (C) I and II
    (D) II and III
    (E) I, II and III

22. In developing the anecdote in paragraph three, the author makes use of all of the following EXCEPT

    (A) adverbs that convey the adamancy and ardor of the dissenter, Cony
    (B) ominous foreshadowings of imminent violence
    (C) a catalog of decisive actions which conveys Cromwell's rise to preeminence
    (D) a derisive pun through which Cromwell mocks the law's inability to restrict his power
    (E) paraphrasings of Cromwell's comments to Cony and the judiciary

23. The passage suggests that which of the following observations about Oliver Cromwell is <u>untrue</u>?

    (A) That he was guarded as to his thought and decisions.
    (B) That he was incapable of being swayed once he had decided upon a course of action.
    (C) That he was able to unify diverse interest groups to his own cause and ends.
    (D) That he was willing to let friendship supersede policy.
    (E) That he was quick to make public examples of those who contradicted him.

24. In light of the author's characterization of Cromwell, which of the following qualifies as understatement?

    (A) "mischief" (line 4)
    (B) "humours" (line 12)
    (C) "designs" (line 13)
    (D) "wickedness" (line 15)
    (E) "resolution" (line 24)

25. In terms of his subject, Oliver Cromwell, the author's tone is one of

    (A) moral indignation
    (B) supercilious contempt
    (C) unctuous veneration
    (D) perplexed humor
    (E) grudging acknowledgment

26. In the passage the author primarily wishes to portray Cromwell as a(n)

    (A) hypocrite
    (B) pragmatist
    (C) reformer
    (D) visionary
    (E) rebel

27. The passage does NOT provide information as to

    (A) what were the conditions of Cromwell's
         birth
    (B) what effect the attainment of power had
         upon Cromwell
    (C) what Cromwell's temperament was like
    (D) what Cromwell felt about law and the
         judicial process
    (E) what Cromwell conceived as his vision for
         the Protectorate

Questions 28-38. Refer to the following passage.

A BLM archaeologist told me, with understandable reluctance, where to find the intaglio. I spread my Automobile Club of Southern California map of Imperial County on
(5)   his desk; and he traced the route with a pink felt-tip pen. The line crossed Interstate 8 and then turned west along the Mexican border.

"You can't drive any farther than about here," he said, marking a small X. "There's
(10)   boulders in the wash. You walk up past them."

On a separate piece of paper he drew a route in a smaller scale that would take me up the arroyo to a certain point where I was to cross back east, to another arroyo. At its head, on
(15)   higher ground just to the north, I would find the horse.

"It's tough to spot unless you know it's there. Once you pick it up…" He shook his head slowly, in a gesture of wonder at its existence.
(20)   I waited until I held his eye. I assured him I would not tell anyone else how to get there. He looked at me with stoical despair, like a man who had been robbed twice, whose belief in human beings was offered without conviction.
(25)   I did not go until the following day because I wanted to see it at dawn. I ate breakfast at four a.m. in El Centro and then drove south. The route was easy to follow, though the last section of road proved difficult,
(30)   broken and drifted over with sand in some spots. I came to the barricade of boulders and parked. It was light enough by then to find my way over the ground with little trouble. The contours of the landscape were stark, without any masking
(35)   vegetation. I worried only about rattlesnakes.

I traversed the stone plain as directed, but, in spite of the frankness of the land, I came on the horse unawares. In the first moment of recognition I was without feeling. I recalled later
(40)   being startled, and that I held my breath. It was laid out on the ground with its head to the east, three times life size. As I took in its outline I felt a growing concentration of all my senses, as though my attentiveness to the pale rose color of
(45)   the morning sky and other peripheral images had now ceased to be important. I was aware that I was straining for sound in the windless air, and I felt the uneven pressure of the earth hard against my feet. The horse, outlined in a standing profile
(50)   on the dark ground, was as vivid before me as a bed of tulips.

I've come upon animals suddenly before, and felt a similar tension, a precipitate heightening of the senses. And I have felt the
(55)   inexplicable but sharply boosted intensity of a wild moment in the bush, where it is not until some minutes later that you discover the source of electricity, the warm remains of a grizzly bear kill, or the still moist tracks of a
(60)   wolverine.

But this was slightly different. I felt I had stepped into an unoccupied corridor. I had no familiar sense of history, the temporal structure in which to think: This horse was
(65)   made by Quechan people three hundred years ago. I felt instead a headlong rush of images: people hunting wild horses with spears on the Pleistocene veld[1] of Southern California; Cortes riding across the causeway into Montezuma's
(70)   Tenochtitlan;[2] a short-legged Comanche, astride his horse like some sort of ferret, slashing through cavalry lines of young men who rode like farmers; a hood[3] exploding past my face one morning in a corral in Wyoming. These
(75)   images had the weight and silence of stone.

When I released my breath, the images softened. My initial feeling, of facing a wild animal in a remote region, was replaced with a calm sense of antiquity. It was then that I
(80)   became conscious, like an ordinary tourist, of what was before me [. . . .].

I still had not moved. I took my eyes off the horse for a moment to look south over the desert plain into Mexico, to look east past
(85)   its head at the brightening sunrise, to situate myself. Then, finally, I brought my trailing foot slowly forward and stood erect. Sunlight was running like a thin sheet of water over the stony ground and it threw the horse into relief.
(90)   It looked as though no hand had ever disturbed the stones that gave it its form [. . . .].

---

[1] grasslands of the archaeological period associated with hunting and scavenging

[2] chief city of the Aztec empire

[3] a covering for a horse's head

28. Based upon the details revealed in the passage, an "intaglio" is a(n)

    (A) cliff dwelling
    (B) wild animal
    (C) tour guide
    (D) border checkpoint
    (E) stone formation

29. The attitude that the archaeologist displays toward the author is likely motivated by a(n)

    (A) personal animus towards uncultured tourists
    (B) understandable reluctance to exaggerate the significance of his discovery
    (C) sincere desire for cultural preservation
    (D) obstinate unwillingness to share credit for finding the intaglio
    (E) mischievous glee at misdirecting strangers

30. The author's delay in departing is a product of his

    (A) confusion over the archaeologist's directions
    (B) fear of the strangeness of the desert locale
    (C) inability to collect his belongings expeditiously
    (D) yearning to divulge the secret of the intaglio to others
    (E) desire to experience the site at a particular time of day

31. The author's observation that he "worried only about rattlesnakes" (line 35) is likely intended to reveal his

    (A) stalwartness in a physically taxing environment
    (B) familiarity with dangers endemic to the landscape
    (C) confidence in locating the intaglio successfully
    (D) attempt to bolster his questionable self-confidence
    (E) disdain for the admonitions of the archaeologist

32. In light of the context in which it appears, the word "frankness" (line 37) is BEST interpreted as

    (A) ruggedness
    (B) starkness
    (C) inaccessibility
    (D) unevenness
    (E) expansiveness

33. The characteristic of the intaglio that first impresses the author is its

    (A) vivid color
    (B) unusual shape
    (C) vast dimensions
    (D) geographical orientation
    (E) intricate detail

34. The impact of the intaglio upon the author triggers all of the following EXCEPT

    (A) a comparative diminution of the other features of the landscape
    (B) a sudden rush of tension and excitement
    (C) an imaginative collage of historical images
    (D) a primal impulse to seek refuge
    (E) an acute consciousness of the desert silence

35. Which of the following does NOT help to establish the discomfiting temporal disorientation of the author?

    (A) the kaleidoscopic images of the hunt and violence
    (B) the metonymy of the "unoccupied corridor" (line 62)
    (C) the allusions to historical conquerors and natives
    (D) the similes of the ferret and the farmers
    (E) the comparison of the images to the ponderous impassivity of stone

36. Which of the following questions about the intaglio remains largely unanswered at the end of the passage?

    (A) Where is it located?
    (B) Who might have created it?
    (C) What is its relative size?
    (D) When was it created?
    (E) What is its significance?

37. The author stylistically conveys the powerful impact of the intaglio upon him through all of the following EXCEPT

    (A) sensory images
    (B) allusions to Western history
    (C) a hyperbolic description of its dimensions
    (D) contrasts with real animal encounters
    (E) a simile comparing its vividness to a bed of flowers

38. The sentences in the final paragraph suggest that the author found the intaglio

    (A) overblown and disappointing
    (B) profound and spiritual
    (C) rudimentary and unrefined
    (D) byzantine and confusing
    (E) totemic and terrifying

Questions 39-52. Refer to the following passage.

Who first reduced lying into an art, and adapted it to politics, is not so clear from history, though I have made some diligent enquiries: I shall therefore consider
(5) it only according to the modern system, as it has been cultivated these twenty years past in the southern part of our own island.

The poets tell us, that after the giants were overthrown by the gods, the
(10) earth in revenge produced her last offspring, which was Fame.[1] And the fable is thus interpreted; that when tumults and seditions are quieted, rumours and false reports are plentifully spread through a
(15) nation. So that by this account, *lying* is the last relief of a routed, earth-born, rebellious party in a state [. . . .].

But the same genealogy can not always be admitted for *political lying*; I
(20) shall therefore desire to refine upon it, by adding some circumstance of its birth or parents. A political lie is sometimes born out of a discarded statesman's head, and thence delivered to be nursed and dandled
(25) by the mob. Sometimes it is produced a monster, and *licked* into shape; at other times it comes into the world completely formed, and is spoiled in the licking. It is often born an infant in the regular way, and
(30) requires time to mature it: and often it sees the light in its full growth, but dwindles away by degrees. Sometimes it is of noble birth; and sometimes the spawn of a stock-jobber.[2] *Here*, it screams aloud at the
(35) opening of the womb; and *there*, it is delivered with a whisper [. . . .]. To conclude the nativity of this monster, when it comes into the world without a *sting*, it is still-born; and whenever it loses its sting, it dies.
(40) No wonder, if an infant so miraculous in its birth, should be destined for great adventures: and accordingly we see it has been the guardian spirit of a prevailing party for almost twenty years. It
(45) can conquer kingdoms without fighting, and sometimes with the loss of a battle: It gives and resumes employments; can sink a mountain to a mole-hill, and raise a mole-hill to a mountain; has presided for many
(50) years at committees for elections; can wash a blackmoor[3] white; make a saint of an atheist, and a patriot of a profligate; can furnish foreign ministers with intelligence,

and raise or let fall the credit of the nation.
(55) This goddess flies with a huge looking-glass in her hands, to dazzle the crowd, and make them see, according as she turns it, their ruin in their interest, and their interest in their ruin [. . . .].
(60) There is one essential point in which a political liar differs from others of the faculty; that he ought to have but a short memory, which is necessary according to the various occasions he meets with every
(65) hour, of differing from himself, and swearing to both sides of a contradiction, as he finds the persons disposed, with whom he has to deal [. . . .].

Some people may think that such
(70) an accomplishment as this, can be of no great use to the owner or his party, after it has been often practiced, and is become notorious; but they are widely mistaken: Few lies carry their inventor's mark; and the
(75) most prostitute enemy to truth may spread a thousand without being known for the author. Besides, as the vilest writer has his readers, so the greatest liar has his believers; and so it happens, that if a lie be
(80) believed only for an hour, it has done its work, and there is no farther occasion for it. Falsehood flies, and Truth comes limping after it; so that when men come to be undeceived, it is too late, the jest is over,
(85) and the tale has had its full effect: like the man who has thought of a good repartee, when the discourse is changed, or the company parted; or, like a physician who has found out an infallible medicine, after
(90) the patient is dead [. . . .].

---

[1] In Book V of Virgil's *Aeneid*, Fame is personified as a winged creature with multiple ears, eyes and mouths who walks on earth but whose head is hidden in the clouds; one who heralds truth and clings to lies.

[2] (Br) A term for a person who exchanges stock with brokers, the word has pejorative connotations, suggesting unscrupulousness and baseness.

[3] A dark-skinned individual of African descent.

39. The passage is BEST labeled a(n)

    (A) parody
    (B) allegory
    (C) diatribe
    (D) satire
    (E) panegyric

40. In the course of the passage a political lie is depicted as all of the following EXCEPT

    (A) a new-born baby
    (B) a hideous monster
    (C) a winged goddess
    (D) a vengeful mob
    (E) a guardian spirit

41. The word "reduced," as it is used in the first sentence, is BEST interpreted as

    (A) transformed
    (B) developed
    (C) subverted
    (D) debased
    (E) refined

42. The allusion to Greek mythology in paragraph two implies which of the following?

    (A) That man's penchant for lying only mimics that of the gods.
    (B) That fame can only be achieved through prevarication.
    (C) That lying often engenders sedition and rebellion.
    (D) That lying is a tactic born of failure and desperation.
    (E) That deceit is more instinctual than rational.

43. In developing his discussion of political lying in paragraph three, the author primarily relies upon

    (A) extended metaphor
    (B) understatement
    (C) simile
    (D) paradox
    (E) allusion

44. The primary purpose of lines 40-44, "No wonder [. . .] for almost twenty years," is to suggest that lying is

    (A) extremely rare in political circles
    (B) commonly practiced by whoever is in power to retain power
    (C) often necessary to preserve a country's security
    (D) effected by only the most artful individuals
    (E) closely allied with heroic exploits

45. In the fourth paragraph the speaker suggests that a particularly pernicious lie can cause all of the following EXCEPT

    (A) the subjugation of a nation
    (B) an understatement or elevation of a particular problem
    (C) an individual's denial of his true beliefs
    (D) a dramatic change in the public taste or fashion
    (E) political espionage and financial ruin

46. In delineating the potentially destructive scope of political lying (lines 44-59), the author MOST frequently employs

    (A) antitheses
    (B) color imagery
    (C) classical allusion
    (D) objective correlative
    (E) paradox

47. The author begins his final paragraph by

    (A) making an affirmation
    (B) speculating on a possibility
    (C) dismissing a misconception
    (D) reiterating an earlier point
    (E) offering a concession

48. The phrase, "such an accomplishment as this" (lines 69-70), likely refers to politicians

    (A) coming from socially prominent families
    (B) promoting the interests of their political party
    (C) fostering employment
    (D) presiding over elections
    (E) performing self-serving acts of deception

49. According to the final paragraph, one of the most damaging things about lies is the

    (A) constant anonymity of their origin
    (B) unsuspecting nature of their target
    (C) astounding alacrity with which they gain credence
    (D) despicable notoriety they bring to their author
    (E) sheer number of falsehoods

50. The phrase "carry their inventor's mark" (line 74) is BEST interpreted as

    (A) identify their source
    (B) gain public credence
    (C) display true originality
    (D) achieve their objective
    (E) display any endurance

51. The characterization of Truth and the similes which follow it (lines 82-90) figuratively convey which of the following?

    I. Truth's inability to overcome an infectious lie.
    II. The slow manner in which truth often comes to light.
    III. The characteristic mendacity of all humans: their tendency to deceive.

    (A) I only
    (B) III only
    (C) I and II
    (D) II and III
    (E) I, II and III

52. In short, the final two paragraphs imply that a political liar must be all of the following EXCEPT

    (A) duplicitous
    (B) conscience-stricken
    (C) hypocritical
    (D) incorrigible
    (E) pragmatic

Section II

Question One

(Suggested time—40 minutes. This question counts as one-third of the total essay section score.)

In his essay, "Circles," Ralph Waldo Emerson argues that all the truly great moments of history have involved "the facilities of performance through the strength of ideas."

Take a moment to reflect on this statement. Then, write a well-organized essay in which you explore the validity of the assertion, using examples from your reading, observation, studies or experience to develop your position.

Question Two

(Suggested time—40 minutes. This question counts as one-third of the total essay section score.)

In the following prose passage, a contemporary writer ponders what motivates writers to write. Read the passage carefully. Then, in a well-organized essay, discuss what assumptions the author makes about writing and about those who labor at it, and illustrate what rhetorical techniques the author uses to convey them.

Why certain individuals appear to devote their lives to the phenomenon of interpreting experience in terms of structure, and of language, must remain a mystery. It is not an alternative to life, still less an escape from life, it *is* life: yet overlaid with a peculiar sort of luminosity, as if one were, and were not, fully inhabiting the present tense. Freud's supposition—which must have been his own secret
(5) compulsion, his sounding of his own depths—that the artist labors at his art to win fame, power, riches, and the love of women, hardly addresses itself to the fact that, such booty being won, the artist often intensifies the effort: and finds much of life, apart from that effort, unrewarding. Why, then, this instinct to interpret; to transpose flickering and transient thoughts into the relative permanence of language; to give oneself over to decades of obsessive labor, in the service of an elusive "transcendental" ideal, that,
(10) in any case, will surely be misunderstood?—or scarcely valued at all? Assuming that all art is metaphor, or metaphorical, what really is the motive for metaphor?—is there a motive?—or, in fact, metaphor?— can one say anything finally, with unqualified confidence, about any work of art?—why it strikes a profound, irresistible, and occasionally life-altering response in some individuals, yet means very little to others. In this, the art of reading hardly differs from the art of writing, in that its most intense pleasures
(15) and pains must remain private, and cannot be communicated to others. Our secret affinities remain secret even to ourselves [. . .] and we fall in love with certain works of art, as we fall in love with certain individuals, for no very clear motive [. . . .].

Is the artist secretly in love with failure, one might ask?

Is there something dangerous about "success," something finite and limited and, in a sense,
(20) historical: the passing over from *striving*, and *strife*, to *achievement*—? One thinks again of Nietzsche, that most profound of psychologists, who tasted the poisonous euphoria of success, however brief, however unsatisfying: beware the danger of happiness! *Now everything I touch turns out to be wonderful. Now I love any fate that comes along. Who would like to be my fate?*

Yet it is perhaps not failure the writer loves, so much as the addictive nature of incompletion
(25) and risk. A work of art acquires, and then demands, its own singular "voice;" it insists upon its integrity; as Gide in his Notebook observed, the artist needs "a special world of which he alone has the key." That the fear of dying or becoming seriously ill in midstream is very real, cannot be doubted: and if there is an obvious contradiction here (one dreads completion; one dreads the possibility of a "posthumous" and therefore uncompleted work), that contradiction is very likely at the heart of the artistic enterprise. The
(30) writer carries himself as he would carry a precarious pyramid of eggs, because he is, in fact, a precarious pyramid of eggs, in danger of falling at any moment, and shattering on the floor in an ignoble mess. And he understands beforehand that no one, not even his most "sympathetic" fellow writers, will acknowledge his brilliant intentions, and see, for themselves, the great work he would surely have completed, had he lived [. . . .].

Copyright © 1992 *Ontario Review.* Reprinted by permission of John Hawkins & Associates, Inc.

<u>Question Three</u>

(Suggested time—55 minutes. This question counts as one-third of the total essay section score.)

Directions:

The following prompt is based on the accompanying six sources.

This question requires you to integrate a variety of sources into a coherent, well-written essay. *Refer to the sources to support your position; avoid paraphrase or summary. Your argument should be central; the sources should support this argument.*

Remember to attribute both direct and indirect citations.

Introduction:

Since Matthew Brady's black and white linotypes first brought home the stark realities of the Civil War, members of the media have documented in print and on film America at war. Though many graphic images and numbing statistics have over the years seared their way into the public consciousness, the U.S. government has occasionally restricted or censored such images, citing reasons such as national security or personal privacy. However, is this censorship of wartime images and information a necessary aegis, or merely a means of protecting the government from unwarranted criticism and negative publicity? Should the media have no restrictions when it comes to reporting war?

Assignment:

Read the following sources (including any introductory information) carefully. **Then, in an essay that synthesizes at least three of the sources for support, take a position that defends, challenges or qualifies the claim that during a time of war the government has a moral responsibility to censor wartime information and images**.

(It is recommended that you spend 15-20 minutes of the allotted time examining the sources and devote the remaining time to writing your essay.)

Young children learn the concept of patterns. They recognize them everywhere—on buildings, in fabric, on a dinner plate.

One child I know recently spotted a pattern in the newspaper: geometrically ordered lines of rectangular boxes, each draped in an American flag.

To me, the pattern was reminiscent of the rows of white grave markers I saw as a child at Arlington National Cemetery, neat and faceless reminders of America's war dead.

More than 700 troops have died in the war in Iraq. Until last week, photographic evidence of those deaths was censored from public view. The Bush administration says that, out of respect for the families, pictures of anonymous coffins are off-limits [. . . .].

While children may identify visual patterns, adults are asking about the metaphorical pattern, specifically, whether the Bush administration believes military policy is more important than constitutionally protected freedom of information.

This isn't a matter of national security. It's about the war of images, the PR battle for the hearts and minds of Americans who increasingly question the wisdom of the war [. . . .].

The ambivalence some feel is part of the historical pattern of queasiness over visual reminders of the cost of war.

"A lot of people saw the symbolism of it," said David Perlmutter, author of two books on war photography and a professor at Louisiana State University. "There were the coffins neatly stacked like economy class, and you're thinking, 'How many airplanes full are arriving each week?' The mass of it was striking."

He calls the original photo, taken by a since-fired cargo worker, "the Cargo of Caskets picture." Photos don't come with names like paintings do, he noted, and in his field it's a privilege to bestow a title.

"The Cargo of Caskets is a very respectful image," with military personnel bending over the coffins almost reverentially, he said. "But it's very hard to say what would hurt anyone."

Document B

Online http://teachpol.tcnj.edu/Amer_pol_hist/thumbnail391.html

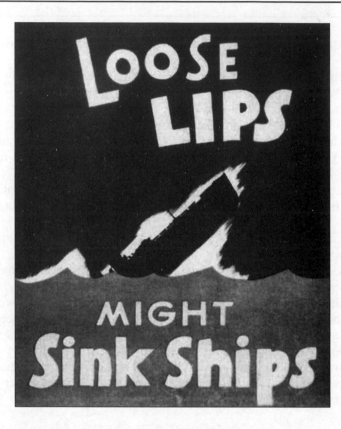

Document C

Ryan, Joan. "Of sensitivity and censorship." *San Francisco Chronicle*. 25 Mar 2003 (Final Ed.): A 17. Online http://proquest.umi.com/pqdweb?index=2&did= 316322271&SrchMode=1&sid=1&Fmt=3&VInst=PROD&VType=PQD&RQT= 309&VName=PQD&TS=1142004542&clientId=6846.

[. . . .] Shouldn't we see the true price of sending our men and women into war? Shouldn't the networks make sure this war doesn't devolve into a palatable mini-series co-produced by the U.S. government? Considering that television shows and movies regularly show graphic, horrifying violence, why is it assumed we are too fragile to face the real thing?

"This is life in a war," said Betsy Aaron, the longtime CBS and CNN war correspondent. "I think you have to show people what's going on with our soldiers. We put them there."

Aaron has covered conflicts in Vietnam, the Middle East, El Salvador, Honduras, Romania, Afghanistan, Chechnya and the first Persian Gulf War, where she reported from Baghdad. She witnessed horrible things that never reached the air and usually agreed with her editors' decisions.

"I'm never for censorship," she said from her home in Tucson. "But I wouldn't run something that's mortifying to the person being shown. And the blanket rule is you don't show anything until the families are notified."

Now that the invasion has turned into a real war, the casualties are mounting and will continue to mount. Is there news value in showing a field of dead soldiers or a city street strewn with the bodies of civilians? Definitely. The American people don't need television executives to protect them from such harsh facts of war.

But is there news value in showing an identifiable soldier with a bullet hole in his head, as in the Al-Jazeera tape? That is more difficult to justify. The networks probably made the right choice in not airing it. From what little I finally saw, the tape humiliates the soldiers, both dead and alive. Airing the footage would inflict even greater pain on the families and add little to our understanding of the conflict.

There is a thin line between news and exploitation, between sensitivity and censorship. The public and the media will be re-evaluating the lines every day until the war is over [. . . .].

<u>Document D</u>

Crossen, Cynthia. "In Every War but One, The Government Had Media Under Control."
Wall Street Journal (Eastern edition): 19 Mar 2003: B.1. Online
http://proquest.umi.com/pqdweb?index=2&did=316322271&SrchMode=1&sid=1
&Fmt=3&VInst=PROD&VType=PQD&RQT=309&VName=PQD&TS=114200 4542&clientId=6846.

In every American war since 1776, there has been a subsidiary battle between the government and media over how much J.Q. Citizen needs to know. The government usually wins.

During World War II, for example, government censors banned man-on-the-street radio interviews lest enemy agents disclose prearranged codes via the open microphone. Even programs that took music requests were asked to desist: "It is evident that a request to play 'Deep in the Heart of Texas,' dedicated to cousin Sarah, might easily be a signal to an enemy agent," wrote Byron Price, director of the Office of Censorship during WWII.

The Office of Censorship, established two weeks after Pearl Harbor, was responsible for the content of every newspaper, magazine and radio station in America. But controlling information was a touchy subject in the early 1940s. The very word censorship reeked of totalitarianism. So journalists were asked to practice "patriotic self-discipline," censoring themselves according to a Code of Wartime Practices.

They shouldn't, for example, report the weather accurately. "Weather news may be of great importance to the enemy," Mr. Price wrote. "Word of a storm in the Midwest may enable him to chart weather conditions over the Atlantic three or four days in advance."

Reporters and editors were also expected to "believe" government leaders when they issued official reports. Stephen T. Early, Franklin Roosevelt's press secretary, said no news denied by the White House should be published. Furthermore, wrote Michael S. Sweeney, author of "Secrets of Victory," reporters could legally sidestep the code only if their stories were approved by an official from the appropriate authority—and that official's name put on record. That reduced chance of violation to about zero.

Meanwhile, the Office of War Information, established in 1942, created and molded information to keep the public united behind the war. Immediately following Pearl Harbor, the American people had a strong sense of why they had entered the war, but by mid-1942, a poll showed 30% had doubts. The Office of War Information began its campaign of "presenting the war in simple terms of good versus evil," wrote George H. Roeder Jr., author of "The Censored War" [. . . .].

Document E

Evans, Harold. "War Stories." *Wall Street Journal* (Eastern edition) 21 Feb 2003: A 10. Online
http://proquest.umi.com/pqdweb?index=4&did=291798541&SrchMode=
1&sid=5&Fmt=3&VInst=PROD&VType=PQD&RQT=309&VName=PQD&TS=1142005717&clientId=6846

A new chapter in the long and furiously contested history of the reporting of war is coming our way with the announcement that somewhere between 500 and 1,000 reporters from all media will be invited to the battlefront in the projected war with Iraq. In the intriguingly friendly language of the Pentagon they will be "embedded" with specific combat units.

What that means precisely, apart from the privilege of getting shot at, is something the news organizations will surely explore. The relationship of journalism to government is complex, one of dependence and antagonism. Without the cooperation of the armed services, the press cannot hope to cover a war. The trade-off is a measure of access for a measure of official control. The U.S. press is still sore about how the balance was struck in the Gulf War, where Walter Cronkite felt provoked to ask: "What are they trying to hide?" The British press felt the same about the Falklands War where 29 correspondents were embedded on Royal Navy warships under the care of liaison officers (minders), the precursor of the system adopted in the Gulf War. "We're from head office, we're here to help" [. . . .].

From authority's point of view, the media has become a major management problem. On the first wave of D-Day landings, there were 27 reporters. In Desert Storm, there were 2,500 and they resented restrictions. Colin Powell maintained that of 1,350 print stories submitted by press pool reporters, only one was changed and that to protect intelligence. Whatever, Gen. Powell was surely right to be angry in the invasion of Panama when bureau chiefs and network executives in New York whined that their correspondents were in danger in the Marriott Hotel and should be rescued. Gen. Powell said no, but Defense Secretary Dick Cheney ordered him to the rescue nonetheless. The 872nd Airborne Division took casualties doing this unnecessary errand. Three GIs were wounded, one seriously, and a Spanish photographer was killed by American fire [. . . .].

Document F

Lichter, S. Robert and Trevor Butterworth. "Commentary: The Press Spins Self-Serving Myths." *Los Angeles Times* (Home Edition) 5 Nov 2001: B.11.
Online http://proquest.umi.com/pqdweb?index=0&did=88217114&SrchMode=1&sid=1&Fmt=3&VInst=PROD&VType=PQD&RQT=309&VName=PQD&TS=1142008208&clientId=6846.

The ground war is finally heating up--no, not the one in Afghanistan, the one in the Pentagon and White House briefing rooms. The brief era of good feelings between the media and the military is already turning sour as journalists complain about being kept in the dark and off the frontlines. They take it as an article of faith that they can be trusted to inform the public without damaging the war effort.

But we need to take a closer look at the good conduct medals they claim to have won in previous wars to see whether they aren't spinning some self-serving myths.

* Myth No. 1: U.S. journalists enjoyed unfettered access to the battlefield in World War II, during which they showed good judgment in the information they chose to reveal or conceal. In reality, many major battles in World War II were never seen, let alone covered, by the press. Of the 461 Allied reporters and photographers accredited to cover the D-Day invasion of France, only a handful went in during the initial assault. Most of the 180-strong U.S. press contingent did their reporting from the rear echelons. Even legendary war correspondent Ernie Pyle, who was assigned to Gen. Omar Bradley's headquarters unit, didn't arrive in Normandy until days after the landing [. . . .].

Reporters were also accompanied everywhere by a military public affairs officer responsible for taking their copy to military censors. These censors had the power to delete a vast range of material, including reports on the effect of enemy attacks, the use of new weapons and tactics and anything "likely to injure the morale of Allied forces." This last stipulation is the reason very few photographs of dead or wounded soldiers ever appeared in print [. . . .].

* Myth No. 2: American journalists won't give away any operational matters that put our soldiers at risk. On the contrary, during the Korean War journalists disclosed so much sensitive information on military operations that they pleaded with Gen. Douglas MacArthur to impose formal military censorship to save them from themselves.

They did not want to be the judge of what might harm Allied troops, especially given the competitive pressures to be first with the story. When MacArthur finally relented, the decision received overwhelming support from journalists.

* Myth No. 3: It was the military that lied in Vietnam, but the press still gets blamed unfairly for telling unpopular truths. This is only partly true. With no censorship whatsoever, the press enjoyed unprecedented freedom to cover the conflict in Vietnam. But the Kennedy and Johnson administrations' constant fudging of the facts in a futile effort to show progress eroded press confidence in the accuracy of military briefings.

Sample Examination IV

Questions 1-17. Refer to the following passage.

A quarter of a century is a phrase
with an epochal ring and these last five and
twenty years have altered the world more
than most. Empires have waxed and waned;
(5) motor cars have altered the whole face of
travel and the whole scale of British
distances; a penny has become a halfpenny
and the char-a´-banc[1] has crashed its way
through the silent austerities of the Scottish
(10) Sabbath. But much of Scotland stands
exactly where it did. Here in the north-east,
whither I have made my sentimental
journey, the land and sea yield the old
harvests of grain and herring. The plough
(15) that has not altered since Homer told its
shape and motion[2] is not to suffer change
while a boy grows up [. . . .], here I can go to
the "games" last visited in 1900 and they will
be held in the same "haugh";[3] the same
(20) dancing-master will sit on the judgment
bench to nod gravely at the same flings and
sword-dances. The pipes will be mournful
and brisk with the same airs and tea-time
will bring the same neat bag of cakes [. . .].
(25)   The conditions, as they say, are
eminently suitable. Here one may indeed go
in search of one's youth and reconstruct in
the tranquility of a sunny afternoon the
emotions of a very small boy. Of course it
(30) is all much smaller than one's memory. A
mile has dwindled to a furlong, a forest to a
copse, a torrent to a trickle. The trout that
were Tritons are now to be seen as
flickering minnows in the shallows under
(35) the bridge. A mountain has shrunk to a
hillock. It doesn't do, this retracing of
boyhood steps. One knew, of course,
that looking backward is like looking through
an opera-glass reversed. But the distortion
(40) is worse than one imagined. One shouldn't
have gone. The return has been a cowardly
assault upon romance, a butchering of
innocent memories. Far better to have left the
old house to be, in mind's eye, grandiose,
(45) mysterious, abounding in dark possibilities;
in short, the half-menacing, half-entrancing

monster that it used to be. Far better to have
left to the gardens their flattering
spaciousness of boyhood's vision, to the
(50) wood its pristine mystery of cavernous and
black allure.
     But one has done the deed. There it
lies, plain-set in smiling sunlight, a
diminished paradise. It is just a piece of
(55) eastern Scotland, that frank and self-
explanatory countryside which rolls an
open bosom to the plain straightforward sea
[. . . .]. Good farming trims the landscape;
grey, orderly walls keep watch over
(60) pasture, roots, and oats. Here and there the
rising ground soars out of man's control
and green fields admit their limitations and
march peaceably with heather [. . . .]. But the
wildness, the strangeness, the beckoning
(65) immensities of those old days have
shriveled and departed. Boyhood was too
small for Ordnance maps[4] and the withering
accuracies of the measuring-rod. It made its
own mileage, forged its own contours,
(70) made and named and ruled its mountain
range. Compute it now coldly at "one inch
to a mile" and a kingdom turns to a
crofter's[5] holding. Yet within this nutshell
moved a king of infinite space. Perhaps not
(75) a king; a princeling were more accurate [. . . .].
     Yet was this visitation altogether a
blundering folly? [. . . .]. No; it has powers of
reassurance, its compensations, and its fair
suggestions. The woods have lost their
(80) wonder, and their darkness is a plain,
unghosted thing. But beauty has crept in.
Boyhood never saw that [. . . .].

---

[1] a large bus used for sightseeing

[2] The plough's function was described by Homer in both the
Iliad and the *Odyssey*.

[3] a meadow in a river valley

[4] extremely precise survey maps

[5] a tenant farmer

1. According to the passage, the aspect of Scotland that has changed the LEAST—in reality or in perception—upon the author's "sentimental journey" back to the land of his youth is the

    (A) balance of political power
    (B) mode and speed of transportation
    (C) purchasing power of currency
    (D) social and agrarian traditions of his homeland
    (E) quiet and secluded nature of the Scottish countryside

2. In defining the char-a´-banc in footnote one, the author wishes to

    (A) avoid any potential misinterpretation of the word in a monetary sense
    (B) lament a noisy intrusion into the Scottish countryside
    (C) illustrate the attractiveness of Scotland as a tourist locale
    (D) demonstrate how transportation has made previously obscure destinations accessible
    (E) comment on the noticeable decline of religious observance in Scotland

3. The loss of the familiar that the author experiences in the second paragraph is stylistically abetted by all of the following EXCEPT

    (A) a series of antitheses that illustrate the disparate perspectives of a youth and an adult
    (B) diction that emphasizes mystery and magic
    (C) a simile that vividly captures the diminished realities of his youth
    (D) images that depict the corrosive effect of industrialization on the natural world
    (E) a metaphor that laments his own decision to revisit this once idyllic world

4. Lines 36-37, "It doesn't do, this retracing of boyhood steps," suggest that the author

    (A) finds his return emotionally moving
    (B) regrets the debunking of the inventions of his youthful fancy
    (C) is dejected by the radically changed landscape
    (D) has discovered he is too old to manage the rugged terrain
    (E) is experiencing a disorientation that frustrates his ability to recognize the familiar haunts of his youth

5. The subtle switch to the indefinite pronoun "one" in the second paragraph does which of the following?

    I. Subtly reinforces the loss of personal connection felt by the author.
    II. Permits the author to chide objectively the fatuousness of his own illusion.
    III. Implies that the desire to return to one's past is both universal and universally disappointing.

    (A) II only
    (B) III only
    (C) I and II
    (D) I and III
    (E) I, II and III

6. The author's second paragraph reverie suggests that his youth was an ironic combination of

    (A) adventure and tedium
    (B) freedom and confinement
    (C) tranquility and violence
    (D) foreboding and attraction
    (E) urbanization and rusticity

7. The simple sentence, "But one has done the deed" (line 52), that marks the transition between the second and third paragraphs conveys a sense of

    (A) prideful accomplishment
    (B) relieved closure
    (C) accusatory reprimand
    (D) amazed disbelief
    (E) regretful resignation

8. The word "diminished," as it is used in line 54, is BEST interpreted as

(A) forfeited
(B) tarnished
(C) scaled down
(D) debased
(E) trivial

9. The description of eastern Scotland in the third paragraph is primarily intended to do which of the following?

(A) suggest the idyllic simplicity and calm of the agrarian landscape
(B) celebrate the unpretentious nature of the region's inhabitants
(C) depict the stark diversity of the region's terrain
(D) empathize with the farmers' difficulty in sowing crops
(E) convey the author's deep regret at having left this region

10. Which of the following does NOT help to convey the author's distaste for the reduction of the seemingly boundless landscape of his youth?

(A) "soars out of man's control [. . .]" (line 61)
(B) "have shriveled and departed" (lines 65-66)
(C) "withering accuracies of the measuring-rod" (lines 67-68)
(D) "Compute it now coldly at 'one inch to a mile' [. . .]" (lines 71-72)
(E) "a crofter's holding" (lines 72-73)

11. In delineating the features of the Scottish countryside in paragraph three (lines 52-75), the author predominantly employs

(A) pathetic fallacy
(B) personification
(C) onomatopoeia
(D) local color
(E) allusion

12. In relation to the author's earlier assertion, that his return "has been a cowardly assault upon romance, a butchering of innocent memories" (lines 41-43), the final paragraph may BEST be seen as

(A) buttressing it
(B) negating it
(C) qualifying it
(D) questioning it
(E) reiterating it

13. The explanation of "Ordnance maps" in footnote four, coupled with the phrase "the withering accuracies of the measuring rod" (lines 67-68), is intended to

(A) demonstrate the British value of efficient measurement
(B) suggest the insignificance of commoners in governmental matters
(C) show that no mere map could effectively record the boundless kingdom of childhood
(D) insure that local farmers did not infringe on their neighbors' plots
(E) bemoan the inability of the government to determine boundaries

14. The author's use of the words "king" and "princeling" in line 75 reflects which of the following?

(A) his fallible memory
(B) his regal lineage
(C) his lust for political power
(D) his sense of youthful empowerment
(E) his admirable humility

15. The "that" which "Boyhood never saw" (line 82) is the fact that

(A) his visit home was folly
(B) his visit had a positive side as well as a negative one
(C) the woods have "lost their wonder"
(D) the landscape has an inherent natural beauty
(E) he has aged substantially since 1900

16. Ultimately, the author's feelings about his return to the landscape of his youth reflect a movement from

    (A) disorientation to acclimation
    (B) shock to denial
    (C) disillusionment to gratification
    (D) yearning to forsaking
    (E) enthusiasm to regret

17. Of the following lines of poetry, which is the most consistent with the overall sentiment of the passage?

    (A) "Come, my friends, / 'Tis not too late to seek a newer world. / Push off and sitting well in order smite / the sounding furrows."
    (B) "O lift me as a wave, a leaf, a cloud! / I fall upon the thorns of life, I bleed!"
    (C) "Then leaf subsides to leaf. / So Eden sank to grief. / So dawn goes down to day. / Nothing gold can stay."
    (D) "The Sea that bares her bosom to the moon; / The winds that will be howling at all hours, / And are up-gathered now like sleeping flowers; / For this, for everything we are out of tune."
    (E) "The Sea of Faith / Was once, too, at the full, and round earth's shore / Lay like the folds of a bright girdle furl'd."

Questions 18-28. Refer to the following passage.

Inside my stoker's singlet,[1] in the armpit, I sewed a gold sovereign (an emergency sum certainly of modest proportions); and inside my stoker's singlet
(5) I put myself. And then I sat down and moralized upon the fair years and fat, which had made my skin soft and brought the nerves to the surface; for the singlet was rough and raspy as a hair shirt, and I am
(10) confident that the most rigorous of ascetics suffer no more than I did in the ensuing twenty-four hours.

The remainder of my costume was fairly easy to put on, though the brogans, or
(15) brogue, were quite a problem. As stiff and hard as if made of wood, it was only after a prolonged pounding of the uppers with my fists that I was able to get my feet into them at all. Then, with a few shillings, a knife, a
(20) handkerchief, and some brown papers and flake tobacco stowed away in my pockets, I thumped down the stairs and said good-by to my foreboding friends [. . . .].

No sooner was I out on the streets
(25) as I was impressed by the difference in status effected by my clothes. All servility vanished from the demeanor of the common people with whom I came in contact. Presto! In the twinkling of an eye,
(30) so to say, I had become one of them. My frayed and out-at-elbows jacket was the badge and advertisement of my class, which was their class. It made me of like kind, and in place of the fawning and too-
(35) respectful attention I had hitherto received, I now shared with them a comradeship. The man in corduroy and dirty neckerchief no longer addressed me as 'sir' or 'governor.' It was 'mate' now, and a fine and hearty
(40) word, with a tingle to it, and a warmth and gladness, which the other term does not possess. Governor! It smacks of mastery, and power, and high authority—the tribute of the man who is under to the man on top,
(45) delivered in the hope that he will let up a bit and ease his weight. Which is another way of saying that it is an appeal for alms.

This brings me to a delight I experienced in my rags and tatters which is
(50) denied the average American abroad. The European traveler from the States, who is not a Croesus,[2] speedily finds himself reduced to a state of self-conscious

sordidness by the hordes of clinging
(55) robbers who clutter his steps from dawn to dark, and deplete his pocketbook in a way that puts compound interest in the blush.

In my rags and tatters I escaped the pestilence of tipping and encountered men
(60) on a basis of equality. Nay, before the day was out I turned the tables, and said, most gracefully, "Thank you, sir," to a gentleman whose horse I held, and who dropped a penny into my eager palm.
(65) Other changes I discovered were wrought in my condition by my new garb. In crossing crowded thoroughfares I found I had to be, if anything, more lively in avoiding vehicles, and it was strikingly
(70) impressed upon me that my life had cheapened in direct ratio with my clothes. When before, I inquired the way of a policeman, I was usually asked, "Bus or 'ansom,[3] sir?" But now the query became
(75) "Walk or ride?" Also, at the railway stations, it was the rule to be asked, "First or second, sir?" Now I was asked nothing, a third-class ticket being shoved out to me as a matter of course.
(80) But there was compensation for it all. For the first time I met the English lower classes face to face, and knew them for what they were [. . . .].

And when last I made it into the
(85) East End, I was gratified to find that the fear of the crowd no longer haunted me. I had become a part of it. The vast and malodorous sea had welled up and over me, or I had slipped gently into it, and there was
(90) nothing fearsome about it [. . . .].

---

[1] a sleeveless undershirt worn by one who tends a furnace

[2] King of Lydia renowned for his enormous wealth

[3] horse-drawn cab

18. The author's account is characterized by which of the following?

    I. Observations that at once capture the local color of the London streets and offer social commentary about the people on them.
    II. Instances of self-deprecating humor and reflection.
    III. A resentment at the new indifference with which he is treated.
    IV. Brief anecdotes that contrast his experiences *before* he changes clothes with his experiences *after* he changes them.

    (A) I only
    (B) III only
    (C) I and III
    (D) I, II and IV
    (E) I, II, III and IV

19. Which of the following does NOT document a change experienced by the author in the course of the passage?

    (A) pride to chagrin
    (B) ignorance to awareness
    (C) contentment to discomfort
    (D) trepidation to tolerance
    (E) superciliousness to fellowship

20. After donning his stoker's singlet, the author

    (A) conceals some emergency funds in the lining
    (B) complains about the texture of the garment
    (C) begins to lose confidence in his venture
    (D) chastens his previous advantages
    (E) becomes impatient to embark upon his foray into the London slums

21. The author most likely labels his friends "foreboding" (line 23) because they are

    (A) embarrassed by his tawdry attire
    (B) angry at his obdurate insistence upon going
    (C) not sanguine about his carrying off the ruse successfully
    (D) endeavoring to restrain him physically
    (E) admonishing his obliviousness to personal peril

22. Which of the following "differences" can the author's change of clothes NOT be said to effect?

    (A) the ardor with which he is embraced by the commoners
    (B) an instantaneous loss of privilege and stature
    (C) an emancipation from the appeals of the needy
    (D) a consciousness of his new expendability
    (E) a limitation in his ability to get around London

23. The author notes that prior to his donning an indigent's attire, the commoners did all of the following EXCEPT

    (A) treat him with exaggerated deference
    (B) address him formally, as a gentleman
    (C) rebuff his attempts to ingratiate himself to them
    (D) assail him for handouts
    (E) fill him with apprehension

24. The author's distaste for the term "governor" (lines 42-47) reflects his

    (A) unpretentious nature
    (B) low self-esteem
    (C) political antipathy
    (D) dislike of colloquial labels
    (E) contempt for strangers

25. It may be inferred from the passage that any American traveler who was a "Croesus" (line 52) would be

    (A) insulated by his money from the indigent masses
    (B) badgered on the sidewalks for alms
    (C) touched by the desperate poverty of the London slums
    (D) offended by the appellation of "Governor"
    (E) accosted and robbed by London toughs

26. Lines 43-46, "[. . .] the tribute of the man who is under to the man on top, delivered in the hope that he will let up a bit and ease his weight," may plausibly be interpreted as which of the following?

    I. A metaphorical depiction of the financial oppression inflicted by the aristocracy.
    II. A literal portrayal of the sidewalk appeals to passing gentry.
    III. A wry allusion to monies paid by weaker nations to more powerful ones to insure their safety.

    (A) I only
    (B) III only
    (C) I and II
    (D) II and III
    (E) I, II and III

27. In the final paragraph the author employs which of the following to depict the impoverished Londoners?

    (A) allusion
    (B) metaphor
    (C) hyperbole
    (D) irony
    (E) personification

28. The passage's final lines—"The vast and malodorous sea had welled up and over me, or I had slipped gently into it, and there was nothing fearsome about it"—do all of the following EXCEPT

    (A) intimate the grave extent of London's poverty
    (B) suggest the author's increased comfort and confidence with a different social class
    (C) offer a tranquil image of submersion
    (D) confirm a significant change in perspective
    (E) imply the author's revulsion at the unhygienic state of the London poor

Questions 29-41. Refer to the following passage.

I am not sure that I can draw an exact line between wit and humor. Perhaps the distinction is so subtle that only those persons can decide who have long white beards. But
(5) even an ignorant man, so long as he is clear of Bedlam,[1] may have an opinion.

I am quite positive that of the two, humor is the more comfortable and livable quality. Humorous persons, if their gift is
(10) genuine and not a mere shine upon the surface, are always agreeable companions and they sit through the evening best. They have pleasant mouths turned up at the corners. To these corners the great Master of marionettes has fixed
(15) the strings and he holds them in his nimble fingers to twitch them at the slightest jest. But the mouth of a merely witty man is hard and sour until the moment of its discharge. Nor is the flash from a witty man always comforting,
(20) whereas a humorous man radiates a general pleasure and is like another candle in the room.

I admire wit, but I have no real liking for it. It has been too often employed against me, whereas humor is an ally. It never points an
(25) impertinent finger into my defects. Humorous persons do not sit like explosives on a fuse. They are safe and easy comrades. But a wit's tongue is as sharp as a donkey driver's stick. I may gallop the faster for its prodding, yet the
(30) touch behind is too persuasive for any comfort.

Wit is a lean creature with a sharp, inquiring nose, whereas humor has a kindly eye and comfortable girth. Wit, if it be necessary, uses malice to score a point—like a cat it is quick
(35) to jump—but humor keeps the peace in an easy chair. Wit has a better voice in a solo, but humor comes into the chorus best. Wit is as sharp as a stroke of lightning, whereas humor is diffuse like sunlight. Wit keeps the season's fashions
(40) and is precise in the phrases and judgments of the day, but humor is concerned with homely eternal things. Wit wears silk, but humor in home-spun endures the wind. Wit sets a snare, whereas humor goes off whistling without a
(45) victim in its mind. Wit is sharper company at table, but humor serves better in mischance and in the rain. When it tumbles wit is sour, but humor goes uncomplaining without its dinner. Humor laughs at another's jest and holds his
(50) sides, while wit sits wrapped in study for a lively answer. But it is a workday world in which we live, where we get mud upon our boots and come weary to the twilight [. . .] and

therefore as I think of my acquaintance, it is
(55) those who are humorous in its best and truest meaning rather than those who are witty who give the more profitable companionship [. . . .].

I sat lately at dinner with a notoriously witty person (a really witty man) whom our
(60) hostess had introduced to provide the entertainment. I had read many of his reviews of books and plays, and while I confess their wit and brilliancy, I had thought them to be hard and intellectual and lacking in all that
(65) broader base of humor which aims at truth [. . . .].

In conversation I found him much as I had found him in his writing although strictly speaking, it was not a conversation, which requires an interchange of word and idea and is
(70) turn about. A conversation should not be a market in which one sells and another buys. Rather, it should be a bargaining back and forth, and each person should be both merchant and buyer. My rubber plant for your
(75) victrola,[2] each offering what he has and seeking his deficiency [. . . .].

But this was a speech and a lecture. He loosed on us from the cold spigot of his intellect a steady flow of literary allusion—a
(80) practice which he professes to hold in scorn—and wit and epigram. He seemed torn from the page of Meredith.[3] He talked like ink. I had believed before that only people in books could talk as he did, and then only when their
(85) author had blotted and scratched their performance for a seventh time before he sent it to the printer [. . . .].

At first I feared there might be a break in his flow of speech which I should be obliged
(90) to fill. Once, when there was a slight pause—a truffle was engaging him—I launched a frail remark; but it was swept off at once in the renewed torrent. And seriously it does not seem fair. If one speaker insists—to change
(95) the figure—on laying all the cobbles of the conversation, he should at least allow another to carry the tarpot and fill in the chinks [. . . .].

---

[1] slang for "Bethlehem," a mental hospital in London founded in the early part of the 15th century.

[2] a phonograph

[3] 19th century novelist and poet

29. The meaning of the word "livable" as it is used in line 8 is

    (A) enduring
    (B) vivacious
    (C) congenial
    (D) ingratiating
    (E) human

30. The phrase "the great Master of marionettes" (line 14) is intended to suggest which of the following?

    I. Humanity's lack of control over its own destiny.
    II. The divine amusement at the human predicament.
    III. The innate sense of humor with which humans have been endowed.

    (A) II only
    (B) III only
    (C) I and II
    (D) II and III
    (E) I, II and III

31. In establishing his preference for humor over wit, the author does all of the following EXCEPT

    (A) personify humor as a constant ally and wit as a frequent foe
    (B) compare humor to something enlightening and wit to something punitive
    (C) characterize humor as a benign and corpulent being and wit as a spare and intrusive one
    (D) imply that humor lies in the province of the commoner and wit in the world of the aristocrat
    (E) associate humor with industry and wit with sloth

32. Which of the following BEST captures the structure of the author's argument?

    (A) Literal and figurative manifestations of humor's superiority followed by an anecdote that confirms it.
    (B) A disclaimer of any ability to determine whether humor or wit is superior followed by a consideration of the attributes of each.
    (C) A central allusion that affirms the humorous nature of man followed by examples of individuals who embody humor.
    (D) A statement of his abhorrence of wit followed by a diatribe against its widespread practice.
    (E) A personal statement of his love of humor followed by a more objective analysis of humor's admirable traits.

33. In contrasting humor with wit, the author uses metaphors drawn from all of the following EXCEPT

    (A) music
    (B) clothing
    (C) social situations
    (D) warfare
    (E) natural phenomena

34. Lines 51-57, "But it is a workday world [. . .] more profitable companionship [. . . .]," imply which of the following?

    I. That life is arduous and enervating.
    II. That the source of human wit is its embitterment with the social condition.
    III. That wit and humor are no panacea for the grim realities of the speaker's era.

    (A) I only
    (B) III only
    (C) I and II
    (D) I and III
    (E) I, II and III

35. In developing the characterization of his dinner companion, the author makes the most use of which of the following?

    (A) extended metaphors
    (B) *ad hominem* argument
    (C) literary allusion
    (D) sardonic diction
    (E) parenthetical commentary

36. The author's inclusion of the parenthetical remark in line 59 is likely intended to

    (A) paint the critic in an immediately unfavorable light
    (B) impress the reader with his social circle
    (C) establish a character who will confirm his belief that wit is not so becoming as humor
    (D) show that true wit must also "be genuine and not a mere shine upon the surface"
    (E) introduce the critic's impressive literary catalog

37. Lines 81-87, "He seemed torn [. . . .] to the printer [. . . .]," imply that the author believed the critic to be

    (A) conceited and highbrow
    (B) monotonous and soporific
    (C) stilted and artificial
    (D) opinionated and didactic
    (E) lively and stentorian

38. Which of the following is the BEST equivalent for the phrase "frail remark" (lines 91-92)?

    (A) feeble retort
    (B) minor objection
    (C) foolish question
    (D) inaccurate observation
    (E) tentative interjection

39. Of the following, which contributes LEAST to the critic's seemingly boundless capacity for self-absorption?

    (A) the transitional sentence "But this was a speech and a lecture." (line 77)
    (B) the metaphor of the "cold spigot" (line 78)
    (C) the allusion to literary characters (lines 81-87)
    (D) the metaphor of the "torrent" (lines 92-93)
    (E) the concluding metaphor of the cobble layer (lines 94-97)

40. Which of the following does NOT contribute to the author's description of the critic's incessant chatter?

    (A) "loosed on us" (line 78)
    (B) "steady flow" (line 79)
    (C) "launched" (line 91)
    (D) "swept off at once" (line 92)
    (E) "torrent" (line 93)

41. Which of the following is NOT characteristic of the style of the author's argument?

    (A) a rich array of metaphorical language
    (B) an anecdote that buttresses his preference for humor
    (C) an insightful contrast of wit and humor that belies his disarmingly modest opening
    (D) a tone that is more familiar and conversational than it is didactic
    (E) allusions to literary exemplars of wit and humor

Questions 42-53. Refer to the following passage.

A circus is both acrobatic and elephantine, wholesome but freakish, and that is partly why we like it so—because we are two-headed, too. A showgirl in the center ring
(5) displays her pretty legs to daddy while his children are engrossed in watching a palomino stallion dance to the band's tempo. But that, of course, is an illusion. The bandmaster, flourishing his silver cornet, is
(10) actually following the horse's mannered, jerky prance, not vice versa, which in turn is being cued by the same short-skirted lady's cracking whip. And in the old days the sideshow used to be called "The Ten-in-One"
(15) because it had "Ten Different Freaks Under One Tent for Only One Dollar! Can you beat that, folks?" as the barkers yelled. Only, I suppose, by looking inside oneself. People too fat or too small, too thin or too tall,
(20) remind us of a certain unwieldy, weird, but shrinking-violet personage whom we know all too well—as does the Knife Thrower, the Escape Artist or Contortionist, the Tattooed or Albino Lady, hefting a boa
(25) constrictor, perhaps, and the knuckle-walking Wild Man, bearded all over, or the Living Skeleton, and the kinky but outwardly clean-cut gentleman who is wed to the swords and fireballs that he swallows a dozen times a day
(30) for our entertainment. Why is it entertainment, if we're not gawking at a caricature of ourselves?

In the big top everybody wears a spiffy uniform, but if yours isn't a one-night stand and
(35) they stay until tomorrow, you'll see some of the circus people sleeping in the horse straw on the ground. And when the costumes come off, baby, don't imagine they'll remember you, no matter how hard you may think you clapped.
(40) Behind the greasepaint is quite a different sort of face and person. You wouldn't necessarily trust one of the clowns or animal handlers who give such intense pleasure to tens of thousands of children with the downright raising of even
(45) a couple; they might already have abandoned a family. Like actors only more so, circus performers are expected to be manic and depressive, and we accept the paradox that a real genius at making little kids laugh, like
(50) Danny Kaye or Charlie Chaplin, could verge on frightening them as a father. The funniness is vertiginous, and the hippodrome food is too sweet. Too much is going on in the rings to absorb it all, and the physical stunts sometimes
(55) edge toward the suicidal. Maybe the grisly part of the bargain is that we, the "lot lice," the Elmers, rubes, towners, hayseeds, hicks, yokels, are paying green money to watch the star troupers risk their lives. If a trapeze artist
(60) falls and hits the ground, he'll lie in front of a grandstand of utter strangers, whimpering, jactitating,[1] and dying alone.

A circus is high and low, piccolos and trombones. The edgy tiger roars and
(65) charges, but then licks her trainer at the end, as if they had been friends all along. A clown meanly tricks his chum, dunks him treacherously in a barrel of water, and gloats for the crowd, but then the high-wire
(70) walker steals all his thunder as soon as the whistle blows. The ringmaster, though he seems the boss, is curiously not the star; the saddest puss gets the biggest laugh; and the innocence is raunchy (those leggy girls who
(75) strut their stuff alongside a whiteface Bozo so that dad has his own reasons to snicker). The clowns teach most memorably that if you trust anybody he will betray you.

We want circus people to be
(80) different from us—homeless and garish, heedless and tawdry (otherwise why pay to watch?)—yet to connect with us in deeper currents that we share. Our fear of heights and ridicule, our complicated fascination
(85) with animals (whips, but kindness), our love of grace and agility, of stylish vanity and splendid boasting, of dressing in spangles yet living in tents and trailers. As an element of rooting our children in a stable
(90) home, we nourish them with this annual spectacle of the elaborately raffish and picaresque. Therefore, we want the show people to be outlandish but never outrageous [. . . .].

---

[1] a restless tossing or twitching of the body

42. The literary devices that pervade the passage and provide the underpinning of the author's argument are

    (A) simile and metaphor
    (B) antithesis and irony
    (C) rhetorical questions and parenthetical remarks
    (D) understatement and allusion
    (E) colloquialisms and jargon

43. In depicting the contrary world of the circus in the third paragraph, the author uses a metaphor drawn from

    (A) weather
    (B) music
    (C) astronomy
    (D) food
    (E) sailing

44. The author's commentary on the animal and human interaction in lines 8-13 suggests which of the following about the circus acts?

    (A) They callously exploit animals.
    (B) They cater primarily to children.
    (C) They are salacious in nature.
    (D) They are elaborately choreographed illusions.
    (E) They shamelessly exploit the public.

45. The relation of the first paragraph to the second is BEST captured by which of the following?

    (A) The first focuses on the showmanship of the circus, the second on the sad realities beneath it.
    (B) The first focuses on the circus performers, the second on the audience.
    (C) The first focuses on the similarities between performers and audience, the second on their differences.
    (D) The first focuses on why people like the circus, the second on why they dislike it.
    (E) The first focuses on animal acts, the second on the human performers.

46. Lines 37-39, "And when the costumes come off, baby, don't imagine they'll remember you, no matter how hard you may think you clapped," suggest which of the following about circus performers?

    (A) Their performance is a grueling reality that the audience fails to perceive.
    (B) Their jesting exterior may mask a melancholy personality.
    (C) Their dualities are similar to those of stage performers.
    (D) Their natures may be shiftless and morally irresponsible.
    (E) Their daredevil behavior suggests an innately suicidal bent.

47. The author's catalog of "'lot lice'" (lines 56-58) is intended to reinforce the

    (A) near universal appeal of circus entertainment
    (B) accessibility of the circus to individuals of diverse income
    (C) tendency of people to waste hard-earned money on escapist entertainment
    (D) naïve and hence vulnerable nature of the traditional circus audience
    (E) large crowds that regularly fill the Big Top

48. According to the passage, which of the following circus entities provides a moral lesson?

    (A) the ringmaster
    (B) the showgirls
    (C) the contortionist
    (D) the trapeze artist
    (E) the clowns

49. The "deeper currents" mentioned in lines 82-83 refer to all of the following EXCEPT

    (A) our aesthetic sensibilities
    (B) our need to maintain a façade
    (C) our deep-seated personal anxieties
    (D) our intellectual capacities
    (E) our desire to be the center of attention

50. Perhaps the cruelest irony in the life of a circus performer concerns the

(A) low level of compensation for such a high-profile job
(B) normalcy that lies behind their colorful circus identities
(C) inability of circus performers to recall the people who applauded them most vigorously
(D) potential for an anonymous and tragic demise before a grandstand of strangers
(E) paradoxical behavior they occasionally direct toward fellow performers

51. Which of the following is NOT a contrast presented in the passage?

(A) the bandmaster's conformity and the ringmaster's command
(B) the innocence of the children watching the palomino and the coquettishness of the showgirls
(C) the dapper costumes of the performers and their sullied backgrounds
(D) the specious hostility of the tiger and its genuine affection for the trainer
(E) the nimbleness of the acrobats and the ponderous step of the circus elephants

52. When one considers the passage as a whole, one may conclude that the author views the circus as all of the following EXCEPT

(A) a collection of exotic and flamboyant performers
(B) an arena of vicarious thrills
(C) a mildly exploitative enterprise
(D) an exemplar of proper conduct
(E) a mirror of human contradiction

53. Which of the following words, in the context in which it appears, may be said to have a double-meaning?

(A) "flourishing" (line 9)
(B) "shrinking" (line 21)
(C) "gawking" (line 31)
(D) "whimpering" (line 61)
(E) "boasting" (line 87)

Section II

Question One

(Suggested time—40 minutes. This question counts as one-third of the total essay section score.)

Read the following passage. Then, in a well-organized essay, indicate what the author's commentary about Epictetus indirectly reveals about himself and the English gentlemen of his social status and show how his language conveys this.

"Have you read Epictetus lately?" "No, not lately." "Oh, you ought to read him. Tommy's been reading him for the first time, and is fearfully excited." I caught this scrap of dialogue from the next table in the lounge of an hotel. I became interested, curious, for I had not read Epictetus, though I had often looked at his works on the shelf—perhaps I
(5)   had even quoted him—and I wondered if here at last was the book of wisdom that I had been looking for at intervals ever since I was at school. Never have I lost my early faith that wisdom is to be found somewhere in a book—to be picked up as easily as a shell from the sand. I desire wisdom as keenly as Solomon did, but it must be wisdom that can be obtained with very little effort—wisdom that can be caught almost by infection. I have no
(10)   time or energy for the laborious quest of philosophy. I wish the philosophers to perform the laborious quest and, at the end of it, to feed me with the fruits of their labours; just as I get eggs from the farmer, apples from the fruit-grower, medicine from the chemist [. . . .]. Still, I have never lost faith in books, believing that somewhere printed matter exists from which I shall be able to absorb philosophy and strength of character while smoking in an
(15)   arm-chair. It was in this mood that I took down Epictetus after hearing the conversation in the hotel lounge.

I read him, I confess, with considerable excitement. He is the kind of philosopher I like, not treating life as if at its finest it were an argument conducted in difficult jargon, but discussing, among other things, how men should behave in the affairs of ordinary life.
(20)   Also, I agreed with nearly everything he said. Indifference to pain, death, poverty yes, that is eminently desirable. Not to be troubled about anything over which one has no control, whether the oppression of tyrants or the peril of earthquakes [. . .]. Yet, close as is the resemblance between our opinions, I could not help feeling, as I read, that Epictetus was wise in holding his opinions and that I, though holding the same opinions, was far from
(25)   wise. For, indeed, though I held the same opinions for purposes of theory, I could not entertain a moment for purposes of conduct. Death, pain and poverty are to me very real evils, except when I am in an armchair reading a book by a philosopher [. . . .].

Even in the small things of life I cannot comfort myself like a philosopher of the school of Epictetus. Thus, for example, when he advises us how to eat "acceptably to the
(30)   gods" and bids us to this end to be patient even under the most incompetent service at our meals, he commands a spiritual attitude of which my nature is incapable. "When you have asked for warm water," he says, "and the slave does not heed you; or if he is not even to be found in the house, then to refrain from anger and not to explode, is not this acceptable to the gods?" [. . . .]. This is all perfectly true, and I should like very much to be a man who
(35)   could sit in a restaurant smiling patiently and philosophically while the waiter brought all the wrong things, or forgot to bring anything at all. But in point of fact bad waiting irritates me. I dislike having to ask three times for the wine-list. I am annoyed when, after a quarter of an hour's delay, I am told there is no celery [. . . .]. And if I cannot achieve his imperturbability in so small affairs as I have mentioned, what hope is there of my being
(40)   able to play the philosopher in the presence of tyrants and earthquakes? [. . . .].

Question Two

(Suggested time—40 minutes. This question counts as one-third of the total essay section score.)

Willa Cather's novel *My Antonia* begins with a Latin epigraph from the Roman poet Virgil: "Optima dies…prima fugit," or "The best days are the first to fade."

Take a moment to reflect on this statement. Then write a well-organized essay in which you explore the validity of this assertion using examples from your reading, observation, studies or experience to develop your position.

<u>Question Three</u>

(Suggested time—55 minutes. This question counts as one-third of the total essay section score.)

Directions:

The following prompt is based on the accompanying six sources.

This question requires you to integrate a variety of sources into a coherent, well-written essay. *Refer to the sources to support your position; avoid paraphrase or summary. Your argument should be central; the sources should support this argument.*

Remember to attribute both direct and indirect citations.

Introduction:

The steady stream of immigrants crossing our Southern border and entering the United States illegally has become a thorny problem. Driven by their own desperate poverty and by the same promise of opportunity that spurred the previous great waves of immigration, these immigrants are further enticed by American businesses that see them as an attractive source of cheap labor. Though the words on our great immigrant beacon, the Statue of Liberty, read, "Give me your tired, your poor, / Your huddled masses yearning to breathe free, / The wretched refuse of your teeming shore [. . . .]," this daily influx of thousands now poses a threat to our national security and our economy. So serious has this problem become that many Americans, from politicians to ordinary citizens, are now advocating closing what Emma Lazarus, the author of the famous welcoming poem, labeled our "golden door."

Assignment:

Read the following sources (including any introductory information) carefully. **Then, in an essay that synthesizes at least three of the sources for support, take a position that defends, challenges or qualifies the claim that the United States can no longer afford the same welcome to immigrants that it has traditionally provided.**

(It is recommended that you spend 15-20 minutes of the allotted time examining the sources and devote the remaining time to writing your essay.)

Document A

"Will we stay a beacon for immigrants." *Knight Ridder Tribune Business News.*
3 Apr 2006: 1. Online http://proquest.umi.com/pdqweb?index=70&did=
1014235101&SrchMode=1&sid=1&Fmt=3.

The current immigration debate in the U.S. Senate is, in a larger sense, a discussion about what kind of country America is going to be.

Will the United States be a welcoming land, a beacon of optimism, opportunity, freedom and tolerance? Will it generously extend the chance for prosperity, which is nearly impossible in many other countries? Will Americans acknowledge, as they have throughout our history, the essential contributions newcomers have made to the fabric of this great land?

Or will America be closed and apprehensive, perceived as selfish and preoccupied with silly arguments over whose land it is? Will genuine concerns about border security translate into boondoggles costing billions and billions of dollars and draconian measures with unintended economic consequences?

The immigration issue is considerable and complex. Yet sometimes lost in the forest of policy questions are the big-picture goals: a secure, but not impenetrable border and a reasonable accounting of the more than 11 million undocumented workers already in the country.

We think President Bush has offered a sensible plan. It calls for increased border security and creates a temporary guest-worker program that recognizes reality: First, that millions of illegal immigrants already are working, paying taxes and raising children, many of whom are U.S. citizens because they were born here. Second, locating them and sending them home is neither feasible, affordable or economically desirable.

Those who keep using terms like "blanket amnesty" are misrepresenting the facts. Neither is it useful to depict all of these immigrants as evil. The House's immigration bill is simply punitive, making felons of people seeking a better life for themselves and their families.

Our plea is for an honest debate, one that refuses to be hijacked by partisan political calculations or nativist paranoia. There are genuine concerns that should be answered with a system that's fair to those who obey the law, yet also is realistic.

This is helped by remembering that the vast majority of Americans came here from somewhere else, and that large part to a history of having open arms.

Document B

Friedman, Thomas L. "High Fence and Big Gate." *New York Times*. Late Edition (East Coast).
5 Apr 2006: A.23: Online http://proquest.umi.com/pdqweb?index=31&did=
1015697631&SrchMode=1&sid=1&Fmt=3.

America today is struggling to find the right balance of policies on immigration. Personally, I favor a very high fence with a very big gate.

So far, neither President Bush's proposal to allow the nation's millions of illegal immigrants to stay temporarily on work visas, nor the most hard-line G.O.P. counterproposal, which focuses only on border security, leaves me satisfied. We need a better blend of the two—a blend that will keep America the world's greatest magnet for immigrants [. . . .].

We shouldn't just welcome educated immigrants, but laborers as well—not only because we need manual laborers, but also because they bring an important energy. As the Indian-American entrepreneur Vivek Paul likes to say: "The very act of leaving behind your own society is an intense motivator. Whether you are a doctor or a gardener, you are intensely motivated to succeed."

We need that steady energy flow, especially with India and China exploding onto the world stage with huge pent-up aspirations. If you want to know what China and India feel like today, just take out a Champagne bottle, shake it for 10 minutes and then take off the cork. Don't get in the way of that cork. Immigrants keep that kind of energy flowing in America's veins.

An amnesty for the 11 million to 12 million illegal immigrants already here is hardly ideal. It would reward illegal behavior. But since we are not going to deport them all, some version of the Arlen Specter bill seems like the right way to go: Illegal immigrants who were in the U.S. before Jan. 7, 2004, could apply for three-year guest-worker visas, each renewable one time if the applicant paid a $1,000 fine and passed a background check. After six years, if the immigrant learned sufficient English and paid another $1,000 fine and back taxes, he or she could start to apply for citizenship.

But because I strongly favor immigration, I also favor a high fence—if not a physical one, then at least a tamperproof national ID card for every American, without which you could not get a legal job or access to government services. We will not sustain a majority in favor of flexible immigration if we can't control our borders.

Good fences make good immigration policy [. . . .].

Document C

Samuelson, Robert J. "The Immigration Impasse: A Way Out." *The Washington Post*
[Final Edition]: 5 Apr 2006: A 23: Online http://proquest.umi.com/pdqweb?index
=31&did=1015712801&SrchMode=1&sid=1&Fmt=3.

Our immigration debate is at an impasse. The House has passed a mean-spirited and delusional bill that focuses heavily on border security and would criminalize some humanitarian acts that aid immigrants. As for the 10 million to 12 million illegal immigrants already here, the supposition is that they should somehow go home. Just how is unclear. Meanwhile, the Senate seems ready to authorize up to 400,000 "guest workers" annually. Guest workers, also endorsed by President Bush, would reduce illegal immigration by giving many of the same people   mainly poor and unskilled Mexicans—work permits. The Senate approach also is delusional and undesirable. It would increase American poverty under the guise of curing worker "shortages" [. . . .].
Let me outline what I think such a consensus might be. It has three elements and borrows from both House and Senate approaches.

Strengthen border and employer enforcement. Unless it's stopped, the present illegal immigration of an estimated 500,000 people annually will overwhelm any system. The main lure is jobs. That's why it's essential to adopt a mandatory requirement for employers to verify new workers—electronic checking of documents. Companies that hire illegal immigrants should be penalized heavily. But it's also essential to dry up the supply. In an earlier column, I supported the construction of fences or walls, 20 to 30 feet high, along the Mexican border. They would, I think, significantly reduce the flow, though some would still come by overstaying student and tourist visas.

Grant amnesty to existing illegal immigrants. President Bush and many Republicans oppose this, but it's essential. We can't run an immigration system that condones mass illegality. Most illegal immigrants deserve legal standing—and a path to citizenship. Although they "broke the law," we (meaning American society) encouraged them by inadequately policing the border and employers. Most won't voluntarily return home, where typical wages are 80 percent lower. Trying to force them back would create a huge backlash. We'd have stories of parents being torn from their American-born children. Companies would complain that government was destroying their firms by removing longtime, diligent workers. Finally, the failure to legalize today's illegal workers would weaken companies' incentives to comply with checks of new workers. If firms were already breaking the law to stay in business, why not take the added risk?

Forget guest workers. Maybe a few job categories (sheepherders) with existing guest worker programs are justified. But businesses' complaints of widespread labor "shortages" mainly put a respectable face on their thirst for cheap labor. Most guest workers won't go home, even if required (see above). They'll become illegal immigrants or citizens. Either way, adding poor people is bad social policy. It would bloat the demand for government social services. And it would hurt today's poor—including other immigrants and many African Americans—by keeping wages down. Jobs attracting lots of immigrants have low wage increases. From 2002 to 2004, median hourly wages rose only 2 percent for construction laborers and 3.6 percent for dishwashers.

On paper, this package has something for everyone [. . . .].

Document D

Bookman, Jay. "Guest worker idea threatens U.S. heritage." *The Atlanta Journal-Constitution*
[Main Edition] 3 Apr 2006: A 13. Online
http://proquest.umi.com/pdqweb?index=31&did=31&did=1014185071
&SrchMode=1&sid=1&Fmt=3.

[. . . .] Under a guest worker policy, we will let the immigrants come here by the millions, but only temporarily. We will let them mangle their hands in our poultry plants and salt our farmlands with the sweat off their brows and break their backs at our construction sites and raise our children as nannies and clean our homes as maids, all at cut-rate wages.

But we will not allow them to dream—for themselves or their children—of sharing in the future they help to build here.

In other words, we are willing to let them serve us but not join us; they must by law be held apart and beneath us. We will import them to serve as a perpetually rotating servant class, and we will do so even while pretending to still honor that most American of principles, "that all men are created equal."

That system of second-class citizenship—far from slavery, but far from the full range of human rights as well—has precedent in American history. In colonial times, more than half of those who immigrated from Europe came here not as free people but as indentured servants.

In return for the cost of passage to the New World, they agreed to be legally bound to an employer for a number of years, unable to marry without permission and with no say over where they lived or how they worked. They could even be sold to another boss.

But even back then, when the period of bonded indenture ended—usually after seven years—the servant was freed and allowed to take his or her place as a full citizen [. . . .].

Document E

Mirta, Olito. "Change in Laws Sets Off Big Wave of Deportations." *New York Times*
(Late Ed. East Coast) 15 Dec 1998: A-1:
http://proquest.umi.com.rocky.iona.edu:2048/pqdweb?index=28&did=37136542&SrchMode=1&sid=1&Fmt=
3&VInst=PROD&VType=PQD&RQT=309&VName=PQD&TS=1153762661&clientId=1907.

In the two years since Congress passed tough laws to stem the flow of illegal immigration to the United States, Federal authorities have deported almost 300,000 immigrants to countries all over the world, more than twice the number who were sent back in the two years before.

The unprecedented number of deportations has been possible because for the first time the Immigration and Naturalization Service has both the Congressional mandate and the money to investigate and prosecute violators of immigration law, arrest immigrants with criminal convictions and would-be immigrants at the border and swiftly deport them from the United States—sometimes in less than 12 hours.

Many of the immigrants who are deported are barred from returning to the country for five years or more. Some are barred for life.

''The rules have changed,'' said Kerry Bretz, a Manhattan immigration lawyer and former I.N.S. prosecutor. ''The agency has become completely enforcement-minded.''

Flush with almost a billion dollars earmarked for the detention and deportation of immigrants, the I.N.S. is now the largest Federal law enforcement agency, the Justice Department says. The immigration service has more than 15,000 officers authorized to carry weapons and make arrests, more than the Federal Bureau of Investigation, the Bureau of Prisons, the Customs Service or the Drug Enforcement Administration.

''It is as if, suddenly, war had been declared on immigrants,'' said Maria Jimenez, director of the Immigration Law Enforcement Monitoring Project of the American Friends Service Committee, a nonprofit organization in Houston that documents abuses on the United States-Mexico border. ''Stopping immigrants from entering the country has become more important than the war against drugs'' [. . . .].

Through a process called expedited removal, for example, the law now allows immigration officials to quickly deport illegal immigrants who show up at airports and at the border. Immigration officials, not judges, determine which of them can be deported and, therefore, barred from the United States for at least five years. The decision can be made in a matter of hours and without a lawyer representing the immigrant.

Before the law changed, immigration officials at the border used to simply send illegal immigrants back without formally deporting them. Undaunted, immigrants tried again and many eventually succeeded at entering the country undetected. Now, any immigrant caught trying to enter the country after having been formally deported can be prosecuted and sentenced to prison [. . . .].

Document F

Bilicki, Justin 2006. "Come to Daddy." New York, NY:
Online http://cagle.com/news/Immigration06/5.asp.

Sample Examination V

Questions 1-13. Refer to the following passage.

[. . .] To imagine a scene, however, does not give us the sense of being, or even of having been, present. Indeed, the greater the glow of the scene reflected, the sharper is the pang of
(5) our realisation that we were not there, and of our annoyance we weren't. Such a pang comes to me with special force whenever fancy posts itself outside the Temple's gate in Fleet Street, and there, at a late hour of the night of May
(10) 10th, 1773, observes a gigantic old man laughing wildly, but having no one with him to share and aggrandise his emotion. Not that he is alone; but the young man beside him laughs in politeness and is inwardly puzzled,
(15) even shocked. Boswell has a keen, exquisitely keen, scent for comedy, for the fun that is latent in shades of character; but imaginative burlesque, anything that borders lovely nonsense, he was not formed to savour. All the
(20) more does one revel in his account of what led up to the moment when Johnson "to support himself, laid hold of one of the posts at the side of the foot pavement, and sent forth peals so loud that in the silence of the night his
(25) voice seemed to resound from Temple Bar to Fleet Ditch."

No evening ever had an unlikelier ending. The omens were all for gloom. Johnson had gone to dine at General Paoli's but was so ill
(30) that he had to leave before the meal was over. Later he managed to go to Mr. Chambers' rooms in the Temple. "He continued to be very ill" there, but gradually felt better, and "talked with a noble enthusiasm of keeping up
(35) the representation of respectable families," and was great on "the dignity and propriety of male succession." Among his listeners, as it happened, was a gentleman for whom Mr. Chambers had that day drawn up a will
(40) devising his estate to his three sisters. The news of this might have been expected to make Johnson violent in wrath. But no, for some reason he grew violent only in laughter, and insisted thenceforth on calling that
(45) gentleman The Testator and chaffing him without mercy. "I daresay he thinks he has

done a mighty thing. He won't stay till he gets home to his seat in the country, to produce this wonderful deed: he'll call up the landlord of
(50) the first inn on the road; and after a suitable preface upon mortality and the uncertainty of life, will tell him that he should not delay in making his will; and Here, Sir, will he say, is my will, which I have just made, with the
(55) assistance of one of the ablest lawyers in the kingdom; and he will read it to him. He believes he has made this will; but he did not make it; you, Chambers, made it for him. I hope you have had more conscience than to
(60) make him say 'being of sound understanding!' ha, ha, ha! I hope he has left me a legacy. I'd have his will turned into verse, like a ballad." These flights annoyed Mr. Chambers, and are recorded by Boswell with the apology that he
(65) wishes his readers to be "acquainted with the slightest occasional characteristics of so eminent a man."

Certainly, there is nothing ridiculous in the fact of a man making a will. But this is
(70) the measure of Johnson's achievement. He had created gloriously much out of nothing at all. There he sat, old and ailing and unencouraged by the company, but soaring higher and higher in absurdity, more and more rejoicing, and
(75) still soaring and rejoicing after he had gone out into the night with Boswell, till at last in Fleet Street his paroxysms were too much for him and he could no more. Echoes of that huge laughter come ringing down the ages.
(80) But is there also perhaps a note of sadness for us in them?

Johnson's endless sociability came of his inherent melancholy: he could not bear to be alone; and his very mirth was but a mode of
(85) escape from the dark thoughts within him. Of these the thought of death was the most dreadful to him, and the most insistent. He was forever wondering how death would come to him, and how he would acquit himself in
(90) the extreme moment. A later but not less devoted Anglican, meditating on his own end, wrote in his diary that "to die in church appears to be a great euthanasia, but not," he quaintly and touchingly added, "at a time to

(95)   disturb worshippers" [. . . .]. But to die of laughter—this, too, seems to me a great euthanasia; and I think that for Johnson to have died thus, that night in Fleet Street, would have been a grand ending [. . . .].

1. The passage is most accurately labeled which of the following?

    (A) a eulogy for a deceased friend
    (B) a denouncement of crass behavior
    (C) a paean to an ebullient personality
    (D) a satire of legal ineptitude
    (E) a meditation on the inevitability of death

2. In the opening two sentences of the passage the author is

    (A) formulating a thesis
    (B) dismissing a conjecture
    (C) qualifying an observation
    (D) establishing a setting
    (E) foreshadowing an action

3. Line 27, "No evening ever had an unlikelier ending," foreshadows the irony of which of the following?

    (A) Johnson's illness at dinner
    (B) Johnson's moroseness as the font of his humor
    (C) Johnson's preoccupation with his mortality
    (D) Johnson's behavior on Fleet Street
    (E) Johnson's actual death

4. The author likely cites Boswell's recording of Johnson's comments on "'the dignity and propriety of male succession'" (lines 36-37) in order to

    (A) emphasize Johnson's trademark misogyny
    (B) reveal Johnson's strong belief in primogeniture
    (C) set up Boswell's anecdote about Johnson and the gentleman's will
    (D) illustrate Johnson's preference for a male monarch
    (E) exemplify a traditional topic of male conversation

5. The modifier "great," as it is used in line 36, is BEST interpreted as

    (A) wonderful
    (B) eloquent
    (C) conciliatory
    (D) staunch
    (E) disputatious

6. Johnson's subsequent reaction to the gentleman who willed his estate to his sisters includes all of the following EXCEPT

    (A) saddling him with an appropriate moniker
    (B) berating him violently for his foolhardiness
    (C) poking fun at his action through insincere superlatives
    (D) envisioning him hastily and foolishly boasting to other men
    (E) intimating he'd like to immortalize his folly in a poem

7. Johnson's overly humorous response to the will implies which of the following?

    I. His ability to elevate something mundane into something entertaining.
    II. His pressing need to suppress his ever-present melancholia.
    III. His skepticism as to the capabilities of women.

    (A) I only.
    (B) II only
    (C) I and II
    (D) II and III
    (E) I, II and III

8. The author likely includes Boswell's observation in lines 63-67 in order to

    (A) laud Boswell's attention to detail
    (B) elaborate upon Boswell's humorous characterization of Johnson
    (C) imply Boswell's chagrin at Johnson's overzealous derision
    (D) poke fun at Johnson's significant girth
    (E) suggest that such ridicule by Johnson is commonplace

9. Lines 72-78—"There he sat, old and ailing and unencouraged by the company [. . .] till at last in Fleet Street his paroxysms were too much for him and he could no more"—are intended to do which of the following?

    I. Stir empathy in the reader for the bored and aging Johnson.
    II. Censure Johnson's public inebriation.
    III. Mirror in their diction and syntax the irrepressible humor of Johnson.

    (A) I only
    (B) II only
    (C) I and III
    (D) II and III
    (E) I, II and III

10. The placement of the dash after "But to die of laughter—" (lines 95-96) creates a tone of

    (A) total incredulity
    (B) sorrowful regret
    (C) censurious ridicule
    (D) wistful longing
    (E) pensive consideration

11. In the passage Johnson's laugh is depicted as which of the following?

    (A) resonant and sonorous
    (B) shrill and cackling
    (C) bitter and sardonic
    (D) scornful and sinister
    (E) muffled and reserved

12. Each of the following helps to establish the capaciousness of Johnson's laughter EXCEPT

    (A) "a gigantic old man laughing wildly [. . .]" (lines 10-11)
    (B) "All the more does one revel in his account [. . .]" (lines 19-20)
    (C) "[. . .] peals so loud that in the silence of the night his voice seemed to resound [. . .]" (lines 23-25)
    (D) "[. . .] till at last in Fleet Street his paroxysms were too much for him [. . .]" (lines 76-78)
    (E) "Echoes of that huge laughter come ringing down the ages" (lines 78-79)

13. Which of the following is NOT a feeling expressed by the author about Dr. Johnson?

    (A) wonder at his creativity and spontaneity
    (B) admiration for his *joie de vivre*
    (C) respect for his deep religious conviction
    (D) empathy for his innate loneliness
    (E) regret at never having experienced him in person

Questions 14-25. Refer to the following passage.

[. . . .] Something will have gone out of us as a people if we ever let the remaining wilderness be destroyed; if we permit the
(5) last virgin forests to be turned into comic books and plastic cigarette cases; if we drive the few remaining members of the last species into zoos or to extinction; if we pollute the last clear air or dirty the last
(10) clean streams and push our paved roads through the last of the silence, so that never again will Americans be free in their own country from the noise, the exhausts, the stinks of human and automotive waste. And so that never again can we have the chance
(15) to see ourselves single, separate, vertical and individual in the world, part of our environment of trees and rocks and soil, brother to the other animals, part of the natural world and competent to belong in it.
(20) Without any remaining wilderness we are committed wholly, without chance for even momentary reflection and rest, to a headlong drive into our technological termite-life, the Brave New World[1] of a
(25) completely man-controlled environment. We need wilderness preserved—as much of it as is still left, and as many kinds— because it was the challenge against which our character as a people was formed. The
(30) reminder and the reassurance that it is still there is good for our spiritual health even if we never once in ten years set foot in it. It is good for us when we are young, because of the incomparable sanity it can bring
(35) briefly, as vacation and rest, into our insane lives. It is important to us when we are old simply because it is there—important, that is, simply as an idea.

    We are a wild species, as Darwin
(40) pointed out. Nobody ever tamed or domesticated or scientifically bred us. But for at least three millennia we have been engaged in a cumulative and ambitious race to modify and gain control of our
(45) environment [. . . .]. Just as surely as it has brought us increased comfort and more material goods, it has brought us spiritual losses, and it threatens now to become the Frankenstein that will destroy us. One
(50) means of sanity is to retain a hold on the natural world, to remain, insofar as we can, good animals. Americans still have that chance, more than many peoples; for while

we were demonstrating ourselves the most
(55) efficient and ruthless environment-busters in history, and slashing and burning and cutting our way through a wilderness continent, the wilderness was working on us. It remains in us as sure as Indian names
(60) remain on the land. If the abstract dream of human liberty and human dignity became, in America, something more than an abstract dream, mark it down at least partially to the fact that we were in subtle
(65) ways subdued by what we conquered.

    As a novelist, I may be perhaps forgiven for taking literature as a reflection, indirect by profoundly true, of our national consciousness. And our literature, as
(70) perhaps you are aware, is sick, embittered, losing its mind, losing its faith. Our novelists are the declared enemies of their society. There has hardly been a serious or important novel in this century that did not
(75) repudiate in part or in whole American technological culture for its commercialism, its vulgarity, and the way in which it has dirtied a clean continent and a clean dream [. . . .]. We need to demonstrate
(80) our acceptance of the natural world, including ourselves; we need the spiritual refreshment that being natural can produce. And one of the best places for us to get that is in the wilderness where the fun houses,
(85) the bulldozers, and the pavements of our civilization are shut out.

    Sherwood Anderson, in a letter to Waldo Frank in the 1920's, said it better than I can. "It is not unlikely that when the
(90) country was new and men were often left alone in the fields and the forest they got a sense of bigness outside themselves that has now in some way been lost [. . .]. Mystery whispered in the grass, played in the
(95) branches overhead, was caught up and blown across the American line in clouds of dust at evening on the prairies [. . . .]."

---

[1] allusion to 1932 dystopian novel by Aldous Huxley

14. Perhaps the MOST significant irony in the passage concerns the author's

    (A) frequent references to man as an animal
    (B) suggestion that though we are "wild" by nature we have tried to tame the continent
    (C) claim that our literature is "sick" when it has always endeavored to raise environmental consciousness
    (D) observation that "we were subdued by what we conquered"
    (E) intimation that the same humans who "slashed and burned" their way across the continent are now charged with saving it

15. Which of the following is NOT a characteristic of the opening sentence?

    (A) parallel conditional clauses that depict environmentally destructive action
    (B) the use of the collective "we" to imply communal responsibility for protecting the environment
    (C) adjectives that convey the noisome effects of air pollution
    (D) active verbs that connote defilement and intrusion
    (E) contrasts between the natural and the synthetic and between the free and the confined

16. In depicting humanity's violation of the wilderness, the author primarily relies upon

    (A) sensory diction
    (B) hyperbolic description
    (C) stream-of-consciousness
    (D) pathetic fallacy
    (E) bitter sarcasm

17. The series of adjectives—"single, separate, vertical and individual" (lines 15-16)—is likely intended to do which of the following?

    I. Acknowledge man's uniquely rational position as *homo sapiens*.
    II. Suggest humanity's lack of community with other species in their environment.
    III. Imply humans' accountability as environmental caretakers.

    (A) I only
    (B) II only
    (C) I and III
    (D) II and III
    (E) I, II and III

18. The phrase "technological termite-life" (lines 23-24) presents an image of

    (A) ascetic seclusion
    (B) patient industry
    (C) blind conformity
    (D) refined destruction
    (E) limited significance

19. Lines 36-38—"It is important to us when we are old simply because it is there—important, that is, simply as an idea"—imply that as humans age they value the wilderness as a symbol of

    (A) spiritual serenity
    (B) unrivaled beauty
    (C) physical challenge
    (D) pristine wildness
    (E) constant endurance

20. The author's allusion to *Frankenstein* in line 49 does which of the following?

    I. Suggest the capricious violence of nature.
    II. Buttress a similar idea as the earlier allusion to *Brave New World*.
    III. Imply that humanity's avarice has created problems that may come back to plague it.

    (A) I only
    (B) III only
    (C) I and II
    (D) II and III
    (E) I, II and III

21. The phrase "Our novelists are the declared enemies of their society" (lines 71-73) suggests that writers have become

    (A) morally decadent individuals
    (B) subservient mouthpieces of the government
    (C) reviled scapegoats for societal ills
    (D) vocal critics of environmentally destructive policies
    (E) unfortunate targets of literary censorship

22. The inclusion of Sherwood Anderson's letter (lines 87-97) is primarily intended to

    (A) impress upon the reader the immensity of the United States
    (B) highlight a spiritual kinship with nature that has been lost
    (C) convey the raw beauty of the American landscape
    (D) capture the lonely toil of the rural farmer
    (E) contrast the 1920's attitude toward protecting the wilderness with the contemporary one

23. The sentiments expressed in Sherwood Anderson's letter are BEST classified as

    (A) existential
    (B) transcendental
    (C) naturalistic
    (D) surrealistic
    (E) ironic

24. In the course of the passage, the author uses personification to depict the

    (A) serendipitous freedom of the American wilderness
    (B) desecration of nature by industrial contaminants
    (C) pervasive malaise in our literature and spirit
    (D) material avarice of the American consumer
    (E) rapid urbanization that is destroying our serenity

25. All of the following are stylistic traits of the passage EXCEPT

    (A) allusions to prominent figures in literature and science
    (B) a polemical and didactic tone
    (C) antithetical images of the pristine and idyllic past, and of the commercialized and technological present
    (D) an extended metaphor that conveys the dehumanization of the individual by rapid technological prowess
    (E) impassioned declarations of the need to preserve our intimacy with the wilderness

Questions 26-37. Refer to the following passage.

I don't remember being born, but opening my eyes for the first time, yes. Under hypnosis many years later, I wandered through knotted jungles of memory to the lost kingdoms of my
(5) childhood, which for some reason I had forgotten, the way one casually misplaces a hat or a glove. Suddenly I could remember waking in a white room, with white walls, and white sheets, and a round white basin on a square
(10) white table, and looking up into the face of my mother, whose brown hair, flushed complexion, and dark eyes were the only contrast to the white room and daylight that stung her with its brightness. Lying on my mother's chest, I
(15) watched the flesh-colored apparition change its features, as if triangles were being randomly shuffled. Then a row of white teeth flashed out of nowhere, dark eyes widened, and I, unaware there was such a thing as motion, or that I was
(20) powerless even to roll over, watched the barrage of colors and shapes, appearing, disappearing, like magic scarves out of hats, and was completely enthralled.

What I couldn't know was how yellow I had
(25) been, and covered with a film of silky black hair, which made me look even more monkey-like than newborns usually do, and sent my pediatrician into a well-concealed tizzy. He placed the cud-textured being on its mother's
(30) chest, smiled as he said, "You have a baby girl," and, forgetting to remove his gloves or even thank the anesthesiologist as was his habit, he left the hospital room to find a colleague fast. Once he had delivered a
(35) deformed baby, which came out rolled up like a volleyball, its organs outside its body, and its brain, mercifully, dead. Once he had delivered premature twins, only one of which survived the benign sham of an incubator, and now was
(40) a confused, growing teenager he sometimes saw concealing a cigarette outside the high school. Stillborns he had delivered so many times he no longer could remember how many there were, or whose. But never had he
(45) delivered a baby so near normal yet brutally different before. He knew that I was jaundiced (which he could treat easily enough), and presumed the hairy coat was due to a hormonal imbalance of some sort, though he understood
(50) neither its cause nor its degree. When he found the staff endocrinologist equally puzzled, he decided the best course was not to worry the mother, who was herself not much more than a

young girl, and one with a volatile marriage,
(55) from what he'd heard from a mutual friend at the country club. He decided he would tell her that the condition was normal—something the baby would outgrow ("like life," he thought cynically)—and prescribed a drug for the
(60) jaundice, lifting the clipboard in the maternity office with one hand and writing the prescription carefully, in an unnecessarily ornate script, which was his only affectation. As he did so, New York State seemed to him
(65) suddenly shabby and outmoded, like the hospital on whose cracked linoleum he stood; like the poor practice he conducted on the first floor of his old, street-front, brick house, whose porch slats creaked at the footstep of
(70) each patient so that, at table or in his study, or even lying down on the sofa in the den wallpapered with small tea roses, he would hear that indelible creaking and be halfway across the room before his wife knew he hadn't
(75) merely taken a yen for a dish of ice cream or gone to fetch a magazine from the waiting room; like the apple-cheeked woman he had married almost twenty-five years ago, when she was slender and prankish and such a
(80) willing chum; like the best clothes of most of his patients, who had made it through the Depression by doing with less until less was all they wanted; like the shabby future of this hairy little baby, on whom fate had played an
(85) as yet unspecified trick. It was that compound malaise that my mother saw on Dr. Petersen's face as she glanced over the clean, well-used crib at her bedside and out of the hospital window just as Dr. Petersen was walking to his
(90) car to drive home for lunch and a short nap before his afternoon hours [. . . .].

26. In the course of the passage, the narrative focus shifts from the author's reverie of her childbirth to the

    (A) doctor's reflection on the growing obsolescence of the medical facility and his own practice
    (B) revulsion of the author's mother at her offspring's deformity
    (C) endocrinologist's puzzlement at the author's hirsute appearance
    (D) reflections of the confused, cigarette-smoking teenager
    (E) catalog of a small town doctor's daily life by his spouse

27. The author figuratively relates her plumbing of the primal memories of her existence to which of the following?

    (A) stepping foot onto a new continent
    (B) being confined to a prison
    (C) being thrust into a bright spotlight
    (D) searching for a buried city of antiquity
    (E) feeling adrift on an ocean

28. The author's initial impressions as a newborn include all of the following EXCEPT

    (A) an initially overbearing sense of whiteness
    (B) an ignorance of the concept of motion
    (C) a consciousness of her physical appearance
    (D) a fascination with the shifting landscape of her mother's face
    (E) a mesmerizing kaleidoscope of shapes and colors

29. The author's reference to the hat and glove (lines 6-7) serves to

    (A) delineate the ladylike refinement of the author's mother
    (B) provide touchstones for a psychological critique
    (C) illustrate the transient nature of human memory
    (D) symbolize the author's desire to cloak her identity
    (E) reveal the author's habitual carelessness with personal effects

30. The author's imagined recollection of the actions of her pediatrician after the delivery paints him as

    (A) relieved and exhausted
    (B) reassuring and solicitous
    (C) hasty and incompetent
    (D) callous and perfunctory
    (E) unnerved and distracted

31. The details of the doctor's experience in delivering babies (lines 34-44) may be said to suggest which of the following?

    I. Dr. Petersen's gross incompetence as a physician.
    II. Dr. Petersen's sincere empathy for his patients.
    III. The staff's general unpreparedness to handle exceptional maternal circumstances.

    (A) I only
    (B) III only
    (C) I and II
    (D) II and III
    (E) I, II and III

32. The doctor's decision as to the "best course" of action regarding the author's "hairy coat" (line 48) is primarily motivated by a(n)

    (A) chagrin, on his part, over his complete ignorance of her condition
    (B) desire to protect the reputation of a professional colleague
    (C) empathy for the youth and marital difficulties of the author's mother
    (D) eagerness to test a new drug therapy
    (E) reluctance fully to submit to his increasingly cynical view of life

33. The long sentence that comprises most of lines 64-85 ("As he did so [. . .] unspecified trick") is stylistically characterized by all of the following EXCEPT

    (A) a series of analogous situations
    (B) an incrementally diminishing focus
    (C) images of the doctor's domestic world
    (D) inverted syntax that mirrors each changing circumstance
    (E) diction suggestive of age and decay

34. The phrase "indelible creaking" (line 73) is intended to suggest which of the following about Dr. Petersen?

    (A) that his body is showing signs of age
    (B) that the arrival of his patients is subconsciously ingrained
    (C) that his house is dangerously dilapidated
    (D) that his wife knows his every movement in the house
    (E) that his practice is financially strapped

35. The phrase "compound malaise" (lines 85-86) refers to the

    (A) author's physical condition as an infant
    (B) multiple medical complications of the deformed baby
    (C) pressing anxiety felt by the author's mother
    (D) consciousness of ubiquitous decline experienced by Dr. Petersen
    (E) rumors conveyed by the physician's country club friend

36. The author's description of the doctor's experiences—both in the hospital and in his own practice—do which of the following?

    I. Expose the urgent need for improved medical care at that time.
    II. Reveal how reduced economic circumstance may engender reduced expectations in people.
    III. Imply that the author's "film of silky black hair" is a portent of future problems.

    (A) I only
    (B) III only
    (C) I and II
    (D) II and III
    (E) I, II and III

37. Which of the following is NOT enhanced by a simile?

    (A) the changing expressions of author's mother's face
    (B) the magical ambience into which author's is born
    (C) the film of hair that envelops author's body
    (D) the contorted shape of a deformed infant
    (E) the doctor's overly elaborate penmanship

Questions 38-51. Refer to the following passage.

Just so hollow and ineffectual, for the most part, is our ordinary conversation. Surface meets surface. When our life ceases to be inward and private, conversation degenerates into mere
(5) gossip. We rarely meet a man who can tell us any news which he has not read in a newspaper, or been told by his neighbor [. . .]. In proportion, as our inward life fails, we go more constantly and desperately to the post office. You may depend
(10) on it, that the poor fellow who walks away with the greatest number of letters, proud of his extensive correspondence, has not heard from himself this long while.

I do not know but it is too much to
(15) read one newspaper a week. I have tried it recently, and for so long it seems to me I have not dwelt in my native region. The sun, the clouds, the snow, the trees say not so much to me. You cannot serve two
(20) masters.[1] It requires more than a day's devotion to know and to possess the wealth of a day.

We may well be ashamed to tell what things we have read or heard in our
(25) day [. . . .]. It is the stalest repetition [. . . .]. Its facts appear to float in the atmosphere, insignificant as the sporules of fungi, and impinge on some neglected thallus, or surface of our minds, which affords a basis
(30) for them, and hence a parasitic growth [. . . .].

Not without a slight shudder at the danger, I often perceive how near I had come to admitting into my mind the details of some trivial affair,—the news of the street; and I am
(35) astonished to observe how willing men are to lumber their minds with such rubbish,—to permit idle rumors and incidents of the most insignificant kind to intrude on ground which should be sacred to thought. Shall the mind be
(40) a public arena, where the affairs of the street and the gossip of the tea-table chiefly are discussed? Or shall it be a quarter of heaven itself—an hypaethral[2] temple, consecrated to the service of the gods? [. . .]. Think of admitting the
(45) details of a single case of the criminal court into our thoughts, to stalk profanely through their very *sanctum sanctorum*[3] for an hour, ay, for many hours! to make a very bar-room of the mind's inmost apartment, as if for so long the
(50) dust of the street had occupied us,—the very street itself, with all its travel, its bustle, and filth, had passed through our thoughts' shrine! Would it not be an intellectual and moral suicide? When I have been compelled

(55) to sit spectator and auditor in a courtroom for some hours, and have seen my neighbors, who were not compelled, stealing in from time to time, and tiptoeing about with washed hands and faces, it has appeared to my mind's eye,
(60) that, when they took off their hats, their ears suddenly expanded into vast hoppers for sound[4] [. . .]. Like the vanes of windmills, they caught the broad but shallow stream of sound, which, after a few titillating gyrations in their
(65) coggy brains, passed out the other side [. . .]. It has seemed to me at such a time, that the auditors and the witnesses, the jury and the counsel, the judge and the criminal at the bar,—if I may presume him guilty before he is convicted,—
(70) were all equally criminal, and a thunderbolt might be expected to descend and consume them all together.

By all kinds of traps and signboards, threatening the extreme penalty of the divine
(75) law, exclude such trespassers from the only ground which can be sacred to you. It is so hard to forget what is worse than useless to remember! If I am to be a thoroughfare, I prefer that it be of the mountain brooks, the
(80) Parnassian[5] streams, and not the town sewers. There is inspiration, that gossip which comes to the ear of the attentive mind from the courts of heaven. There is the profane and stale revelation of the barroom and the police court.
(85) The same ear is fitted to receive both communications. Only the character of the hearer determines to which it shall be open, and to which closed [. . . .].

---

[1] Matthew 24.6—"No man can serve two masters: for either he will hate the one, and love the other; or else he will hold to the one, and despise the other. Ye cannot serve God and Mammon."

[2] Wholly or partly open to the sky

[3] Lat.—holiest of holies, or innermost shrine

[4] Perhaps an allusion to Midas who was given the ears of an ass as a punishment for his foolhardy wish to turn everything into gold

[5] Gk—sacred mountain associated with the Muses and the Oracle of Delphi

38. The overall tone and content of the passage suggest that it comes from a(n)

    (A) religious tract
    (B) newspaper editorial
    (C) reflective essay
    (D) court record
    (E) political satire

39. In making his case against news and gossip, and for the integrity of the mind, the author employs all of the following EXCEPT

    (A) comparisons to organisms that are associated with disease or leech-like dependence
    (B) exemplary items from the newspapers of his era
    (C) classical allusions that convey the inviolable nature of the mind
    (D) images of domestic and public life that are readily associated with conversation
    (E) figurative language that humorously depicts both the vacuity of most conversation and his neighbors' ironic compulsion to attend to it

40. When the author suggests that he has "not dwelt in [his] native region" (line 17), he is confessing to a(n)

    (A) nostalgia for a previous locale
    (B) unfamiliarity with local people and events
    (C) alienation from the natural world
    (D) disorientation due to an excess of mundane information
    (E) inability to understand the significance of political events

41. According to the author, which of the following is a direct consequence of humanity's failure to engage in contemplative activity?

    I. An ignorance of significant worldly events.
    II. An erosion of their sensitivity to nature.
    III. A dearth of intellectual conversation.

    (A) I only
    (B) III only
    (C) I and II
    (D) II and III
    (E) I, II and III

42. In the passage the author employs diction that likens preserving the integrity of one's mind to

    (A) chastity
    (B) asceticism
    (C) imprisonment
    (D) sanitation
    (E) husbandry

43. Which of the following plays the MOST prominent role in stylistically underscoring the deleterious effects of the tea-table, street, or courtroom?

    (A) the author's anecdote of the "poor fellow" who received the most letters (lines 9-14)
    (B) the author's tone in confessing that he feels it too much to read even one newspaper a week (lines 14-17)
    (C) the author's use of the collective "we" (lines 23-25)
    (D) the author's physical revulsion at almost "admitting into [his] mind the details of some trivial affair" (lines 33-34)
    (E) the author's diction that contrasts the sacredness of the mind with the profanity of the trivial and sensational (lines 44-52)

44. In light of the account in lines 54-72, which BEST captures the author's attitude towards his neighbors?

    (A) derisive condemnation
    (B) overt jealousy
    (C) arrogant condescension
    (D) bemused disapproval
    (E) general indifference

45. The author's attitude towards his neighbors' fascination with courtroom testimony is buttressed by all of the following EXCEPT

    (A) his belief that letting such details into our minds is "intellectual and moral suicide" (lines 53-54)
    (B) his choice of the verb "compelled" (line 57)
    (C) his blanket condemnation of all the involved parties as "equally criminal" (line 70)
    (D) his ire at the Constitutional separation of church and state
    (E) his satiric depiction of his neighbors' physical features

46. The simile of the windmills (lines 62-65) is intended to reinforce the

    (A) author's own discomfort in the formal courtroom setting
    (B) insubstantial nature of courtroom discourse
    (C) circuitous nature of legal maneuvering
    (D) slow moving wheel of justice
    (E) public's quixotic faith in the legal system

47. In light of the argument that precedes them, lines 78-80, "If I am to be a thoroughfare [. . .] not the town sewers," suggest all of the following contrasts EXCEPT

    (A) the man-made and the natural
    (B) the defiled and the pure
    (C) the public and the secluded
    (D) the stagnant and the fluid
    (E) the profane and the divine

48. The likely purpose of the lines that close the passage—"Only the character of the hearer determines to which it shall be open, and to which closed [. . . .]" (lines 86-88)—is to

    (A) recall the exaggerated ears of his neighbors
    (B) introduce two antithetical types of communication
    (C) imply a connection between intellectual integrity and morality
    (D) suggest that *all* people are compelled to gossip
    (E) intimate that those not punished on earth will suffer divine retribution

49. Which of the following words or phrases does nothing to help establish the author's low opinion of trivia and gossip?

    (A) "trivial affair" (line 34)
    (B) "rubbish" (line 36)
    (C) "idle rumors and incidents" (line 37)
    (D) "shallow stream" (line 63)
    (E) "traps and signboards" (line 73)

50. In light of the theme and the tone of the passage, which of the following does NOT belong grouped with the others?

    (A) the tea-table (line 41)
    (B) the hypaethral temple (line 43)
    (C) the bar-room (line 48)
    (D) the street (lines 50-52)
    (E) the courtroom (lines 55-72)

51. Taken together, the footnotes of the passage help to establish which of the following?

    I. The author's belief in an intimate communion with nature.
    II. The strength of the author's religious conviction.
    III. The breadth and depth of the author's erudition.

    (A) II only
    (B) III only
    (C) I and II
    (D) I and III
    (E) I, II and III

Section II

<u>Question One</u>

(Suggested time—40 minutes. This question counts as one-third of the total essay section score.)

The following passage, taken from Jane Addams' <u>Twenty Years at Hull House</u>, recounts her daunting struggle to address the acute poverty of late-nineteenth century Chicago. Read the passage carefully. Then, in a well-organized essay, discuss how the author uses language as a powerful tool of social advocacy.

That neglected and forlorn old age is daily brought to the attention of a Settlement which undertakes to bear its share of the neighborhood burden imposed by poverty, was pathetically clear to us during our first months of residence at Hull-House. One day a boy of ten led a tottering old lady into the House, saying that she had slept for six weeks in their kitchen on a bed made up next to the stove; that she had
(5)   come when her son died, although none of them had ever seen her before; but because her son had "once worked in the same shop with Pa she thought of him when she had nowhere to go." The little fellow concluded by saying that our house was so much bigger than theirs that he thought we would have more room for beds. The old woman herself said absolutely nothing, but looking on with that gripping fear of the poorhouse in her eyes, she was a living embodiment of that dread which is so heartbreaking that the
(10)   occupants of the County Infirmary themselves seem scarcely less wretched than those who are making their last stand against it.

This look was almost more than I could bear for only a few days before some frightened women had bidden me come quickly to the house of an old German woman, whom two men from the county agent's office were attempting to remove to the County Infirmary. The poor old creature had thrown herself
(15)   bodily upon a small and battered chest of drawers and clung there, clutching it so firmly that it would have been impossible to remove her without also taking the piece of furniture. She did not weep nor moan nor indeed make any human sound, but between her broken gasps for breath she squealed shrilly like a frightened animal caught in a trap. The little group of women and children gathered at her door stood aghast at this realization of the black dread which always clouds the lives of the very poor when
(20)   work is slack, but which constantly grows more imminent and threatening as old age approaches. The neighborhood women and I hastened to make all sorts of promises as to the support of the old woman and the county officials, only too glad to be rid of their unhappy duty, left her to our ministrations [. . . .]. To take away from an old woman whose life has been spent in household cares all the foolish little belongings to which her affections cling and to which her very fingers have become accustomed, is to
(25)   take away her last incentive to activity, almost to life itself. To give an old woman only a chair and a bed, to leave her no cupboard in which her treasures may be stowed, not only that she may take them out when she desires occupation, but that their mind may dwell upon them in moments of revery, is to reduce living almost beyond the limit of human endurance.

The poor creature who clung so desperately to her chest of drawers was really clinging to the last
(30)   remnant of normal living—a symbol of all she was asked to renounce [. . . .].

Even death itself sometimes fails to bring the dignity and serenity which one would fain associate with old age. I recall the dying hour of one old Scotchwoman whose long struggle to "keep respectable" had so embittered her that her last words were gibes and taunts for those who were trying to minister to her. "So you came in yourself this morning, did you? You only sent things yesterday. I guess you knew
(35)   when the doctor was coming. Don't try to warm my feet with anything but that old jacket that I've got there; it belonged to my boy who was drowned at sea nigh thirty years ago, but it's warmer yet with human feelings than any of your damned charity hot-water bottles." Suddenly the harsh gasping voice was stilled in death and I awaited the doctor's coming shaken and horrified [. . . .].

Question Two

(Suggested time—40 minutes. This question counts as one-third of the total essay section score.)

In Jane Austen's novel, *Persuasion*, the protagonist observes, "Here and there, human nature may be great in times of trial, but generally speaking it is its weakness and not its strength that appears in the sick chamber; it is selfishness and impatience rather than generosity and fortitude, that one hears of [. . .]."

Take a moment to reflect on this statement. Then, write a well-organized essay in which you explore the validity of this assertion using examples from your reading, observation, studies or experience to develop your position.

<u>Question Three</u>

Directions:

The following prompt is based on the accompanying six sources.

This question requires you to integrate a variety of sources into a coherent, well-written essay. *Refer to the sources to support your position; avoid paraphrase or summary. Your argument should be central; the sources should support this argument.*

Remember to attribute both direct and indirect citations.

Introduction:

The specter of terrorism in America has prompted a legislative demand for heightened security. As a result, Americans have come under close, invasive, and perhaps unconstitutional scrutiny that includes random searches, call monitoring, and increased access to personal information. This need to secure Americans has also been used to defend methods of interrogation in addition to methods of surveillance. While many feel that the security of the whole outweighs the privacy of the individual, others believe that increased security measures legitimize the invasion of personal privacy and allow our government to exceed moral boundaries that *no* government should be permitted to cross.

Assignment:

Read the following sources (including any introductory information) carefully. **Then, in an essay that synthesizes at least three of the sources for support, take a position that defends, challenges or qualifies the claim that the need to protect individual rights is paramount regardless of the political circumstance or climate**.

(It is recommended that you spend 15-20 minutes of the allotted time examining the sources and devote the remaining time to writing your essay.)

Document A

Bice, Ed. "Dear Homeland Security, We Have Found the Enemy. He is Us."
Online http://www.commondreams.org/views04/0615-03.htm: 15 Jn 2004.

The finest legal minds in Washington presumably found reason to advise President Bush in March of 2003 that the President need not concern himself with international or federal anti-torture laws when the security of the nation was at stake. If we were to torture a detainee for a parking ticket it would be wrong, but because our nation is threatened we need not concern ourselves with laws that were clearly written for matters less significant than matters of national security. What nation? It is not clear to me that, at the point we decide our nation is above the laws that codify decency and humanity, we remain a nation worthy of our history. There is much in America that is worth dying for—this weasel opinion and the related abhorrent actions that are starting to seem more pervasive than exceptional are not.

I think it is time to dust off the word 'un-American.'

In fact, I can't think of anything less in keeping with the moral and political idealism that this country purports to stand for. The premise of our constitution is that the means are the ends. The constitution was created not toward but from the idea of certain inalienable rights. The argument forwarded to our President in this memo is the same argument that has been whispered into the ears of torturers and dictators throughout history. The hope for a civilized world rests in our ability to reject this argument, to reject that we can achieve anything noble through such ignoble means [. . . .].

Document B

Ranum, Marcus J. *The Myth of Homeland Security.* Indianapolis: Wiley, 2004: 231.

With terrorism or in a cold war, the only viable answer is active counterterror. It's a nasty dirty business, but so far it is the single most effective tool against organized attacks. We've avoided it for years. Indeed, we've had a number of laws against domestic counterintelligence since the FBI targeted individuals who were opposed to the administration's policies but were not an immediate military or civil threat. The big problem remains: How do we infiltrate organizations, which have known associations with assassins and terrorists, without also compromising the next Dr. Martin Luther King? We need to be realistic about allowing counterintelligence against self-declared threats without instantiating a police state.

Personally, I don't think the balance between staying alert and a police state should be particularly difficult. Many of the organizations we're talking about have members that do indiscrete things such as standing in the street chanting "Death to America." I don't think it's a moral leap to justify investigating their after-hours behaviors and hobbies. The challenge is to keep administrators from using espionage services to their political ends, as Richard Nixon attempted to do.

Our founding fathers understood the importance of separation of powers, and I believe that the threat of abuse of authority can be mitigated through careful planning [. . . .].

From "The Myth of Homeland Security" by Marcus J. Ranum (www.ranum.com) mjr.

Document C

Garfinkel, Simson. *Database Nation: The Death of Privacy in the 21st Century*.
Sebastopol, CA: O'Reilly & Associates, 2000: 258.

The campaign against liberty, identity, and autonomy in the twenty-first century is being carried out around the world, but nowhere are the attacks more evident than in the United States. It's a campaign that is being pursued, hand in hand, by government, businesses and ordinary citizens. We are all guilty. Privacy is suffering the death of a thousand cuts.

Free societies turn their backs on privacy at their own risk, for privacy is one of the fundamental human rights from which all other human rights are derived:

- Without the ability to prevent or control intrusions, life itself cannot exist. Simple organisms use their cell walls to protect their bodily integrity from intrusions. We humans rely on our skin, our homes, our fences, and our weapons to protect our integrity and our privacy.

- Without privacy of thought—the freedom that allows us to form our own opinions, and the secrecy that allows us to keep our opinions private until we choose to reveal them—there can be no identity and no individuality.

- Without privacy of communications, there can be no politics and ultimately no true relationships. People can't have honest discussions with one another if they think their words are being overheard and possibly recorded. Just as privacy is a fundamental requirement for the development of the self, privacy between individuals is a fundamental requirement for the creation of true and lasting relationships.

from *Database Nation: The Death of Privacy in the 21st Century*, by Simson L. Garfinkel.

Document D

"Code of Fair Information Practices." Electronic Privacy Information Center.
Online http://www.epic.org/privacy/consumer/code_fair_info.html.

The Code of Fair Information Practices was the central contribution of the HEW (Health, Education, Welfare) Advisory Committee on Automated Data Systems. The Advisory Committee was established in 1972, and the report released in July. The citation for the report is as follows: U.S. Dep't. of Health, Education and Welfare, Secretary's Advisory Committee on Automated Personal Data Systems, Records, computers, and the Rights of Citizens viii (1973).

The Code of Fair Information Practices is based on five principles:

1. There must be no personal data record-keeping systems whose very existence is secret.
2. There must be a way for a person to find out what information about the person is in a record and how it is used.
3. There must be a way for a person to prevent information about the person that was obtained for one purpose from being used or made available for other purposes without the person's consent.
4. There must be a way for a person to correct or amend a record of identifiable information about the person.
5. Any organization creating, maintaining, using, or disseminating records of identifiable personal data must assure the reliability of the data for their intended use and must take precautions to prevent misuses of the data.

Document E

Krauthammer, Charles. "How Do You Think We Catch the Bad Guys?" *Time* 9 Jan 2006: 35.

Recent revelations about the actions of the Bush Administration in the war on terror have given it the image of a cross between Big Brother and Torquemada.[1] Most recently comes the story of the National Security Agency (NSA) intercepting and monitoring communications from overseas to al-Qaeda operatives in the U.S. This followed reports of "black sites" in Eastern Europe and elsewhere, where high-level al-Qaeda operatives were kept incommunicado and under stress in conditions well below even Motel 6 standards [. . . .].

This has all been variously portrayed as trampling on civil liberties, violating the Constitution, jeopardizing the very idea of freedom and otherwise destroying all that is sacred in America. Well, that's one way to look at it. But there's another way to look at it—as a triumph of counterterrorism, the beginning of the answer to the question that for the past four-plus years has been on everyone's mind but that no one could figure out: Why haven't we been hit again?

On Sept. 12, 2001, there wasn't a person in Washington who did not think that it was only a matter of days or weeks or at most months before the jihadists would strike again. It has been more than four years. Al-Qaeda knows its inability to repeat 9-11 is a blow to its prestige and pretensions of leading a global jihad. Anyone can put a bomb in a Bali discothèque. But in more than four years, al-Qaeda has not been able to do anything in America even on the scale of Madrid or London.

Why? It turns out there were people who knew the answer but couldn't say, lest they blow the secret programs that were behind our current interval of safety. But now that the programs are blown, the Administration should stop being defensive about its secreted prisons and intercepted communications. It should step forward and say, "O.K. You got us. We didn't want to talk about this stuff openly, but now you know [. . . .].

---

[1] Leading figure in the Spanish Inquisition, whose name is immediately associated with punishment and torture.

Document F

Ramirez, Michael. *Los Angeles Times Online*
Online http://cagle.msnbc.com/news/AirportSecurity2/main.asp.

Sample Examination VI

Questions 1-13. Refer to the following passage.

About the intrinsic value of science, its value as a factor in our civilization, there can be but one opinion; but about its value to the scholar, the
(5) thinker, the man of letters, there is room for very divergent views. It is certainly true that the great ages of the world have not been ages of exact science; nor have the great literatures, in which so much of the
(10) power and vitality of the race have been stored, sprung from minds which held correct views of the physical universe. Indeed, if the growth and maturity of man's moral and intellectual stature were a
(15) question of material appliances or conveniences, or of accumulated stores of exact knowledge, the world of to-day ought to be able to show more eminent achievements in all fields of human activity
(20) than ever before. But this it cannot do. Shakespeare wrote his plays for people who believed in witches, and probably believed in them himself; Dante's immortal poem could never have been produced in a
(25) scientific age. Is it likely that the Hebrew Scriptures would have been any more precious to the race, or their influence any deeper, had they been inspired by correct views of physical science?
(30) It is not my purpose to write a diatribe against the physical sciences. I would as soon think of abusing the dictionary. But as the dictionary can hardly be said to be an end in itself, so I would
(35) indicate that the final value of physical science is its capability to foster in us noble ideals, and to lead us to new and larger views of moral and spiritual truths. The extent to which it is able to do this
(40) measures its values to the spirit,—measures its value to the educator.
That the great sciences can do this, that they are capable of becoming instruments of pure culture, instruments to
(45) refine and spiritualize the whole moral and intellectual nature, is no doubt true; but that

they can ever usurp the place of the humanities or general literature in this respect is one of those mistaken notions
(50) which seem to be gaining ground so fast in our time.
Can there be any doubt that contact with a great character, a great soul, through literature, immensely surpasses in
(55) educational value, in moral and spiritual stimulus, contact with any of the forms or laws of physical nature through science? Is there not something in the study of the great literatures of the world that opens the mind,
(60) inspires it with noble sentiments and ideals, cultivates and develops the intuitions, and reaches and stamps the character, to an extent that is hopelessly beyond the reach of science? They add something to the
(65) mind that is like leaf-mould to the soil, like the contribution from animal and vegetable life and from the rains and the dews. Until science is mixed with emotion, and appeals to the heart and imagination, it is like dead
(70) organic matter; and when it becomes so mixed and so transformed it is literature [. . . .].
"Microscopes and telescopes, properly considered," says Goethe, "put our human eyes out of their natural, healthy,
(75) and profitable point of view." By which remark he probably meant that artificial knowledge obtained by the aid of instruments, and therefore by a kind of violence and inquisition, a kind of
(80) dissecting and dislocating process, is less innocent, is less sweet and wholesome, than natural knowledge, the fruits of our natural faculties and perceptions. And the reason is that physical science pursued in and for
(85) itself results more and more in barren analysis, becomes more and more separated from human and living currents and forces,—in fact, becomes more and more mechanical, and rests in a mechanical
(90) conception of the universe. And the universe, considered as a machine, however scientific it may be, has neither value to the spirit nor charm to the imagination [. . . .].

John Burroughs, "Great Essays in Science", January 1, 1901.
Copyright(c) 1901 by Houghton Mifflin Company.

1. The "one opinion" to which the author refers in line 3 is that

   (A) science serves a more valuable purpose than the arts
   (B) science has always offered the "correct" view of the universe
   (C) science has played an integral role in the development of civilization
   (D) the contributions of science have been sorely undervalued
   (E) material conveniences prove the extensive impact of science on all fields

2. Lines 13-20 —"Indeed, if the growth and maturity [. . .] in all fields of human activity than ever before"—express the author's belief that

   (A) scientists have made smaller technological strides than they are capable
   (B) technological advances are not the most accurate measure of human progress
   (C) material conveniences are "exact" measures of human accomplishment
   (D) literature has surpassed the sciences in the significance of its accomplishments
   (E) humans are not as active as they need to be

3. The antecedent of the word "it" in line 20 is

   (A) "growth" (line 13)
   (B) "question" (line 15)
   (C) "world" (line 17)
   (D) "achievements" (line 19)
   (E) "activity" (line 19)

4. The references to Shakespeare, Dante and the Hebrew Scriptures are intended to imply which of the following?

   I. That the world of the mythical and the miraculous offers values beyond the reach of science.
   II. That these works of literature do not exemplify the tenets of "exact science."
   III. That the impact of these literary texts is decreased because of their misconceptions and inaccuracy.

   (A) I only
   (B) III only
   (C) I and II
   (D) II and III
   (E) I, II and III

5. The author's observation that he would "as soon think of abusing the dictionary" (lines 32-33) does which of the following?

   (A) offers a suggestion
   (B) poses a question
   (C) employs an analogy
   (D) proposes a solution
   (E) provides a disclaimer

6. Despite their difference in length, the first and third paragraphs of the passage are similar in all of the following ways EXCEPT

   (A) their reflection of the author's conviction that science can effect social change
   (B) their rhetorical structure of a strong affirmation followed by a qualification of it
   (C) their contrast of the relative impact of science and literature
   (D) their focus on similar periods of time
   (E) their implication that the spiritual and intellectual natures of man still need refinement

7. The BEST equivalent of the word "stamps" (line 62) is

   (A) validates
   (B) mars
   (C) impresses
   (D) moulds
   (E) tramples

8. The comparison of the great literatures of the world to "leaf-mould" (line 65) implies literature's

   (A) outmoded state
   (B) inferiority to natural beauty
   (C) capacity to enrich
   (D) gradual decline
   (E) characteristic mustiness

9. In lines 75-83 the author's diction reveals that

   (A) scientific technology has afforded us new and exciting insights into the natural world
   (B) the invasive nature of technology is inferior to the natural perceptions of our senses and intellect
   (C) science has been forcibly diverted to serve militaristic and violent ends
   (D) naturally grown produce is preferable to an organically grown product
   (E) human knowledge has been corrupted ever since Eden

10. In the concluding paragraph, the author's primary point is underscored by contrasts between all of the following EXCEPT

   (A) progress and stasis
   (B) human vision and instruments of magnification
   (C) natural knowledge and artificial knowledge
   (D) barrenness and fecundity
   (E) human and machine

11. In the final paragraph the author may be said to

   (A) foreshadow a potentially dehumanizing consequence of science
   (B) discourage the practice of scientific inquiry
   (C) advocate a return to idyllic simplicity
   (D) criticize a scientific claim by a literary persona
   (E) question the reliability of human perceptions

12. Of the following, which is NOT characteristic of the author's rhetoric?

   (A) rhetorical questions that persuade the reader of the power of literature
   (B) the use of scientific data to buttress his philosophical argument
   (C) an analogy that links natural growth to intellectual development
   (D) allusions to writers of great stature
   (E) a tendency to begin sentences with a coordinating conjunction

13. Which of the following is NOT used by the author to effect a transition between two paragraphs?

   (A) an assertion
   (B) a disclaimer
   (C) a citation
   (D) a question
   (E) a refutation

Questions 14-27. Refer to the following passage.

I cannot call riches better than the baggage of virtue. The Roman word is better, *impedimenta*, for as the baggage is to an army, so is riches to virtue; it cannot
(5) be spared nor left behind, but it hindereth the march; yea, and the care of it sometimes loseth or disturbeth the victory. Of great riches, there is no real use, except it be in the distribution; the rest is but conceit. So
(10) saith Solomon:[1] *Where much is, there are many to consume it; and what hath the owner but the sight of it with his eyes?* The personal fruition in any man cannot reach to feel great riches: there is a custody of
(15) them; or a power of dole and donative of them; or a fame of them; but no solid use to the owner. Do you not see what feigned prices are set upon little stones and rarities? And what works of ostentation are
(20) undertaken, because there might seem to be some use of great riches? But then you will say, they may be of use, to buy men out of dangers or troubles. As Solomon saith: *Riches are as a stronghold in the*
(25) *imagination of the rich man.* But this is excellently expressed, that it is in imagination, and not always in fact. For certainly great riches have sold more men than they have bought out. Seek not proud
(30) riches, but such as thou mayest get justly, use soberly, distribute cheerfully, and leave contentedly [. . . .]. The poets feign that when Plutus (which is Riches) is sent from Jupiter, he limps and goes slowly; but when
(35) he is sent from Pluto, he runs and is swift of foot; meaning, that riches gotten by good means and just labor pace slowly; but when they come by the death of others (as by the course of inheritance, testaments, and the
(40) like), they come tumbling upon a man. But it mought[2] be applied likewise to Pluto, taking him for the devil. For when riches come from the devil (as by fraud and oppression, and unjust means), they
(45) come upon speed.
The ways to enrich are many, and most of them are foul. Parsimony is one of the best, and yet it is not innocent; for it withholdeth men from works of liberality and charity. The improvement of the
(50) ground is the most natural obtaining of riches; for it is our great mother's blessing, the earth's; but it is slow. And yet, where

men of great wealth do stoop to husbandry,
(55) it multiplieth riches exceedingly. I knew a nobleman in England, that had the greatest audits of any man in my time; a great grazier,[3] a great sheepmaster, a great timberman, a great collier, a great
(60) cornmaster, a great leadman, and so of iron, and a number of the like points of husbandry; so as the earth seemed a sea to him, in respect of the perpetual importation [. . . .].
(65) Believe not much them that seem to despise riches: for they despise them that despair of them; and none worse when they do come to them. Be not penny-wise; riches have wings, and sometimes they fly away
(70) of themselves, sometimes they must be set flying to bring in more. Men leave their riches either to their kindred, or to the public; and moderate portions prosper best in both. A great state left to an heir is as a
(75) lure to all the birds of prey round about to seize him, if he be not the better stablished in years and judgment. Likewise glorious gifts and foundations are like sacrifices without salt; and but the painted sepulchers
(80) of alms, which soon will putrefy and corrupt inwardly. Therefore measure not thine advances by quantity, but frame them by measure; and defer not charities till death; for certainly, if a man weigh it
(85) rightly, he that doth so is rather liberal of another man's than of his own [. . . .].

---

[1] Old Testament king renowned for great wisdom and wealth

[2] might

[3] a person who feeds cattle for market

14. The opening paragraph of the author's discussion of riches is characterized by all of the following EXCEPT

    (A) an extended analogy
    (B) irony
    (C) negation
    (D) questions and admonitions
    (E) allusions

15. The author argues that the true value of significant wealth to an individual is its

    (A) contribution to social prominence
    (B) visual appeal
    (C) function as a tangible measure of achievement
    (D) potential to help the less fortunate
    (E) usefulness as ransom

16. The difference in meaning between "feigned" (line 17) and "feign" (line 32) is BEST expressed by which of the following pairs of words?

    (A) "inflated" and "fancy"
    (B) "significant" and "imagine"
    (C) "ridiculous" and "state"
    (D) "unrealistic" and "pretend"
    (E) "obscene" and "deduce"

17. Which of the following is the LEAST persuasive interpretation of the phrase "leave contentedly" (lines 31-32)?

    (A) relinquish without qualms
    (B) bequeath to another
    (C) wash one's hands of
    (D) part with willingly
    (E) suffer someone to take

18. The implication of the mythological allusion that concludes paragraph one is that

    (A) the gods are capricious
    (B) wealth attained quickly is frequently tainted
    (C) hard-working individuals are seldom rewarded
    (D) inheriting money makes people lazy
    (E) anyone wealthy is evil

19. In relation to attaining riches, the phrase "one of the best" (lines 47-48) means one of the most

    (A) surefire
    (B) respectable
    (C) gratifying
    (D) practical
    (E) rapid

20. In his anecdote about the English nobleman (lines 55-64), the author suggests that the earth "seemed as a sea, in respect of the perpetual importation [. . . .]" in order to

    (A) conjure up the fecund bounty returned by seafaring men or vessels
    (B) deplore the fickleness of the harvest
    (C) celebrate the great variety of edible crops
    (D) note how the great expanse of crops seems limitless
    (E) acknowledge the wave-like nature of the furrows

21. In the final paragraph, the author offers admonitions against all of the following EXCEPT

    (A) people without riches who are scornful of them
    (B) people who are overly cautious and refrain from investing
    (C) people who leave great financial legacies that plague the inheritor
    (D) people who leave money to public institutions
    (E) people who wait until they die before being charitable

22. In depicting the ease with which inheritance can be snatched from the young and uninformed, as well as the unscrupulous individuals who purloin it, the author uses metaphors drawn from

    (A) fireside and family
    (B) birds and flight
    (C) statesmanship and law
    (D) art and aesthetics
    (E) ritual and religion

23. All of the following are characteristic of the author's argumentative style EXCEPT

    (A) posing questions to his audience
    (B) citing the wisdom of a wealthy Biblical personage
    (C) anticipating and rebutting counter-arguments
    (D) using imperatives to buttress his counsel
    (E) satirizing wealthy men of his era

24. Which of the following verbs has both literal and figurative possibilities?

    (A) "spared" (line 5)
    (B) "limps" (line 34)
    (C) "stoop" (line 54)
    (D) "prosper" (line 73)
    (E) "weigh" (line 84)

25. In the course of the passage, the author uses a series of appositives to

    (A) recount the impediments brought about by great wealth
    (B) celebrate the diverse successes of a wealthy acquaintance
    (C) catalog the many dishonest means by which men become rich
    (D) list the number of ways people can lose money
    (E) list the various entities to whom men bequeath their fortunes

26. For which of the following does the author reference a more sapient authority?

    I.   The powerful and seductive allure of wealth.
    II. The perils of a too easily acquired fortune.
    III. The vulnerability of youthful heirs.

    (A) I only
    (B) III only
    (C) I and II
    (D) II and III
    (E) I, II and III

27. The overall tone of the passage is BEST classified as

    (A) condescending
    (B) excoriating
    (C) didactic
    (D) solemn
    (E) skeptical

Questions 28-40. Refer to the following passage.

The following is an excerpt from a longer essay that has previously established the setting (England) and the time (the first half of the 19th century).

Until a few years ago I had no idea that if you sent a letter out of town—and if you weren't a nobleman, a member of Parliament, or other VIP who
(5) had been granted the privilege of free postal franking—the postage was paid by the recipient. This dawned on me when I was reading a biography of Charles Lamb,[1] whose employer, the East India
(10) House, allowed clerks to receive letters gratis until 1817: a substantial perk, sort of like being able to call your friends on your office's 800 number [. . . .].

Sir Walter Scott[2] liked to tell the
(15) story how he had once had to pay "five pounds odd" in order to receive a package from a young New York lady he had never met: an atrocious play called *The Cherokee Lovers*, accompanied by a
(20) request to read it, correct it, write a prologue, and secure a producer. Two weeks later another large package arrived for which he was charged a similar amount. "Conceive my horror," he told his
(25) friend Lord Melville, "when out jumped the same identical tragedy of *The Cherokee Lovers*, with a second epistle from the authoress, stating that, as the winds had been boisterous, she feared that
(30) the vessel entrusted with her former communication might have foundered, and therefore judged it prudent to forward a duplicate." Lord Melville doubtless found this tale hilarious, but Rowland Hill would
(35) have been appalled. He had grown up poor, and, as Christopher Browne notes in *Getting the Message*, his splendid history of the British postal system, "Hill had never forgotten his mother's anxiety when
(40) a letter with a high postal duty was delivered, nor the time when she sent him out to sell a bag of clothes to raise 3*s*[3] for a batch of letters."

Hill was a born Utilitarian[4] who,
(45) at the age of twelve, had been so frustrated by the irregularity of the bell at the school where his father was principal that he had instituted a precisely timed bell-ringing schedule. In 1837 he published a report
(50) called "Post Office Reform: Its Importance and Practicability." Why, he argued,

should legions of accountants be employed to figure out the Byzantine[5] postal charges? Why should Britain's
(55) extortionate postal rates persist when France's revenues had risen, thanks to higher mail volume, after its rates were lowered? Why should postmen waste precious time waiting for absent
(60) addressees to come home and pay up? [. . . .].

After much debate Parliament passed a postal reform act in 1839. On January 10, 1840, Hill wrote in his diary, "Penny Postage extended to the whole
(65) kingdom this day!....I guess that the number despatched [sic] tonight will not be less than 100,000…".On January 11 he wrote, "The number of letters despatched exceeded all expectation. It was 112,000
(70) of which all but 13,000 or 14,000 were prepaid." In May, after experimentation to produce a canceling ink that could not be surreptitiously removed, the Post Office introduced the Penny Black, bearing a
(75) profile of Queen Victoria: the first postage stamp. The press, pondering the process of cancellation, fretted about the "untoward disfiguration of the royal person," but Victoria became an enthusiastic philatelist,[6]
(80) and renounced the royal franking privilege for the pleasure of walking to the local post office from Balmoral Castle to stock up on stamps and gossip with the postmaster. When Rowland Hill—by that
(85) time Sir Rowland Hill—retired as Post Office Secretary in 1864, *Punch*[7] asked "SHOULD ROWLAND HILL have a statue? Certainly, if OLIVER CROMWELL[8] should. For one is
(90) celebrated for cutting off the head of a bad King, and the other for sticking on the head of a good Queen [. . . .]."

---

[1] late 18th-early 19th century British essayist

[2] late 18th-early 19th century Scottish author

[3] shillings—a unit of money

[4] a philosophy which defined good as whatever brings the greatest happiness to the greatest number of people

[5] highly complex (as in the ornate nature of Byzantine architecture and art)

[6] stamp collector

[7] famed British magazine of humor and satire

[8] 17th century British statesman and one of the men responsible for the execution of King Charles I

"Mail" by Anne Fadiman. Originally published in *The American Scholar*, Winter 2000, Volume 69, Number 1. Copyright © by Anne Fadiman. Reprinted by permission of Lescher & Lescher, Ltd. All rights reserved.

28. The primary purpose of the passage is to

    (A) condemn a practice
    (B) laud an individual
    (C) chronicle an improvement
    (D) validate a theory
    (E) debunk a myth

29. According to the opening paragraph, which of the following would have had to pay a fee upon receiving a letter?

    (A) a member of Parliament
    (B) an aristocrat
    (C) an employee of the East India House
    (D) an individual who had been made exempt from postal fees
    (E) an ordinary citizen

30. The author's second paragraph anecdote about Sir Walter Scott and the young playwright suggests all of the following EXCEPT

    (A) Scott's bemusement at the playwright's presumptuous demands
    (B) Scott's distaste for the poor quality of the playwright's drama
    (C) Scott's surprise upon receiving a second copy of the playwright's manuscript
    (D) Scott's difficulty in paying the required postal tariff
    (E) Scott's delight at recounting the episode for his circle of friends

31. The author likely provides details of Rowland Hill's youth and schooling in order to

    (A) depict his precociously meddlesome nature
    (B) document his habitual tardiness
    (C) presage his desire for order and economy
    (D) connect his inventiveness to his religious upbringing
    (E) convey his spoiled attitude

32. In arguing for postal reform as an adult, Hill was critical of all of the following EXCEPT

    (A) mail delivered to the wrong address
    (B) confusing rate schedules
    (C) excessive charges
    (D) poor time-management
    (E) extraneous bookkeepers

33. Which of the following likely motivated Parliament to agree to enact postal reform legislation?

    I. Delays in collecting revenue.
    II. The simplicity of the penny stamp.
    III. The potential to increase revenue by downsizing staff.

    (A) I only
    (B) III only
    (C) I and II
    (D) I and III
    (E) I, II and III

34. Which of the following is used by the author to document the meteoric success of Hill's postal vision?

    (A) the anecdote about Hill's mother
    (B) Hill's 1837 report on post office reform
    (C) entries from Hill's diary
    (D) the enthusiasm for philately later displayed by Queen Victoria
    (E) the article about Hill in *Punch*

35. The passage implies that a key difference between Sir Walter Scott and Rowland Hill was

    (A) nationality
    (B) religious belief and affiliation
    (C) sense of humor
    (D) financial circumstance in youth
    (E) public recognition of their accomplishments

36. Which of the following claims about the issuance of the first postal stamp is supported by the passage?

    (A) It resulted in Hill's promotion to Post Office Secretary.
    (B) It raised media concern over potential defacement of the royal image.
    (C) It increased the number of letters being mailed nationally.
    (D) It resulted in the knighthood of Rowland Hill.
    (E) It resulted in the dedication of a statue commemorating Hill's innovation and service.

37. Which of the following BEST epitomizes the author's characterization of Rowland Hill?

    (A) ingenious inventor
    (B) visionary pragmatist
    (C) dabbling dilletante
    (D) confrontational firebrand
    (E) enthusiastic philatelist

38. Which of the following is NOT characteristic of the author's style?

    (A) allusions to figures of literary and historical importance
    (B) parenthetical references
    (C) direct citation of primary sources
    (D) the use of questions to depict the inquiring spirit of Rowland Hill
    (E) a didactic but droll tone

39. The importance of the fourth footnote is that it helps to explain Hill's

    (A) appalled reaction to Sir Walter Scott's story
    (B) admirable devotion to his mother
    (C) passionate commitment to improving efficiency
    (D) clear enthusiasm over the number of dispatched letters
    (E) public recognition via a commemorative statue

40. Which of the following footnotes provides an explanation of something that the context could not otherwise clarify for the reader?

    (A) footnote two
    (B) footnote three
    (C) footnote four
    (D) footnote five
    (E) footnote seven

Questions 41-52. Refer to the following passage.

When there has been brought home to any one, by conclusive evidence, the greatest crime known to the law; and when the attendant circumstances suggest no
(5) palliation of the guilt, no hope that the culprit may even yet not be unworthy to live among mankind, nothing to make it probable that the crime was an exception to his general character rather than a
(10) consequence of it, then I confess it appears to me that to deprive the criminal of the life of which he has proved himself to be unworthy—solemnly to blot him out from the fellowship of mankind and from the
(15) catalogue of the living—is the most appropriate as it is certainly the most impressive, mode in which society can attach to so great a crime the penal consequences which for the security of life
(20) it is indispensable to annex to it. I defend this penalty, when confined to atrocious cases, on the very ground on which it is commonly attacked—on that of humanity to the criminal; as beyond comparison the
(25) least cruel mode in which it is possible adequately to deter from the crime [. . . .]. Few, I think, would venture to propose, as a punishment for aggravated murder, less than imprisonment with hard labor for life;
(30) that is a fate to which a murderer would be consigned by the mercy which shrinks from putting him to death. But has it been sufficiently considered what sort of mercy this is, and what kind of life it leaves to
(35) him [. . . .]. What comparison can there really be, in point of severity, between consigning a man to the short pang of a rapid death, and immuring him in a living tomb, there to linger out what may be a long life in the
(40) hardest and most monotonous toil, without any of its alleviations or rewards—debarred from all pleasant sights and sounds, and cut off from all earthly hope, except a slight mitigation of bodily restraint, or a small
(45) improvement of diet? Yet even such a lot as this, because there is no one moment at which the suffering is of terrifying intensity, and, above all, because it does not contain the element, so imposing to the
(50) imagination, of the unknown is universally reputed a milder punishment than death [. . . .]. As my hon. Friend the Member for Northampton (Mr. Gilpin) has himself

remarked, the most that human laws can do
(55) to anyone in the matter of death is to hasten it; the man would have died at any rate; not so very much later, and on the average, I fear, with a considerably greater amount of bodily suffering. Society is asked, then, to
(60) denude itself of an instrument of punishment which, in the grave case to which alone it is suitable, effects its purposes at a less cost of human suffering than any other; which, while it inspires
(65) more terror, is less cruel in actual fact than any punishment that we should think of substituting for it. My hon. Friend says that it does not inspire terror, and that experience proves it to be a failure. But the
(70) influence of a punishment is not to be estimated by its effect on hardened criminals. Those whose habitual way of life keeps them, so to speak, at all times within sight of the gallows, do grow to care less
(75) about it; as, to compare good things with bad, an old soldier is not much affected by the chance of dying in battle. I can afford to admit all that is often said about the indifference of professional criminals to the
(80) gallows. Though of that indifference one-third is probably bravado and another confidence that they shall have the luck to escape, it is quite probable that the remaining third is real. But the efficacy of a
(85) punishment which acts principally through the imagination, is chiefly to be measured by the impression it makes on those who are still innocent; by the horror with which it surrounds the first promptings of guilt;
(90) the restraining influences it exercises over the beginning of the thought which, if indulged, would become a temptation [. . . .].

41. The length of the passage's opening sentence could be a result of which of the following?

   I. The author's attempt to convince his audience that he would not favor capital punishment but in the most exceptional cases.

   II. The author's desire to evade clarifying his position on the matter.

   III. The expansive oratorical nature of the discourse.

   (A) I only
   (B) II only
   (C) I and III
   (D) II and III
   (E) I, II and III

42. In the interspersed phrase—"solemnly to blot him out from the fellowship of mankind and from the catalogue of the living" (lines 13-15)—the author is trying to

   (A) convey his hesitancy over supporting a measure that favors capital punishment
   (B) emphasize the blunt finality of execution
   (C) provide a more formal recapitulation of the prisoner's sentence
   (D) express his personal animus for those who kill
   (E) defer an unavoidable concession to the opposing viewpoint

43. In lines 35-45 the author explodes the claim that capital punishment is the "least cruel mode in which it is possible adequately to deter from the crime" by doing all of the following EXCEPT

   (A) utilizing diction that emphasizes the tedium of incarceration
   (B) effecting a contrast between the immediacy of death and the duration of terminal confinement
   (C) using an oxymoron to depict the moribund nature of a life sentence
   (D) alluding to a well-known scene in Greek tragedy
   (E) employing a key word that denotatively and connotatively reinforces the totality of exile for a prisoner

44. In choosing such phrases as "the greatest crime known to the law" (lines 2-3), "atrocious cases" (lines 21-22) and "grave case" (line 61), the author wishes to

   (A) lament the murderous bent of depraved individuals
   (B) deplore the ineffectiveness of written laws
   (C) reaffirm his belief in the limited exercise of capital punishment
   (D) exaggerate the criminals' transgressions to increase the likelihood of their execution
   (E) suggest a pattern to seemingly random homicides

45. The author argues that the *real* reason most people perceive life imprisonment as more lenient than capital punishment is because it

   (A) precludes any arduous labor
   (B) offers the possibility of parole
   (C) is more humane than the alternative, execution
   (D) is a social, not isolated, experience
   (E) lacks the terrifying specter of post-life judgment

46. Which of the following most appropriately describes the author's attitude toward his opponent, Mr. Gilpin?

   (A) cordial and deferential
   (B) terse and acerbic
   (C) empathetic and embarrassed
   (D) bored and indifferent
   (E) sarcastic and derisive

47. Upon what point would the author and Mr. Gilpin most likely agree?

   (A) That society should maintain capital punishment as a deterrent against crime.
   (B) That incarceration is an effective means of moral rehabilitation.
   (C) That capital punishment should only be invoked in the most egregious cases of homicide.
   (D) That incorrigible criminals are inured to the threat of capital punishment.
   (E) That capital punishment instills terror in all members of society.

48. Lines 77-80, "I can afford to admit all that is often said about the indifference of professional criminals to the gallows," are intended to confirm the

(A) disdain of hardened criminals for the threat of the gallows.
(B) likelihood that most criminals will escape punishment
(C) rectitude of Mr. Gilpin's opposing argument
(D) stalwart conviction of the author that execution is a deterrent to crime
(E) author's insufferable conceit

49. What aspect of the author's defense of the death penalty is MOST surprising and ironic?

(A) his insistence on "conclusive evidence" prior to its assessment
(B) his belief that it is the most "impressive" penalty society can levy
(C) his perception of it as the most humane of all sentences
(D) his observation that the criminal would have died anyway
(E) his unwillingness to admit its failure to intimidate serial offenders

50. Which of the following BEST captures the author's perspective on the issue of capital punishment?

(A) blanket endorsement
(B) limited advocacy
(C) moral objection
(D) general indifference
(E) rabid opposition

51. Under which of the following circumstances would the author stalwartly maintain his position on capital punishment?

(A) if the crime committed was deemed manslaughter, not homicide
(B) if the evidence of wrongdoing was not sufficiently definitive to convict
(C) if the murder was committed in self-defense
(D) if the party charged had a long history of violent behavior
(E) if the transgressor exhibited remorse and potential for redemption

52. Which of the following is NOT characteristic of the author's rhetoric?

(A) limited use of the first-person to affirm his position or concur with society
(B) the admission of an opposing claim followed by a challenge of its validity or logic
(C) sprawling, complex sentences lengthened by instances of emphasis and explanation
(D) images that understate the finality of execution
(E) questions which challenge the prevailing opinion about punishment

Section II

Question One

(Suggested time—40 minutes. This question counts as one-third of the total essay section score.)

Read the following passage carefully. Then, in a well-organized essay, discuss how the author uses elements of language to convey the dilemmas that individuals face in determining what they should read.

Since we are all moribund, and since reading books is time-consuming, we must devise a system that allows us a semblance of economy. Of course, there is no denying the possible pleasure of holing up with a fat, slow-moving, mediocre novel; still, we all know that we can indulge ourselves in that fashion only so much. In the end, we read not for reading's sake but to

(5) learn. Hence the need for concision, condensation, fusion—for the works that bring the human predicament, in all its diversity, into its sharpest possible focus; in other words, the need for a shortcut. Hence, too—as a by-product of our suspicion that such shortcuts exist (and they do, but about that later)—the need for some compass in the ocean of available printed matter.

The role of that compass, of course, is played by literary criticism, by reviewers. Alas, its

(10) needle oscillates wildly. What is north for some is south (South America, to be precise) for others; the same goes in an ever wilder degree for east and west. The trouble with a reviewer is (minimum) threefold: (a) he can be a hack, and as ignorant as ourselves; (b) he can have strong predilections for a certain kind of writing or simply be on the take with the publishing industry; and (c) if he is a writer of talent, he will turn his review writing into an independent art

(15) form—Jose Luis Borges is a case in point—and you may end up reading reviews rather than the books themselves.

In any case, you find yourself adrift in the ocean, with pages and pages rustling in every direction, clinging to a raft whose ability to stay afloat you are not so sure of. The alternative, therefore, would be to develop your own taste, to build your own compass, to familiarize

(20) yourself, as it were, with particular stars and constellations—dim or bright but always remote. This, however, takes a hell of a lot of time, and you may easily find yourself old and gray, heading for the exit with a lousy volume under your arm. Another alternative—or perhaps just a part of the same—is to rely on hearsay: a friend's advice, a reference caught in a text you happen to like. Although not institutionalized in any fashion (which wouldn't be such a bad idea), this

(25) kind of procedure is familiar to all of us from a tender age. Yet this, too, proves to be poor insurance, for the ocean of available literature swells and widens constantly, as this book fair amply testifies: it is yet another tempest in that ocean.

So where is one's terra firma, even though it may be but an uninhabitable island? Where is our good man Friday,[1] let alone a Cheetah?[2]

---

[1] native befriended by the castaway protagonist in Daniel Defoe's 18th century novel, *Robinson Crusoe*

[2] chimpanzee companion of pulp-fiction jungle hero Tarzan, created by Edgar Rice Burroughs in 1912

"How to Read a Book" from ON GRIEF AND REASON by Joseph Brodsky. Copyright (c) 1995 by Joseph Brodsky.

<u>Question Two</u>

(Suggested time—40 minutes. This question counts as one-third of the total essay section score.)

"It's an unnerving thought that we may be the living universe's supreme achievement and its worst nightmare simultaneously."

—Bill Bryson, *A Short History of Nearly Everything*

A Short History of Nearly Everything by Bill Bryson from Random House, Inc.

Take a moment to reflect on this statement. Then, write a well-organized essay in which you explore the validity of this assertion using examples from your reading, observation, studies or experience to develop your position.

<u>Question Three</u>

(Suggested time—55 minutes. This question counts as one-third of the total essay section score.)

Directions:

The following prompt is based on the accompanying six sources.

This question requires you to integrate a variety of sources into a coherent, well-written essay. *Refer to the sources to support your position; avoid paraphrase or summary. Your argument should be central; the sources should support this argument.*

Remember to attribute both direct and indirect citations.

Introduction:

Much as previously passed civil rights' legislation prohibited discrimination due to race, the Americans with Disabilities Act, signed into law by President George H. Bush on July 26, 1990, banned discrimination against the disabled in the workplace, in public accommodations, and on transportation. However, to what degree has such legislation been effective? Has it genuinely protected the rights and enhanced the opportunities of those who are disabled?

Assignment:

Read the following sources (including any introductory information) carefully. **Then, in an essay that synthesizes at least three of the sources for support, take a position that defends, challenges or qualifies the claim that legislation intended to insure the rights of the disabled has had its desired effect in protecting and advancing the rights of the disabled.**

(It is recommended that you spend 15-20 minutes of the allotted time examining the sources and devote the remaining time to writing your essay.)

Document A

"Disability." U.S. Census Bureau.
http://www.census.gov/hhes/www/disability/disabstat2k/disabstat2ktxt.html.

Disability Status: 2000
Census 2000 Brief
Highlights

Census 2000 counted 49.7 million people with some type of long lasting condition or disability. [1] They represented 19.3 percent of the 257.2 million people who were aged 5 and older in the civilian noninstitutionalized population—or nearly one person in five (see Table 1). [2] Within this population, Census 2000 found:

- 9.3 million (3.6 percent) with a sensory disability involving sight or hearing.
- 21.2 million (8.2 percent) with a condition limiting basic physical activities, such as walking, climbing stairs, reaching, lifting, or carrying.
- 12.4 million (4.8 percent) with a physical, mental, or emotional condition causing difficulty in learning, remembering, or concentrating.
- 6.8 million (2.6 percent) with a physical, mental, or emotional condition causing difficulty in dressing, bathing, or getting around inside the home.
- 18.2 million of those aged 16 and older with a condition that made it difficult to go outside the home to shop or visit a doctor (8.6 percent of the 212.0 million people this age).
- 21.3 million of those aged 16 to 64 with a condition that affected their ability to work at a job or business (11.9 percent of the 178.7 million people this age).

FOOTNOTES

[1] The estimates in this report are based on responses from a sample of the population. As with all surveys, estimates may vary from the actual values because of sampling variation or other factors. All statements made in this report have undergone statistical testing and are significant at the 90-percent confidence level, unless otherwise noted.

[2] In this report, the population universe for people with disabilities excludes people in the military and people who are in institutions.

Document B

Olson. Walter A. "Under the ADA, We May All Be Disabled." *The Wall Street Journal*. 17 May 1999:1.

To understand the latest controversy concerning the Americans With Disabilities Act, the word to keep in mind is "unmitigated."

Karen Sutton and Kimberly Hinton want to be classed as legally disabled on account of their poor eyesight. There's just one catch: it seems the two sisters can see pretty much as well as the rest of us. Ah, their lawyers say, but that's when they're wearing glasses! Ditch the specs, and they're badly nearsighted. Last month, the Supreme Court heard arguments on whether the physical condition of persons wishing to sue under the ADA should be considered in its "unmitigated" state; that is, before any remedial steps have been taken.

The issue has plenty of applications. A second case before the court involves a United Parcel Service driver who wishes to qualify as "disabled" because he'd have a serious problem with high blood pressure if he stopped taking his medication—though in fact he does take it. Also watching with interest are people who'd be in medical trouble if not for their joint or heart-valve replacements [. . . .].

To be fair, the tangle of disability-definition gets a lot more complicated than this. Economist Carolyn Weaver says the government has used more than 20 different definitions of disability for various purposes. And the ADA's is among the vaguest of all. At the Supreme Court last month, you might say the theme was unmitigated confusion. "I don't see how to get this statute to work," said Justice Stephen Breyer. "I'm at sea," confessed Justice David Souter. As Justice Antonin Scalia waved his glasses in the air—seven of the nine Justices wear glasses—the court seemed to realize in one magic moment that under the more liberal interpretations of the ADA every one of them could count as protected-class members as could "a majority of Americans," as Justice Scalia said. That's a result at odds with the law's preamble, which cited 43 million as the number regarded as disabled then.

By this point, to be sure, it would seem late in the day to stop the majestic progress of disabled-rights law from bestowing a right to accommodation on everyone who differs physically, mentally, or behaviorally from the norm. Last year the *Hartford Courant* reported that nearly one in three high schoolers in affluent Greenwich, Conn., are now officially regarded as disabled, entitling them to various benefits ranging from individualized tutoring to laptop computers. Soon we may achieve a Lake-Wobegon effect in reverse, in which we will all get to be below average [. . . .].

Document C

Rosen, S.L. "A Survivor's Manual." *Reflections: The Early Rags*.
Online http://www.raggcdedgemagazine.com/departments/reflections/000652.html.

In 1976, I "survived" an automobile accident. Some would say that I shouldn't have—meaning by that all sorts of curious things. Since then, I have spent all my waking hours learning the curious rituals set down by America for becoming a proper "survivor."

Some call me "handicapped"; others—at both ends of the spectrum (those who would view me only in terms of a Social Security statistic and those who would have me join the pseudo "disabled rights" movement)—called me disabled. And I read about the thinkers up at Michigan State who have thought up some new reasons why I should call myself a "handicapper."

Well, to me, all the terms are offensive. I am, first of all and always (unable to get away from the fact), a survivor. For me, and I imagine for most others like me, "survivor" is the real term that holds meaning. We are surviving, indeed; to the embarrassment of a society that can't figure out what to do with us, ghastly successes of that medical skill of patching together shards of people who, twenty years ago, wouldn't have survived at all. What to do with us survivors has never been of much interest to anyone except the survivors themselves. And I don't care what is said about all this "handicapped rights" stuff. That's all very fine and good, but it's not doing much to change society's view of disability itself. And until that's changed, us survivors will continue to eke out an existence at the fringes of society, a society that nobody really wants us to join [. . . .].

After thinking about it a good long time, I've come to see through this "overcoming a handicap" stuff. I've come to the conclusion that my body doesn't handicap me at all compared to the handicapping created by society. I have overcome the problems I had at first with feeding myself, getting into bed, and learning to move about in a wheelchair. But I'll tell you what I can't overcome: I can't overcome society's barriers; this country's discriminatory practices, this country's apparent unconcern for getting to the root of this problem. And furthermore, I think it's a damn crime that we're expected to. But that is really what they mean when they expect us survivors to overcome our handicaps. I'll tell you what does handicap me: the lack of a job handicaps me; the lack of money handicaps me; the lack of adequate housing handicaps me; the lack of transportation handicaps me. And yet I'm supposed to "overcome my handicap [. . . .]."

<u>Document D</u>

Wade, Betsy. "Airlines Face Scrutiny Over Wheelchair Policies." *New York Times*. Late Edition (East Coast). 26 Sept 1999: 5.3. Online http://proquest.umi.com/pqdweb?index=1&did=45133551&SrchMode=1&sid =1&Fmt=3&VInst=PROD&VType=PQD&RQT=309&VName=PQD&TS=1140887996&clientId=56233.

The rights of disabled airline travelers under Federal laws are getting renewed attention from the Department of Transportation.

In mid-August the department served Continental Airlines with a complaint saying that the airline had treated three wheelchair passengers illegally, and seeking fines of $250,000. Action against other airlines is likely soon, according to Nancy E. McFadden, general counsel in the department. The department has been looking into the complaint letters it has received, she said, and is preparing much broader moves against five airlines. Ms. McFadden would not identify the airlines, but the department has begun breaking down by airline its monthly tabulation of complaint letters from disabled passengers [. . . .].

The case against Continental began when Paul Tobin, Angelo Bianco and Gerard M. Kelly reported that they were not able to get their wheelchairs stored in cabins, as the law required, instead of with the luggage, did not get seats in rows with movable armrests and were bumped while being placed in seats with fixed armrests, were stranded aboard long after other passengers had debarked or were not able to get appropriate answers to their complaints. They were represented by the Eastern Paralyzed Veterans Association, an advocacy group that has played a major role in getting lift-equipped buses onto municipal routes. In 1998, it filed formal charges for its three clients, saying Continental violated the Air Carrier Access Act [. . . .].

Continental, in response, unequivocally denies that it discriminated against people with disabilities. Noting that the department had found Continental's training of employees in dealing with disabled passengers to be adequate, the airline said "occasional inadvertent mistakes by an individual do not constitute discrimination on the part of the corporation [. . . .]."

> ### Document E
>
> Barnartt, Sharon and Richard Scotch. *Disability Protests: Contentious Politics, 1970-1999*. Washington: Gallaudet UP, 2001: 172.

There are a number of problems with the ADA, especially in relation to enforcement. For one thing, the ADA requires that people who feel their rights have been violated under the ADA file a complaint themselves, which requires a degree of knowledge and resources that many people do not have, especially those with impairments, who tend to have lower incomes than people without disabilities. Another difficulty is that it does not permit government agencies to initiate investigations or lawsuits or to be proactive in seeking out instances of violations. Finally, it permits no compensatory damages to be awarded by a successful lawsuit, unlike the situation in civil rights laws for women or racial minorities [. . .]. Thus, lawyers have less interest in taking Title III cases, especially on a contingency basis (which is the only way someone without money can convince a lawyer to take a case), because there is little possibility of financial reward for them. In addition, evidence about the success of the ADA, especially in the area of employment, has been somewhat mixed. Some researchers or reporters see improvement; others do not. These evaluations are fraught with conceptual and methodological problems, however, and thus may not give us a true picture of its effects [. . . .].

To some extent, it does not matter whether the ADA was a real victory for the deaf and disability communities (or if it should become so in the future) or if it was simply a symbolic one [. . . .]. A sociological maxim says that things perceived as real are real in their consequences. It is absolutely clear that the ADA was *perceived* to be a victory by people with disabilities, as well as by outsiders [. . . .].

Document F

Holland, Gina. "High Court Dodges Right Over Seating for Disabled." *Columbian* 29 Jun 2004: A-8.
Online http://proquest.umi.com/pqdweb?index=2&did=656879401&SrchMode=1&sid=1
&Fmt=3&VInst=PROD&VType=PQD&RQT=309&VName=PQD&TS=114088 8555&clientId=56233.

The Supreme Court refused Monday to consider whether disabled moviegoers must be given better seats than the front-row accommodations they're provided in many new stadium-seating theaters.

Justices had been asked to decide if a landmark disabilities law requires better accommodations, and if theater owners can be ordered to make after-the-fact changes.

Instead, at the urging of the Bush administration, they left undisturbed rulings against two theater companies while the government reviews its guidelines for movie theater owners.

Stadium-riser seating gives unobstructed views to most everyone in the theater. Critics, however, complain that those in wheelchairs are often left to awkwardly crane their necks from the less-desirable front rows.

In some theaters, the wheelchair accessible area is 11 feet from the screen "essentially the worst seats in the house," lawyers for three disabled women in one of the Supreme Court cases said in court filings.

Remodeling the auditoriums would cost hundreds of millions of dollars, movie theater companies told justices, and is unnecessary because the seats up front provide "clear and unobstructed views" of screens.

Movie theater accommodations have become the latest battleground over rights for the disabled. A dozen different courts have dealt with lawsuits over theater seating, and sour tension has developed between the federal government and screen owners.

The Justice Department "chose to sit on its hands while thousands of stadium-style movie theater auditoria were constructed based upon the reasonable and universal understanding among design professionals" that wheelchair patrons only had to be given an unobstructed view, justices were told by the National Association of Theatre Owners.

The group estimates there are about 10,000 individual theaters with stadium-seating most in large multiplexes. It would cost $100,000 to install elevators in each of those or $50,000 each, for wheelchair lifts, the association said [. . . .].

NOTES

NOTES

NOTES

NOTES

NOTES

NOTES

NOTES

NOTES